Cooking Lessons

Cooking Lessons

The Politics of Gender and Food

Edited by
Sherrie A. Inness

ROWMAN & LITTLEFIELD PUBLISHERS, INC.
Lanham • Boulder • New York • Toronto • Plymouth, UK

ROWMAN & LITTLEFIELD PUBLISHERS, INC.

Published in the United States of America
by Rowman & Littlefield Publishers, Inc.
A wholly owned subsidiary of The Rowman & Littlefield Publishing Group, Inc.
4501 Forbes Boulevard, Suite 200, Lanham, Maryland 20706
www.rowmanlittlefield.com

Estover Road
Plymouth PL6 7PY
United Kingdom

British Library Cataloguing-in-Publication Information Available

Library of Congress Cataloging-in-Publication Data

Cooking lessons : the politics of gender and food / edited by Sherrie A. Inness.
    p. cm.
  Includes bibliographical references and index.
  ISBN 978-0-7425-1574-1
    1. Food habits—United States—History. 2. Food habits—United States—Sex differences.
  3. Food in popular culture—United States. 4. Sex role—United States. 5. Cookery,
  American. I. Inness, Sherrie A.

GT2853.U5 C66 2001
394.1'222—dc21

2001019733

Printed in the United States of America

∞™ The paper used in this publication meets the minimum requirements of
American National Standard for Information Sciences—Permanence of Paper
for Printed Library Materials, ANSI/NISO Z39.48-1992.

For Heather Schell

A good thing is the encouragement of a friend.
—Homer, *Iliad*

Contents

Part III: Class, Race, and Food

Acknowledgments

I wish to thank all the contributors to this anthology. They never failed to be polite, cheerful, and prompt. I appreciate everyone's effort. I am equally thankful for the other people who helped make this book possible. Robi Malone deserves a special thank you for reading the entire manuscript with such a meticulous editorial eye.

I also appreciate my friends who kept me going through this book's publication. I especially have to thank Hallie Bourne, Faye Parker Flavin, Jane Dusselier, Barbara Emison, Julie Hucke, Stephanie Levine, Michele Lloyd, Deb Mandel, Lisa Sommer, and Liz Wilson. I wish to thank all my colleagues at Miami University for being supportive, considerate, and encouraging. They are wonderful people. I also wish to thank Christine Gatliffe, Ginger Strader, and all the other people at Rowman & Littlefield who helped to make this book a reality.

I would also like to thank a network of food scholars whose prior work has inspired this collection: Arlene Voski Avakian, Warren Belasco, Amy Bentley, Anne L. Bower, Carole Counihan, Jane Dusselier, Barbara Haber, Harvey A. Levenstein, Lucy M. Long, Laura Shapiro, Janet Theophano, Penny Van Esterik, and many others.

I wish to express my deepest gratitude to two especially important people in my life, my mother and father, Ruth and Lowell Inness. I have the best parents in the world, and they inspire me every day. Even though my mother is no longer with us in person, not a day passes that I don't think of her.

Finally, this book is dedicated to Heather Schell, a dear friend and a talented writer. I love and admire Heather for her keen sense of humor, sharp intellect, and genuine good heart. She is someone who adds immeasurably to my life, and I appreciate her friendship. Thank you, Heather.

Introduction: Of Meatloaf and Jell-O . . .

Sherrie A. Inness

$\mathcal{A}$pple pie, meatloaf, Jell-O, macaroni and cheese, fried chicken, hamburgers, hotdogs—these are just a few of the hundreds of foods that play important roles in American culture. We find these foods everywhere from the kitchen table, to the backyard grill, to the fast-food restaurant. Perhaps because such foodstuffs are so very common, we rarely think about them in much depth. But these foods and others deserve more critical scrutiny since they reveal lessons about American society and its values—lessons as important as those in books, newspapers, or magazines. *Cooking Lessons: The Politics of Gender and Food* explores what we can learn from going no further than our dinner plates; analyzing common foodstuffs, this book suggests, can give as valuable a lesson about American beliefs as any textbook.[1]

In particular, the authors in *Cooking Lessons* examine the relationship between women, gender, and various foods, including meatloaf, fried chicken, cake, and Jell-O, exploring how such foodstuffs have offered women a way to gain power and influence in their households and larger communities. For women without access to other forms of creative expression, preparing a superior cake or batch of fried chicken has been a way to display their talent in an acceptable venue. But foods and the stereotypes attached to them also have been used to keep women (and men, too) from different races, ethnicities, and social classes in their places. By teasing out the ways that foodstuffs are used to constitute women and their lives, *Cooking Lessons* offers its readers a better understanding of one of the significant forces that shapes the lives of women and men in America.

This is not the first study to focus on the importance of individual foods and their impact on American culture. Other works focus on everything from the unusual—Cincinnati chili—to the universal—the hotdog.[2] Probably the most famous of these studies is Sidney W. Mintz's *Sweetness and Power: The Power of Sugar in Modern History* (1985). Like Mintz's, many of these works focus on a single food (steak or hamburgers,[3] for instance). Unlike Mintz's, *Cooking Lessons: The Politics of Gender and Food* studies not a single food, but a wide variety of different foods in order to gain a broader understanding of the interaction between gender and food.

The importance of food to every human in the world is obvious. It is one of the few substances that all humans require to stay alive and thrive. At the cultural level, food has deeper significance than simple survival. Every society invests symbolic importance to food. Food scholar Carole M. Counihan notes in her book, *The Anthropology of Food and Body: Gender, Meaning, and Power* (1999), that "Food is a product and mirror of the organization of society on both the broadest and most intimate levels" (6). The foods we eat or do not eat, who prepares them, and how they are served reveal a tremendous amount of information about how a society is structured; food is one of the most visible and omnipresent symbols of everything from class to race to age, and it provides a powerful symbolic message of who we are and who we aspire to be.

Studying the cultural contexts of single foods, from bananas to fried chicken, reveals a great deal about how gender is constituted in America. For example, one of the most well-known examples of how a single food suggests the consumer's identity is steak. It is widely recognized that steak is the penultimate male dish. A man who eats steak makes himself appear symbolically more masculine, powerful, and manly, which is one reason that steak restaurants continue to thrive in the United States. Since steak (and meat in general) is so strongly associated with men and masculinity, it is not surprising that men are still the ones in the United States who usually do the grilling in countless backyards across the nation. Like steak, Jell-O is another food that is strongly gender-coded—it is associated with femininity. Women (and young children) are supposed to delight in Jell-O. For decades, Jell-O has been advertised as a feminine food, something that the ladies would appreciate. Men, however, were supposed to avoid Jell-O as too ladylike. (Despite Bill Cosby's advertising for Jell-O, it continues to be a food associated with women.) Steak and Jell-O are two examples of many that show the gendered messages conveyed in the making and consuming of different foods.

As *Cooking Lessons: The Politics of Gender and Food* argues, single food items, from meatloaf to Jell-O, do more than fill our stomachs. Sarah E. Newton observes in her essay "'The Jell-O Syndrome': Investigating Popular Culture/Foodways" (1992), "the study of popular commercial food products can have value . . . in uncovering the intimate, important, and sometimes symbolic relationships people develop between themselves, their world, and the foods they eat" (266). Taking Newton's words one step further, it is not only commercial food products that reveal important lessons about people and their relationship to the world, it is any food. For instance, meatloaf stands for Mom's home cooking and conjures up a powerful nostalgia for, presumably, a simpler time. But meatloaf also represents a time of rigid conformity—the fifties—in the United States. Meatloaf carries with it a complex cultural iconography, and it is only one food of thousands that possess such an iconography. Our relationship to foods, as we shop, cook, or eat them, is one method by which race, ethnicity, class, and gender are constructed in U.S. society. In many ways, our identities are shaped by our relationships to foods.

The chapters in *Cooking Lesson*'s first section focus on how food has offered and continues to offer women a means for self-expression. As I have mentioned earlier, many American women in the past and present have not had access to "traditional" venues for self-expression, such as painting or writing. For some of these women, cooking, rather than being something that confined and limited them to the kitchen, was a way to gain personal power both in and outside the home. Paul Christensen begins our exploration of how food and cooking have offered women influence. He focuses on the role that a cup of tea had for his own mother and for countless other women in the post–World War II era. For his mother and others, he argues, a cup of tea was not only a pause in a dreary day of housework and domestic routines, but a chance to meditate, to dream, to imagine forbidden worlds where women were free of their entrapments and obligations. The tea break lasted only briefly and was often interrupted by hungry children coming home from school demanding their milk and cookies. It was a stolen time before dinner was to be prepared, but in its glow one entered a fleeting paradise of solitude and rest shared by other women, each alone in her kitchen at the quiet hour.

Like Christensen, the other three writers in this section, Traci Kelly, Benay Blend, and Patricia M. Gantt, also focus on how foods give women a source of power. Each of these writers examines how preparing a traditional foodstuff offers women a form of self-expression and a way to gain influence and recognition both in the domestic realm and the larger community outside the home. Kelly examines the role of lefse-making in North Dakota and Minnesota. She suggests that making these labor-intensive potato griddlecakes has long offered status to some Lutheran-Norwegian American women, as the most talented lefse makers were openly lauded within their families, churches, and towns. Blend focuses on tortilla- and tamale-making and the role that they have in the lives of Hispanic women in the Southwest.

She explores the important traditional place of these foods in the Hispanic household and suggests that Chicana feminist authors have challenged traditional notions of domesticity by showing how women use tortilla- and tamale-making to question the dominant culture and its values. Gantt focuses on cake in the American South and demonstrates how it long has had a special significance for Southern women. She argues that cake has become a way for Southern women to demonstrate their power, influence, and prestige both inside and outside of the home.

While the chapters in *Cooking Lesson*'s first section focus on how food offers women a way to gain influence inside the house and in the larger community, the chapters in the second section examine how the media shape women's relationship to food. These chapters show how the media spread cultural values about women, food, and gender roles. Jessamyn Neuhaus writes about meatloaf, a menu item that has been a staple on the American kitchen table for decades. Analyzing cookbooks and cooking magazines from 1920 to 1960, she shows how meatloaf recipes for women and men were tailored differently in popular cooking literature, demonstrating that cooking for women was a distinct and separate process than it was for men. Women were instructed to make the simplest meatloaves, while men were encouraged to make more exotic ones, in order to demonstrate their talents as gourmet chefs. Even something as simple as a recipe for meatloaf, Neuhaus argues, conveys important messages about how society expects men and women to relate to food.

The next two chapters focus on how foods have been sold and marketed specifically to women. Virginia S. Jenkins argues that one way bananas in the United States were transformed from an expensive specialty to an inexpensive staple found at every grocery store was by marketing them as an ideal food for women. Jenkins depicts the powerful role that advertising and marketing have in making some foods more acceptable for one gender or the other. Like Jenkins, Kathleen LeBesco writes about the marketing of a common everyday food: Jell-O. She explores how this food has become a signifier of a woman's class status, with a working-class woman being far more likely to serve the gelatin dessert than someone from a higher-class background. LeBesco, however, also shows that factors other than social class must be considered when analyzing Jell-O and its consumption, including race, ethnicity, and age.

The chapters in *Cooking Lesson*'s final section show a darker side of food's place in U.S. culture. The book's first four chapters focus on how food offers women influence and control; the final two chapters examine how foods and their creation help to perpetuate class, ethnic, and race divisions. Elizabeth S. D. Engelhardt focuses on class. In Appalachia at the turn of the century, the beaten biscuit and cornbread conveyed two different messages about class, with the biscuit being perceived as upper class and cornbread as lower class. She focuses on how Progressive Era women reformers encouraged working-class women in Appalachia to switch from cornbread to the supposedly more refined beaten biscuit. The reformers were trying to improve Appalachian women's class status but often the reformers made dietary changes without regard to whether making cornbread might be less expensive and easier to make.

The final chapter analyzes fried chicken. Psyche A. Williams-Forson explores how the stereotype of African Americans as chicken lovers perpetuated racism through the nineteenth and twentieth centuries. She also demonstrates, however, that African American women have resisted this stereotyping by transforming fried chicken into a source of power and influence both in the family and community.

Whether Jessamyn Neuhaus's on meatloaf, Virginia S. Jenkin's on bananas, or Patricia M. Gantt's on Southern cake, all this book's chapters are designed to give readers a broader appreciation of the ways that food and food culture shape the lives of American women and men. The foods we consume, how we prepare them, and who prepares them reveal important information about our race, class, ethnicity, and gender.

Gender, in particular, is heavily intertwined with food, since food preparation is so frequently assumed to be women's primary domestic responsibility. In order to understand how gender is created in the United States (and around the world), it is essential to understand how food and food culture have shaped and continue to shape our lives. From grocery shopping, to preparing the food, to cleaning up afterward, every aspect of food is intermingled with issues of gender. We need to understand these gendered messages to understand better the gender differences and inequities in American society.

Finally, this book is designed to encourage its readers to analyze more closely how food shapes their own personal lives. It is an essential part of all of our lives, but how many of us really stop to think about the food that we eat, except to worry about its calorie or fat content? We need to examine its place more carefully. Too frequently we do not stop to think about the foods we consume. Who produces them? What messages about gender, class, race, and ethnicity do their advertisements promote? Why are some foods either more or less appealing to us and what does this suggest about our cultural background? We will discover that our breakfast of either Cheerios or eggs, grits, and bacon suggests more than we might assume about our place in American society.

NOTES

1. For general studies of American food culture and history, see Avakian; Belasco; Bower; Gabaccia; Inness, *Dinner Roles and Kitchen Culture*; Long; Root and de Rochemont; and Shapiro.

2. Other studies of single foods include Bria; Dusselier; Fiddes; Fuller; Garber; Kim and Livengood; Kurlansky; Lloyd; Lockwood and Lockwood; Naj; Neustadt; Pendergrast; A. Smith, *Popped Culture* and *Pure Ketchup*; C. Smith; and Wyman.

3. A number of studies have been written about the success of the hamburger in the United States and how the lowly ground-meat sandwich has changed the culinary landscape. See Hogan; Tennyson.

WORKS CITED

Avakian, Arlene Voski, ed. *Through the Kitchen Window: Women Explore the Intimate Meanings of Food and Cooking.* Boston: Beacon, 1997.

Belasco, Warren J. *Appetite for Change: How the Counterculture Took on the Food Industry, 1966–1988.* New York: Pantheon, 1989.

Bower, Anne L., ed. *Recipes for Reading: Community Cookbooks, Stories, Histories.* Amherst: University of Massachusetts Press, 1997.

Bria, Rosemarie Dorothy. "How Jell-O Molds Society and Society Molds Jell-O: A Case Study of an American Food Industry Creation." Ph.D. diss., Columbia University Teachers College, 1991.

Counihan, Carole M. *The Anthropology of Food and Body: Gender, Meaning, and Power.* New York: Routledge, 1999.

Dusselier, Jane. "Bonbons, Lemon Drops, and Oh Henry! Bars: Candy, Consumer Culture, and the Construction of Gender, 1895–1920." Pp. 13–49 in *Kitchen Culture in America: Popular Representations of Food, Gender, and Race*, ed. Sherrie A. Inness. Philadelphia: University of Pennsylvania Press, 2001.

Fiddes, Nick. *Meat: A Natural Symbol.* New York: Routledge, 1991.

Fuller, Linda K. *Chocolate Fads, Folklore, and Fantasies.* New York: Haworth, 1994.

Gabaccia, Donna R. *We Are What We Eat: Ethnic Food and the Making of Americans.* Cambridge: Harvard University Press, 1998.

Garber, Marjorie. "Jell-O." Pp. 11–22 in *Secret Agents: The Rosenberg Case, McCarthyism, and Fifties America*, ed. Marjorie Garber and Rebecca L. Walkowitz. New York: Routledge, 1995.

Hogan, David Gerard. *Selling 'em by the Sack: White Castle and the Creation of American Food.* New York: New York University Press, 1997.

Inness, Sherrie A. *Dinner Roles: American Women and Culinary Culture.* Iowa City: University of Iowa Press, 2001.

———, ed. *Kitchen Culture in America: Popular Representations of Food, Gender, and Race.* Philadelphia: University of Pennsylvania Press, 2001.

Kim, Sojin, and R. Mark Livengood. "Ramen Noodles and Spam: Popular Foods, Significant Tastes." *Digest: An Interdisciplinary Study of Food and Foodways* 15 (1995): 2–11.

Kurlansky, Mark. *Cod: A Biography of the Fish that Changed the World.* New York: Walker, 1997.

Long, Lucy M. "Culinary Tourism: A Folkloristic Perspective on Eating and Otherness." *Southern Folklore* 55.3 (1998): 181–204.

Lloyd, Timothy Charles. "The Cincinnati Chili Culinary Complex." *Western Folklore* 40 (1981): 28-40.

Lockwood, Yvonne R., and William G. Lockwood. "Pasties in Michigan's Upper Peninsula: Foodways, Interethnic Relations, and Regionalism." Pp. 3–20 in *Creative Ethnicity: Symbols and Strategies of Contemporary Ethnic Life*, ed. Stephen Stern and John Allan Cicala. Logan: Utah State University Press, 1991.

Mintz, Sidney W. *Sweetness and Power: The Place of Sugar in Modern History.* New York: Penguin, 1985.

Naj, Amal. *Peppers: A Story of Hot Pursuits.* New York: Knopf, 1992.

Neustadt, Kathy. *Clambake: A History and Celebration of an American Tradition.* Amherst: University of Massachusetts Press, 1992.

Newton, Sarah E. "'The Jell-O Syndrome': Investigating Popular Culture/Foodways." *Western Folklore* 51 (July 1992): 249–67.

Pendergrast, Mark. *Uncommon Grounds: The History of Coffee and How It Transformed Our World.* New York: Basic Books, 1999.

Root, Waverley, and Richard de Rochemont. *Eating in America: A History.* New York: Morrow, 1976.

Shapiro, Laura. *Perfection Salad: Women and Cooking at the Turn of the Century.* New York: Farrar, Straus, and Giroux, 1986.

Smith, Andrew F. *Popped Culture: A Social History of Popcorn in America.* Columbia: University of South Carolina Press, 1999.

———. *Pure Ketchup: A History of America's National Condiment.* Columbia: University of South Carolina Press, 1996.

Smith, Christopher Holmes. "Freeze Frames: Frozen Foods and Memories of the Postwar American Family." Pp. 175–210 in *Kitchen Culture in America: Popular Representations of Women, Gender, and Race*, ed. Sherrie A. Inness. Philadelphia: University of Pennsylvania Press, 2001.

Tennyson, Jeffrey. *Hamburger Heaven: The Illustrated History of the Hamburger.* New York: Hyperion, 1993.

Wyman, Carolyn. *I'm a Spam® Fan: America's Best-Loved Foods.* Stamford: Longmeadow, 1993.

The Cup of Comfort

Paul Christensen

The smell I recall most about my childhood is tea. The tangy, lemony bitter smell of my mother's tea steeping in a cheap red pot on the stove in the kitchen. I might be ill upstairs, another bout of asthma, home from school with the day dreary and cloud-covered, and rising up the narrow staircase with its white posts and brown banister would be that evil smell, the sour smell of loneliness, a vague sense of bitter regret and disappearing hopes. It would enter my head and blow through me like a wind, and I would feel myself falling off the delicate ledge I was on—with my stopped-up nose and wheezing, my headache and hot legs, I would be falling down deeper and deeper into my mother's own depression. We would be falling together, hand in hand, with the day coming to a wheezy, rusty stop at 2:30 in the afternoon.

Sometimes I would come in from school and find my mother slumped over the table with her cup of tea before her. She would have put out some macaroons or Fig Newtons in a bowl and have one in her reddened fingers, and before her, in the chipped cup that was hers alone to use, would be the ocher-tinted water with one or two gray wisps of steam coming up. She would have that tired, droop-eyed look of one who had spent the day at tedious chores—maybe the laundry was hanging wet on the line in the basement. Or she had been pushing the Electrolux up and down the halls upstairs, getting under the beds with that complaining grunt of hers. She might be a little red-eyed after stirring all that dust. It was her moment of respite, a private time she begrudged herself, which I might spoil by bee-lining home instead of taking my usual jagged course to the candy store, a friend's house.

Once I was inside the house, she felt compelled to rise to serve me something. Not tea, which I hated, but maybe a glass of milk or the coffee she had poured off into another little pot from the morning. I would hasten to get to

1

the cupboards before she could rise, and make something to eat. But her little rest period was already spoiled by someone being there. It meant she couldn't escape; she was mother again. So I busied myself, talked a little, and went off with my plate of cookies and milk to sit alone in my bedroom. No matter. The faucet would gush and she was back to work again, laying out the food for supper.

Forty years later, I can't help but fall off a cliff of memory when I pass someone in a diner or cafeteria sipping tea. I go into one of those spells where the tea's singeing aroma enters me and I am dragged back to that narrow box of a kitchen, inside the red brick box of our house, which sat there anonymously as the fourth or fifth door in a row of such houses in a nondescript Philadelphia neighborhood. I would be parachuted in to my helpless state as the third boy in front of a mother whose tea I now disturbed. My gut told me I would never get over it.

For some reason, growing up meant expecting by some unknown law that my mother, a good housekeeper and a compulsive cleaner, should be busy. I don't know why I accepted this principle. But anything else seemed wrong. If she sat too long with a book or magazine, it meant she was going into one of her blue periods, it meant trouble. Any kind of idleness in her was morally disturbing to me, as it was to my brothers. My father imposed the law, maintained it by his own erratic energies on weekends, but it was she who seemed to embody the rightness of the law by always moving around with dirty shirts, a broom, a piece of the vacuum tube in her hand.

To this day, I recall with a little shudder the hour or so when she would go upstairs to take her afternoon nap. I was the youngest child, and therefore the last to leave the house to begin schooling. The first six years of my life were lived to the smell of her ironing, to the sound of the radio in the kitchen muttering over the hiss of the frying pan. I studied her through the wooden bars of my crib as she came and went with bottles of detergent, rags for window cleaning. I took my own rhythm from the sound of her footsteps in the bedrooms above, making beds, putting away clothes.

Her dull industry everywhere around me as I sat there with thumb in mouth, or with an old linty juice bottle in my lap, was hypnotic. I accepted this form of mother as the only one. It was beyond me to think of her idling over a phone or laughing with other women in the dining room. She did go out occasionally; she had a friend or two who came over once in a great while. And those jags of thirty minutes of mere chat were unnerving to me. I counted the clouds, I followed trucks as they drifted past the living room window, I watched for any visitors to the cemetery across the street. When the chairs scraped back and farewells began, I felt a warm thrill go up my arms. It meant she would return to work, and the house would go along again, as it must—toward evening on the wheels of her mop ticks, her coughs.

Then she would head down to the kitchen at the hour when reality seemed to drown in glue. You could feel the energy dying away; you knew something was off balance now, like a motor downsurging at a precarious uphill moment. She was about to fold towels or push the bed away from the wall for the monthly corner dust mopping, and then that blackness of fatigue would drop over her. She would hesitate, look up, and put the mop against a dresser. Silence would pour in all around her solitary figure in the thin winter light. She would want to go on, but couldn't. She would draw breath and come down the stairs slowly, her mouth set. She would make tea and talk herself into another hour of cleaning afterward.

What did she think in those idle minutes while the water boiled in the dented little pan? Did she venture out beyond the wire fences of an authority she didn't agree with, but nonetheless obeyed? Who said she should work like this all day and every day, anyway? Why was it engraved in stone over the women of America that they must use up their lives in this kind of monotonous labor? It would be twenty years before women would reenter the workplace in large numbers and demand their fair share of leisure and enjoyment. For now, in the early 1950s, no one dared to question the victory men had created in two wars. Even I knew that my father enjoyed an authority that was more than himself, more than his sex or his fatherhood. It came with a sense of almost universal victory from World War II. The house was filled with its memories, though we were not especially patriotic or zealous about America.

But we did have a flag, and it went into the bracket under the front window each Veterans' Day. And across the street were rows of crooked white crosses behind a rusty iron fence where the martyrs lay, each of them demanding homage once a year when a few straggling soldiers got up in their old ill-fitting uniforms came out to fire their rifles in the air to the thrill of neighborhood boys. The brass shell casings were our saints' relics to be enshrined in cigar boxes at the foot of our beds. My father carried the full glory of a war inside him, and his one or two soldier pictures were part of the elastic of that glory, part of the old connections to this vague but powerful atmosphere of male triumph.

No one can deny this war had built up men unlike any other event since American independence, and that it had come upon the heels of masculine disgrace suffered in the Great Depression. My father had stood in breadlines, had eaten his two raw eggs one suffering day without any other food. He had been fed by my mother's family when he came to court my mother. He ate ravenously and held out his plate for as long as there was food in the kitchen. He couldn't get enough. He needed a victory in his life, something to win back the losses of a collapsed economy, a failing system of male values. And the war came on a platter, with Hitler as the demon, and other fascist leaders as the excuse to remove all trace of male responsibility for events of the last decade. And out of victory would come a vast new era of heroes and unimpeachable masculine prowess, an era in which women would be indentured servants.

So, in my mother's hesitation in the moments before tea became a necessity, she tested her bonds, her invisible chains to this war. If she felt done in, she came down. Otherwise, she might grit her teeth and go on without the tea, working away at some resistant island of gray dust slipping beyond reach into ever-receding dark corners. And all the women of the neighborhood followed her through their own rooms, pushing a mop or broom, the nozzle of a whining vacuum. They obeyed the hidden law, while men were milling about in corridors downtown.

Everywhere you looked in America, the triumphant war was present. At the movies, those grim-faced men of the 1950s were the veteran heroes now conquering civilian life—in the same way they had won the war over Germany and Japan. By male grit, by logic and calculated aggression. They were the taciturn, unemotional types like John Wayne, Alan Ladd, the Orson Welles of *Citizen Kane*, big, rough-edged warrior males like Robert Mitchum and Marlon Brando, or quiet, steel-ribbed pragmatists like Fred McMurray and James Stewart. They were all trooping the colors in Hollywood postwar hymns to the male gods. And my mother would sit beside my father in the dark as the flickering lights of the screen poured their silver propaganda into everyone's gullible faces. We had no escape from these advertisements for male conquest, and behind the heroes was a new imperial America spreading its Coca-Cola and Pepsi and popcorn and Spam and Texaco gas across the old boundaries of human difference, powered by democracy's triumphs.

My mother was a foreigner in the all-male courts of American privilege. She was the dutiful charwoman in a man's house, and as the observer in his crib, I could not know to doubt the ultimatum to work under which she lived. I simply timed my heart beats and hunger cycle to the sound of her old vacuum cleaner above me.

As I grew up, my impression of her complicated into several versions of who she might be. The custodial woman remained bedrock to my image of her; she was cook, cleaner, mender first. Somewhere behind that grayly docile silhouette existed a female with her own needs. So the closet in which her homemade dresses hung belonged to this more mysterious dimension of her life. Tenderly folded into shelves were a few scarves, pairs of gloves, a few unopened packages of hose, the bottles of perfume my father gave her, which she was saving for the "right occasion." The smell of those garments and luxuries was as thin as the aroma of a church—remote, sacred in a passionless sort of way. She had put these things aside as the raw potentials of a life she wouldn't live.

I understand my mother now as a human being who found herself in a cultural era in which her sex was demoted by the terms of American victory abroad. She could not claim anything but a domestic participation in the effort, a maintenance role that would have gone on in peace as in war. Therefore, she was not a warrior, and could not claim anything but a little of the prosperity men had made possible. So she stinted, and cut out her food coupons, made her skirts and blouses, mastered the art of making dinner stretch to two, sometimes three leftover nights.

But tea was the thing she had claimed as her island, her one sandbar in the sea of housework. She would descend the steps in that haggard face and old clothes; she was stripped of any make-believe. The girl was gone, the woman was merely the drudging housemate and mother. No lipstick, no eye shadow, nothing but pins in the hair, an old skirt stained by all the previous years of cleaning and waxing. Her shoes were old canvas mules or maybe flats she had bought in a basement sale. She was headed for the kitchen, where the water would run into the pot, the stove would give off its evil little smell of sulfur, and the vinyl dinette chair would be pulled back over the linoleum, and then silence.

She would be thinking, perhaps fidgeting over the green Formica tabletop. Her hands would be very tired by now. At a certain low hissing noise behind her she would rise and open the cupboard, take down the Lipton's Tea box and pull out a teabag. She would look around for her chipped cup and saucer in the next cabinet, then open the bread box and take out the macaroons or Fig Newtons, pull down a small pie dish and load it up. She would take out a half lemon, already pinched and dried out, from the crisper and squeeze the last few drops into the pot. Then she would pour the boiling water over the teabag in her cup, and sit down again. If there were no lemons left, she poured a good dollop of milk into the tea, which turned it muddy white.

She would drink with an audible slurp from the scalding cup, and dip her cookie. Her eyes would roam around the little kitchen, with its window over the back alley driveway. The backs of the next row of houses faced in to the alley, where women like her were hanging up wet laundry on the lines. They were hoping the dark clouds did not mean rain. It was cold for March, still a winter day even though the calendar said spring. Inside all the kitchens were women sitting down to tea and cookies, and a quiz show on the radio. Everyone was doing the same thing, going through the precise rituals she observed. Some faces were looking out at her from across the alley, with teacup or milk glass raised. All the women were sitting down with her, though she did not want to talk to any of them, or be their friends. She was alone in the world, and preferred it that way.

Tea came from something blissfully foreign and undefined; it was a liquor squeezed from resistant little bushes, whose perfume could only be beaten from it and which released into the water dreams of islands and tropical hillsides, and a lush, passive, idle sense of time. My mother allowed herself this pool of highlights and cloudy water as a small reward, and once drunk she could rise again and reenter a world she had been born to serve.

My mother would quit her work the way a writer might get up from a snag in the language, or a painter from some stroke of the brush that was clearly unintended or just wrong. You got up from cleaning because the rug was dirty and too heavy to roll up. You came away with a headache and a tight stomach, and the heat of the tea water eased that away. You could spread your knees a little, put your feet down flat now. You could peel off the anxiety, mild as it was, and feel some coolness on the skin.

Tea in America was a woman's drink. It seemed to come with the idea of womanhood into this open arena of democracy and commerce. No matter where you came from, or what sort of immigrant you or your parents were, tea was a shared ritual. When Mary Cabot Wheelwright, a Boston Brahmin born in 1878, traveled to the Southwest at the age of forty to start a new life among Navajos and ranchers, she was determined, she said, "that one of my missions was to convince cowboys that it was possible for a person to be a sport and also drink tea."[1]

Even as a child, I associated coffee with my father, who counted off the level measuring spoons aloud, in hoarse whispers, as he prepared the morning pot. My mother was much too casual about making coffee and made it either too weak or too strong—rarely measuring or counting the amount she dropped into the basket. It simply came out one way or another, and we drank it. But my father would measure and count, and hold out his pocket watch for the precise time when he felt the percolating was done. Then he would savor it as his special beverage. As if he knew it was a male tradition to drink coffee properly prepared. My mother drank it without comment. She reserved the right to drink tea when she was alone.

Recently I came across a remark made by the Texas writer J. Frank Dobie, who said somewhere that he resented the women poets of the 1930s, those who had done most of the lyric writing in the state up until the end of World War II as the "pink tea poets," meaning that all those reading clubs that hosted poetry contests and annual reviews whirled around a teapot and frilly napkins, and whose literary labors couldn't be taken for more than a woman's culture in Texas. It made me think about my own mother's life and how hard it was, how gloomy it could be at times, and how this beverage above all others was a solace and a special rite of females. It also made me look into the source of tea and its long, often winding history as a sacred liquor. Here are some of the things I have uncovered in looking into the background of what my mother used to slake a thirst that was not merely physical but emotional, and that sprang from psychological needs felt by everyone who partook of it, right back to its origins.

Tea is a dreamy sort of liquid; to drink it rouses fantasies in one's head not awakened by anything else. It comes from the camellia family of shrubs, the *camellia sinensis* or Chinese camellia. The place where the wild tea shrubs first grew was in southern China, but it is likely tea leaves were cultivated in a lush rainy triangle of cultures that included Burma, China, and Thailand, the same or nearly the same ground where opium and cocaine come from now. Tea is first of all a stimulant, rich in caffeine, an alkaloid that affects heart rate and blood pressure. Its flavor arises from its particular combination of polyphenols, the aromatic benzene compounds that vary according to which highland soils of Southeast Asia it is grown in. Each area has its own distinctive flavoring, like the soils of French vineyards. A taster can even recognize tea harvested from different bushes.[2]

Tea cultivation spread early into Japan, and as far north as Nepal, and south into India and Sri Lanka. It was first consumed as a medicine for curing certain nervous ailments. Kazuko Okakura, once the collaborator of Ernest Fenellosa, the most formidable of early American Orientalists whose notes on Chinese language found their way into American poetry, wrote a small classic called *The Book of Tea*, first published in 1906 and still widely read as an authoritative guide to the Japanese tea ceremony. In it, he remarks that tea "was highly prized for possessing the virtues of relieving fatigue, delighting the soul, strengthening the will, and repairing eyesight."[3] It was even used as a compress for relieving rheumatism. But from about the fifth century on, it became associated with religion. Buddhist monks used it "to prevent drowsiness during their long hours of meditation."[4] Taoists and Zen Buddhists incorporated tea into their rituals and prayers, where it still occupies a central place.

Perhaps it was the making of the tea that seemed a metaphor for the workings of the mind. The leaf is wounded and made to sweat its inner fluids out through the bruised pores. To make the leaf yield its secrets—its essences from a rainy, shadowy highland earth—the leaf is withered over special dryers, then cooled in rooms before being shredded and packaged. The leaf is then torn or broken down into a fine powder for steeping in hot water, the Japanese "whipping method" for tea preparation, before being consumed. The process by which tea was prepared in Japan especially seems to venerate the idea that tea is a form of spiritual earth—a carrier of certain essences of the mountains where it grows. One tea master praised tea as "flooding his soul like a direct appeal, that its delicate bitterness reminded him of the aftertaste of a good counsel."[5]

The great tea ritualists spent their lives learning a special set of motions with their utensils and firepits, with the guests observing a rigorous practice of responses and patient sitting before consuming, and then meditating over the influences of the tea. All this represents a kind of Eastern mysticism surrounding tea, roughly parallel to Christian communion and wine.

The relation between wine and tea is subtle, richer than that between wine and coffee. Coffee came out of Arab culture, a fluke of a sixteenth-century war when Turkish troops retreated before an Austrian assault and left behind a few sacks of roasted beans. Call it a war victory at the end of the Middle Ages, when the Austrians made a few of their Turkish prisoners demonstrate the art of making coffee. The Viennese bakers celebrated the victory over Turkey by baking croissants as a mockery of the crescent moon on the Turkish flag. Cafes sprouted up in Vienna serving both items, and a new kind of male social life formed and spread throughout Europe.

All through the centuries of coffee culture, this beverage was mainly a man's drink. Coffee was associated with male intellectuals, with male leaders—drawn to cafés such as Procope's in Paris—and, in this century, with cops and detectives up all night with a crisis or hard case to solve. The newspaper office would not be real without its mugs of coffee on every desk. And what boiler room could survive in New York without the delivery of coffee and doughnuts at 10:00 and 3:00 of the workday?

Wine and tea seem bound together by certain laws of origin and distribution in the world, and by their religious contexts, even though the word coffee (*qahwah*) is actually Arabic for wine. The word *tea* is a corruption of the Chinese word *Ch'a*, or *Tcha* in Anglicized transliteration. And while monks may have been the first harvesters of the plant, by the late Middle Ages women became the chief pluckers, as they are called. From then on, women came to have a prominent role in the world of tea. A woman's hands seemed peculiarly adept at gathering the required "two leaves and a bud" of each flush or vintage.

There has even been an effort to separate tea from coffee by sometimes labeling the caffeine in tea as theine. But the distinction is not universal, and most reference writers refer to the stimulant in tea as caffeine. Even so, the blending of modern teas, especially the black teas of India and Sri Lanka, are intended to conform with western tastes for strong morning beverages like coffee. The black tea of China is more delicate, and is rarely taken with sugar or milk. The black teas of India are stronger and tend toward bitterness, and are therefore treated almost as coffee substitutes, especially the cheaper blends.

Tea in Japanese culture rose to the heights of Buddhist ritual as the means for intensifying and honing meditation. The art of its preparation became the specialty of highly trained monks whose implements and gestures in the making of tea were considered essential steps in releasing the full powers of the drink. The exhilaration that followed from drinking the strong tea gave one the feeling of being opened, raised up out of the body's limits and carried before the divine.

But as Okakura is careful to point out, the tea ceremony, elaborate beyond almost every other kind of religious rite, nonetheless found its proper domain in simple, even bare rooms or huts reserved for the purpose:

> The tea room (the *Sukiya*) does not pretend to be other than a mere cottage— a straw hut, as we call it. The original ideographs for Sukiya mean the Abode of Fancy. Latterly the various tea-masters substituted various Chinese characters according to their conception of the tea-room, and the term Sukiya may signify the Abode of Vacancy or the Abode of the Unsymmetrical. It is an Abode of Vacancy inasmuch as it is devoid of ornamentation except for what may be placed in it to satisfy some aesthetic need of the moment. It is the Abode of the Unsymmetrical inasmuch as it is consecrated to the worship of the Imperfect, purposely leaving some thing unfinished for the play of the imagination to complete. (30–31)

The original Japanese tearoom seems remarkably like my mother's kitchen, where only the window offered a slight diversion from inward thought. Even her chipped kettle and old pot accorded with the tea master's implements, highly valued for having been owned by great tea servers of the Japanese. But when you see them now, reproduced in the photographs in Ryoichi Fukioka's *Tea Ceremony Utensils*, most are nothing more than old bits of crockery without much aesthetic value.[6] I would put my mother's warming pan alongside the more battered pots of the Zen tea masters any day.

Tea followed the coffee road into the west at roughly the same time, the early seventeenth century, at the peak of European expansion into Asia. With trade routes and colonies well established, products from the eastern cultures began to make their way into France, where tea arrived around 1630, and then to England at about 1650. When tea arrived, it was first treated as a drink for aristocrats. Like every other privilege of high society, the use of tea began to filter its way down to the middle and lower classes, a process that required two centuries to complete. But by the 1880s, in the so-called tea boom of Europe and England, merchants were demanding large quantities of packaged tea to sell in the shops, and a few importers with access to the colonies in India and Ceylon were eager to provide.

One such man was Thomas Lipton, born in Glasgow in 1850 and a careful student of American merchandising techniques.[7] He not only clerked in an American department store, he spent time on southern cotton plantations learning how large-scale production was supervised. When he returned to Scotland, his father refused to use his new franchising savvy at his own little store. Lipton went on his own and by 1890, he owned and operated three hundred shops selling general merchandise. He was a success story and carefully watched, so well hounded by rivals and the press that he had to pretend he was sailing to Australia when he headed off for Ceylon in 1890. When he arrived, a disease had wiped out the coffee plantations of the highlands and land was selling cheap. It was his genius to realize that the same ground could support large-scale tea production, and he bought up four highland plantations around Dambatene, a coveted growing area.

If he was already a millionaire, he soon became the equivalent of a billionaire with tea sales. Ceylon soon became known as not so much an English colony but as a Lipton colony. And the presence of Lipton's name was on everything from harvesting bags to factory buildings to the steamers bearing the cured tea back to England and the rest of the world. Lipton, who had learned only too well from his American merchant teachers, soon began to underprice and freeze out the other tea importers. But he also advertised heavily, and plastered the walls of London with his notices, his logo and all the colorful posters advertising the green hills of Ceylon. Even his delivery vans bore on their roofs full-scale advertising for anyone who happened to be looking down from the new office buildings.

When asked by a journalist what his secret to success was, he replied that he had none. But his key was advertising, and knowing how to accommodate the love of strong, coffee-like flavors to western drinkers. His tea, a blend of orange pekoe grown especially strong, was not only cheap to produce but was perfect for either morning or afternoon tea, and seemed to improve when milk was added. By 1894, Lipton's payroll included five hundred office workers in London and ten thousand factory hands in Ceylon. He was the largest merchant of tea in the world, and his tea became synonymous with the working class break in the workday. One didn't order tea anymore, one asked for a cup of Lipton's.

When he turned to the American tea market, he ordered samples of successful brands and discovered they were ordinary Chinese green tea varieties, sold in open bins without much effort to preserve freshness. Even before he was fully invested in his distribution, Lipton's tea won coveted tasting awards at the 1893 Chicago World's Fair. Soon after, the familiar red and yellow box of Lipton's tea, with a bearded Lipton raising his smoking cup, was the American brand of choice. It was not fancy tea, and it appealed more to women than to men. It had hit the magic formula of a stimulant with appeal to women as a separate, distinct, gendered form of drink during breaks. Lipton could then turn to sailing, a childhood passion, and spend the rest of his life reaping the rewards of having discovered a woman's pleasure. The teabag, a recent innovation in making tea, simply speeded up the process and did away with the tea strainer, or tea ball.

My mother was a child when the Lipton tea box stared down at her from the shelves of the little store opposite her house on the corner of Barracks and Bourbon streets in New Orleans. She must have purchased a few of those boxes for her own mother, who may or may not have acquired the habit of drinking a cup in the afternoon. Italian culture is not much taken with tea; it remains rooted in the coffee habit. But my mother was soon to leave the confines of her Italian heritage and travel north and east with my father, and would need to find some form of personal identity outside her family and her past. She would endure many years of vagabonding around the United States while my father rose up the government ranks, and along the way, someone, a neighbor? a friend? a confidant? would introduce her to this female elixir, this singular form of American woman's drink—over which, like heirs to the Zen and Taoist tradition, she would learn to breathe in the vapors and imbibe little glimpses of heaven.

My mother was susceptible to mood swings. I can recall many times when she would slump over her table and nibble at a sugary doughnut or a piece of leftover pie and brighten up on this sugar snack and the tea she had drunk. She would spring up from her chair, rush the dishes under the faucet, let out a few bars of her favorite French song, "*La Vie en Rose*" ("Life through rose-colored glasses"), and then head back to work. The moment she was bent over her dust mop again, she was off down the hall like something driven, scaring cats away and shooing all the little dust balls toward her pan. But after thirty minutes of arduous quick-time labor, she would throw the handle of the mop against the wall and sit down in the bedroom, head bowed, hands folded in her lap.

She might turn bitter, she might start cursing under her breath. If anyone were lurking about, she would turn on him in a scolding, molten eloquence. God help him if my father should be around at that hour, which he rarely was. Instead, it was usually my oldest brother who got the whip of her tongue. He would stand there nobly, looking a bit like Mitchum in a jam, his big well-muscled neck and shoulders holding his head steady, his hooded, slightly sleepy eyes observing this small, rather plump figure before him gesturing madly, haranguing him for all the ills of her life. She was fighting off a real sword blade of depression stuck in her back, mainly brought on by fatigue, hunger, and withering frustration.

She would spend herself in a long tirade, at me if I were the only one around, and then sulk a good long while in her bedroom behind a closed, often locked door. It was the withdrawal period, and though I didn't fully understand these trapeze-like emotions she swung on high above my head, I knew it was serious. She was a smiling, good-hearted woman, with a very large Italian generosity, but she was also tortured by the inequalities of her marriage, her life. Her scorching eloquence was the anticipation of all the recriminations and rage that would pour out of Sylvia Plath and Ann Sexton a decade hence in the movement known as confessionalism. She never read these poets, but if she had she might have had a good long hearty laugh—she had been there, said that.

In that gloomy upper story of the house, you could feel the upheavals of her unconscious. Her character seemed to be splitting up like a fishing boat in a hurricane. There was not enough for her to live on in that narrow, miserly row house of ours. We were not enough for her, either. Our lives were almost equally narrow in their constraints. We were predictable, mechanical, given to certain obvious desires followed by certain male-ordained ambitions. And nothing we did welcomed her along or encouraged her to follow our path. She was just there, that ancillary figure made smaller by the military victories that now filled all the cultural spaces of America. She couldn't come along, but she could work for us. She knew that was the deal, the only terms on which her life was based.

Even so, she would worm out of her underground tunnels and come back to us in the end. The light in the upstairs hall would flash on, and there would be the sound of her shoes in the bathroom as she prepared herself for my father's return. The kitchen, a cold narrow grave of winter twilight, would soon become a brilliant center of action when she came down to it. She would survive and come back home like a veteran of private wars of the soul. And she was generous enough to accept defeat every time she stared into her future. She knew it was bad, empty, cold where she had been, but she came down anyway to fix the meal, to save the night from her own desperation. We would make it another day into the future.

In a recent illustrated book called *The Book of Tea*, named after Okakura's classic essay, a photograph opens the text showing a cleaning woman with her cup of tea laughing uproariously in eyeglasses and a floppy work hat. It was taken in Cambridge in 1939, the start of World War II. Cambridge, we presume, is the university, the male enclave of the rich and powerful. There she sits, dust wrap gathered around her waist and ample breasts by a pin, her arms covered by an undershirt of black cotton, her mouth soft and drawn back in a fabulous expression of laughter, with the heavy cup now empty of its tea.

She is in her first throes of rejoicing over this beverage. It is not only the tea that delights her, but also the company, the social coherence of this moment when someone had spoken to her and another person shot her picture. It is a candid shot, not posed in any sense. But it is the perfect icon of tea in the modern world. Behind her are the paneled walls of a serious sort of place, painted a matte white and casting strict shadows, as if it were the background of the Enlightenment. She is there in her humble capacity as custodian, female worker. No pretensions, no claims to anything higher. She accepts. She obeys. She goes on with her life, and here, in this momentary relief from the chores, she blooms.

The English absorbed tea in a way that no other culture has done since the Chinese discovered it. According to *The Book of Tea*, the average English male or female consumes six cups of tea a day, the level of China's consumption. And both the Chinese and the English have demythologized their drink of all the gods and mysteries once given to it by the monks. Now it is an ordinary drink of small pleasures and few or no wonders. What the English conferred upon the stained water in their cups was a certain conviviality and joy that arrived intact when Lipton and his rivals popularized tea for the modern age. The English made it a Protestant drink, and when it arrived in America, it acquired something of its pragmatic and utilitarian aspects. But its history came to the New World trailing old clouds of aristocratic glory, which a fancy cup of tea can still invoke in most American minds.

Even my mother could not escape the desire to imitate some of the ways of the English. As a daughter of immigrants she longed for a new identity, and it is highly possible that she found part of her American self by borrowing from English conventions. My mother's indulgence in tea was connected in some way with her desire to be respectable, to rise up the social strata into a place she had not defined but knew existed, where her presence would not be questioned or contained. And an English woman conferred something of that elegance or freedom she could not find in the neighborhoods and among the women we knew. They had not risen or enriched their minds. They lacked manners or taste; their judgments were faulty. When she heard them screaming and fighting in public, having it out with husbands in the car, she winced. She was among the common lot, and it wasn't good enough.

I know the English were in her because her dining closet was packed with the imitations of English upper-class symbols—the tea service with matching snack plates, the fancy silverware in its cherry wood case, the delicate napkins for "nice." All that was a treasure she had accumulated and held in reserve for occasions that never fully materialized. The best china and silverware were carted out for family occasions, because the family never quite received the important guests, the aristocrats, she expected and was ready for. She had to cheat. She used the good stuff for birthdays and anniversaries, for a few milestones like our graduations or my father's promotions. And she, like many women of her kind, kept an "Irish parlor" in the living room, full of untouchable and often gaudy furniture and lamps with their cellophane wrappings left on—where none of us were permitted to sit without a newspaper under us.

But she would not allow herself the luxury of using any of this precious porcelain for herself. She chose instead to join the Cambridge charlady for a spot of tay and a crumpet, and to hell with airs. Alone, she could allow herself the privilege of being a common woman with labor to do. She joined an invisible legion of such bedraggled, tired women taking a pause. If that was her identity, she resented being interrupted and made aware of herself in that undefended mood. She was forgiving herself for her life, I think. That is why it was necessary to be alone at her table at such times. The two sides of her nature were being placated at once—the desire to strip away all longing and hope and be herself, the plain mortal woman that she was, and to also levitate out of that sack of blood and bone, her begrimed and desacralized body into her dreams, where she was free to roam, free to believe the most delicate of whimsies and laugh at herself. Free, perhaps, to rise into some social ideal where she was fulfilling all the desires of American Cinderellas stuck with the dirty house to clean. And I heard this laughter often from my sick room upstairs, or from my crib. I remember its sound coming from the quiet end of the house, a sound so private that you could not ask her what was so funny.

She was most alone with her tea; nothing could so closet her soul and free it as when she sat down to tea with her cookie untouched on the plate. She was there, and wasn't there. She was very likely a woman without being mother in that moment. I could feel her leaving me behind in that laugh, so soft and knowing, so wisely ironic and conscious. And what enriched her moment was this other sense that she was not merely the drudge of the house, but belonged in some subtle, intangible way to whatever it was that made the English crucial to American identity.

The servant end of her was a bearable penalty for being female in the New World; but in taking the tea, she sat down with a tradition of women who had made a display of their gender and importance. She knew the castles of England had rooms reserved for this ceremony, and that the highest orders of female society gathered to drink this same exotic beverage. It was a liquor that had passed down through many hands and stood for something that did not dissolve into mere humanity. It remained a womanly spiritual drink. It had its latent content and meanings.

Sometimes she would turn on the radio to a music show and use that as a surrogate for others. She would sing along to a familiar tune, "Tea for Two" if she was lucky. Most of the time it was men crooning over lost love or trying to find new love, and she would join in with her slightly nasal soprano, which had good pitch but not much range or timber. She would run out of the real words, tag behind a bit, catch up on the refrains, and then hum the rest of the way to the end. My mother, alone in her twilit winter kitchen, teacup in hand, radio turned to a kind of shadowy voice, while she lifted her spirits. The afternoon unrolled in the streets and over the city, with the moon rising over the rooftops and the kids beginning to filter back into the neighborhood. *Tea for two, and two for tea.* . . .

Sometimes I would come along and find the teabag sopping in a dish by the sink, useable another time, perhaps. She would sometimes leave her teabag in the kettle for a second cup later on. But she rarely came back to it, and I or someone else would throw it out and wash the kettle.

Even now, I sometimes find in a house I am visiting a little box of Lipton's in the corner of a kitchen cabinet and smell the odor of dry tea, the pungent odor of stale, but useable tea. It is a sign, a wonder of a vanished time. When my wife goes down to the kitchen to make tea, it's usually an herb tea, chamomile or mint tea, and lacks the dark hunger of the smell of Lipton's. I am not so moved, but I am fascinated all the same. No woman drinks tea in quite the same despair or longing as my mother and her generation did.

Vietnam ended my mother's world more finally than did any other event in her life. She seemed to know it, too. It ended with Watergate and Nixon kissing us all farewell on the steps of his helicopter, and with the desperate hands of people reaching up to a final rescue helicopter on the roof of the American embassy in Saigon. We didn't talk about it; history and grand subjects did not come easily to us in conversation. Though she read a lot and wondered aloud about the larger scheme of things, still my father's presence in the room made us cautious about history. He might demand the proof of our thoughts in a reference book, and so we kidded more than traded ideas. But the Vietnam War entered her mind in a fashion that told me she felt its great shock in the earth beneath her.

What made her feel so certain the century had ended early was that the men came home defeated, unwanted and unsung. And she was glad I was a peacenik and a street protester. She told me to go to Canada if I were drafted. We had seen Saigon, had lived there for two years before the war, from 1959 to 1961, and she knew the war was dirty, brutal, illogical. It was not a war you could win for the moral good. It was a bitter and unethical conflict in her eyes. When the men came back, they were rootless and cut off. They came home in disgrace and had taken on the nation's burdens unfairly. Now they would shrivel up in the years ahead and be nothing.

She felt that, and by now she was politically disillusioned. But she also sensed that if she had been a girl in this era, it would have meant a different life. She might have grown up in a house where men were not the lords they once were. Men were in disarray, me included. I felt the road disappearing ahead of me. I knew that I would have difficulty finding my life as a man. And all around us were the movements beginning to liberate women from what my mother had been. We could sense it in the news, in the churning of society, in the upheavals at school. It was over, the indentured years. The men had lost a war, finally. The lordship had ended in defeat.

My father retired soon after, and they went away to Georgia to live by the sea. When I visited next, my mother was no longer the crone or the dark woman of my past. She seemed frail and almost artificial in her new era—a woman of means, certainly, older and now more sophisticated and resolved. She cared more about the life of her children, after losing her middle son to cancer. She loved him most, and he had withered away in a year and died in a coma. It was the first real death close to her in the Vietnam years, and he was a metaphor of the frail male, the easily broken man. I was also fragile in her eyes, given to a little too much drink, a bit of a flake in taking hold of my life. She turned to me as if I had inherited her old life. She had come through, and now one merely had to live to the end. It wasn't so bad. She had me to worry about, and she chose to worry even though I wasn't all that bad off. I was okay, just struggling. Lost.

But the real epiphany is that the tea didn't taste the same, or work its wonders upon her in the same way. Now that she was liberated, she couldn't taste the magic. It had gone up into the heavens, a genie-less liquor already drifting toward instant tea and then bottled soft drinks. Tea had closed its doors and taken down its shingle. It wasn't the elixir of the east, the cure-all of women in their blues. She had other things to drink, and she went out more often, she opened up her life a little more. She wasn't fully liberated; she still washed clothes, and cleaned, and complained. But it wasn't the same anymore. She chose to do it. She *chose* to do things, and the tea was no longer tea.

NOTES

1. Mary Cabot Wheelwright, "Journey towards Understanding," in *A Quilt of Words: Women's Diaries, Letters & Original Accounts of Life in the Southwest, 1860–1960,* ed. Sharon Niederman (Boulder, Colo.: Johnson Books, 1990), 1.

2. This and other information on tea cultivation in the chapter are taken from C. R. Harler's *The Culture and Marketing of Tea*, 3rd ed. (London: Oxford University Press, 1964), 17.

3. Okakura, Kazuko, *The Book of Tea*, ed. Everett F. Bleiler (New York: Dover, 1964), 11.

4. Okakura, *The Book of Tea*, 11.

5. Okakura, *The Book of Tea*, 15.

6. Ryoichi Fukioka, *Tea Ceremony Utensils* (New York: Weatherhill/Shibundo, 1973).

7. The story of Lipton's success is taken from the chapter "Tea Barons," in *The Book of Tea*, trans. Deke Dusinberre (Paris: Flammarion, 1992), 94–99.

2

Honoring Helga, "The Little Lefse Maker": Regional Food as Social Marker, Tradition, and Art

Traci Marie Kelly

"*The* first thing you gotta know is that Lutefisk and Lefse are *not* a Norwegian law firm."

It was July 1992, and I was in a bar in Twin Falls, Idaho. The man across from me, heavy with too much drink, was giving me "Nort' Dakota/Minnesota lessons." A mutual friend had paired us up because I was moving to Grand Forks, North Dakota, on the border between the two states, and this odd man had once lived there.

"Well, what is it?"

"It's food. Lutefisk is a nasty fish thing. You'll never eat it. But lefse . . . lefse is something else. There was this neighbor lady who made it down the street, and she always gave me some if I shoveled her walk. Mmmm . . . lefse."

"But what is it?"

"Oh, it's just like a tortilla, but thinner and made of potatoes. You always eat it with sugar. Always."

***

The mosquitoes were eating me alive. It was six years later, and I was in the Lutheran graveyard near Fisher, Minnesota. The town of Fisher, which is ten miles east of Grand Forks, has a post office, a hardware store, a gas station, an American Legion, a café that serves breakfast and lunch (each table has dice and a cup, and the elders throw dice, rolling to see who pays for the meals), schools, and a couple of churches. I was renting a large farmstead outside of town that had been established at the turn of the twentieth century. My landlady had asked me to help tend the graves of her family homesteaders. We were going to split some peonies, fertilize the bushes near her family graves, and weed.

At some point, I wandered around, reading the graves next to the head-stones of my adopted homesteaders . . . Ole Hanson, another Ole Hanson, the Aakhusses, and their neighbors the Svengusons, the Petersons. It is truly a homesteading graveyard, marking the stories of premature deaths, hardy individuals and enduring families. But the most interesting grave marker simply said this: "Grandma Helga Skomdahl / 1892–1984 / The Little Lefse Maker." Good heavens, I thought. For all eternity, this woman will be known for her lefse. A complete and full life of a ninety-two-year-old woman, summed up in one dish. I didn't know how to think about this message from the grave. Should I be sad that this woman was known for her lefse so completely, or should I celebrate her culinary talents, as her family obviously did?

* * *

Lefse is no joking matter in North Dakota and Minnesota. While it may be nothing more than a "potato tortilla" to the uninitiated, the paper-thin griddlecakes were, and still are, culinary and social powerhouses in these small, mostly Lutheran, rural communities. In the generation just before mine, I am told that everyone worth her salt made lefse, and her recipe was distinct from everyone else's. Men, too, took pride in their lefse-making skills, but for women, the ability to turn out perfectly round, brown-speckled, millimeter thin sheets of potato mash was something that the entire community noticed. Small towns have easily identifiable citizens who hold certain talents or skills: carpenter, house painter, crop duster, pastor, volunteer firefighter, and so on. The lefse makers of these communities hold no less a place than any of these folks, and their value multiplies exponentially at holiday time when nostalgia's grip is most tight. The lefse makers, while they may downplay their own importance, are essential culinary links to the Norwegian immigrant histories.

Like the grave marker for the Little Lefse Maker, food eventually identifies all of us. Patterns of consumption define boundaries of acceptability, place in a community, and social ritual.[1] Codified and symbolic culinary structures abound in every social group: what we eat, who makes the food, when and how it is consumed—all of this reveals the historical and habit-based associations with certain foods. Lefse has become "holiday" food, imbued with nostalgia, rules of production, and even playful "factions" that argue over its proper form and delivery. To some, lefse is an art form. Simply put, for these Lutheran Norwegian American communities, lefse is far more than merely a food item.

A QUICK HISTORY OF LEFSE

Lefse is Norwegian fare, and it holds a special place on holiday tables and as a special winter holiday food. In the Old Country, Norwegian women made lutefisk and lefse as a staple for winter diets.[2] Women would pool their energies and spend three or four days traveling to neighbor homes making enough lefse for a year and storing it stacked in a wooden barrel.[3] After their introduction sometime in the mid-1700s, potatoes became a staple in Norway. Soon every family had potato patches and relied on the root for nutrition year round. Potatoes made a cheap food extender, too, to hold against the hard times. And since necessity is the mother of invention, differing methods for potato-based dishes abounded.

Norwegians emigrated to America for some of the same reasons as any other population: a better economic chance was one of those reasons. In the years spanning 1820 and 1975, roughly 855,000 Norwegians came to America to start anew.[4] Homesteaders were a tenacious group, and they knew that once they left Norway, they would probably never see their homeland again. Norwegian immigrants, like so many others, came to America for a fresh start, leaving behind small plots of overworked land and poverty. For most, scraping together money enough for the ocean passage was a trial. Often, hopeful immigrants would exchange promises of labor in exchange for payment of passage. Once in America, it was not monetarily feasible to return to Norway, although it wasn't unheard of. Most homesteading families could not think of returning to Norway, even to visit; there was too much to do on their new parcels of land.

Because the upper Midwest was the site for both opportunity and isolation at the same time, reminders of the Old Country for these homesteaders were essential. "Exile food," the food that those leaving home take with them, tends to stand still in time. Exile food is the culinary reminder of home; in the wilds of an adventure where everything is new and strange, homestyle food is a nod toward that which is still constant and reassuring. For the Norwegian population that came to the upper Midwest, lutefisk and lefse were the staples of a frugal, hard life. Those foodstuffs transferred to the New World easily. Seafood in Norway was often fresh, but lutefisk was an economically sound way of preserving cod. The transfer of lutefisk as a foodstuff to the upper Midwest was, therefore, easy. Lefse required no fresh ingredients beyond the hardy potato.

The homesteaders were basically isolated from Norway except for the occasional letter. As such, they were also unaware that in Norway, slowly but surely, lutefisk and lefse were being left behind as standard fare. Old Norway was solid and stable and never changing in the minds of the American immigrants who longed for home; the food, too, was the same. Heritage-minded cooks still pass on the recipes as traditional fare, disregarding the fact that the same dishes are not habitually eaten in modern times.[5] Today, as we step into the twenty-first century, lutefisk and lefse are prized Norwegian American holiday foods, even showing up in easy-to-microwave packages in the grocer's freezer case. However, those foods are difficult to find in today's dynamic Norway. For example, it is told that when the wife of a recent Norwegian ambassador, Gro Hedemann, saw lutefisk and lefse on a menu, she remarked that the dishes were no longer put to table in Norway.[6] Many people who I know now visit Norway to reestablish contact with long-lost relatives, and upon their return, they always remark about how nobody there eats lefse any more (or lutefisk, for that matter). Norwegian cooking has evolved, but Norwegian American cooking seems to have grinded to a halt when it comes to traditional foods; Norwegian American holiday/festival food is a snapshot of Old Country cooking one hundred years ago. Kittler and Sucher note that while Scandinavians in general assimilated quickly and well into the emerging American milieu, their diet did not change significantly.[7]

Lefse falls neatly into the category called "regional foods" as defined by Elaine N. McIntosh: "Regional foods are fostered and nurtured by isolation. They are most likely to develop and persist, without significant changes, in small pockets or localities with little contact with the outside world."[8] In no manner of thinking are citizens of northern Minnesota and North Dakota still so completely isolated. Nevertheless, the pride of heritage is an active ingredient in preserving the culinary traditions that served the early isolated homesteaders so well. Norwegian Americans in this area are proud of their impact on the upper Midwest, and they celebrate the heritage that gave them a work ethic strong enough to tackle an endless prairie and its moody weather. These people embrace their differences from other immigrant populations, but they are not blinded by it. Sharing a smorgasbord with all members of the community is a common occurrence, and it speaks to their desire to welcome and be welcomed. Such a camaraderie was essential for the survival of the homesteaders, and the traditions of community feasts, with lefse, lutefisk, Jell-O salads, meats, pies, and pastries continue today.

For their preparations for coming to America, packing up recipes as well as furniture, implements, and clothing was important to would-be homesteaders. Eating familiar food in a new and wild place has a civilizing effect for those in new territory. In the regional cookbook *A Tribute to North Dakota Families* (a compendium of stories, recipes, remedies, and quotations), among the three recipes for lefse, June Dokken contributes this remembrance: "This lefse recipe is a favorite of our family. Before my grandmother left Norway to come to America and homestead in rural North Dakota, she bravely packed her trunk and copied some of her mother's recipes before leaving."[9] Marian Johnson of Cogswell, North Dakota, has contributed her version of lefse,[10] with a preface attached that clearly associates the food with both Norway and America:

My Grandma Iverson's Lefse

This recipe was made by my Grandmother Anna Iverson many times during my growing up years on the farm near Brampton, North Dakota. This farm is now 100 years old and is still in the family. It was homesteaded in September 1889 by my grandfather and is now owned and operated by his great-grandson (my son).

8 c. mashed potatoes
1 c. whipping cream
1/4 c. shortening
1/4 c. sugar
1 1/2 tsp. salt
1 1/2 c. whole wheat flour

While potatoes are hot, add cream, shortening, sugar, and salt. Let cool. Add flour, whole wheat first and then enough white flour to make stiff dough (about 3 c.). Form into small balls about size of a large walnut. Roll out thin on floured cloth with a lefse rolling pin. Bake on lefse grill until brown on both sides.

Homesteaders brought with them what they could, but much was left behind. The mind, however, is the best traveling trunk of all, retaining language, memories, and catalogues for the senses. Torbjorn Norvoll, a Minnesota elder, said, when responding to a query about why lefse was so important to the emigrants, "whenever they left, it was goodbye forever. So they would cling to anything—old diets, memories—anything that reminded them of the old country."[11] Lefse survives (as do other traditional dishes) because of this need for a connection to home. Traditions from the old countries die hard because those who are removed from home comfort themselves with seasonal and religious cycles.[12] Even after language is lost, the food traditions remain. Elizabeth (Morken) Tollefson, whose mother grew up in Fisher, Minnesota, said it to me best: "It's as if, when mom made lefse, it was memory solidified by repetition."

When I ask my younger friends about lefse and why they eat it, inevitably they say something like this: "I dunno. We always have. Gramma always makes it. It's just part of Christmas dinner. I don't like the lutefisk, but lefse is ok." In contrast to the youth's casual association, there is something undeniable about the earnestness that some people express about absolutely *having* to have lefse for the holiday table. People in stretch of the prairie beg, banter, and bargain for homemade lefse. Neatly folded into quarters, it is sold during the winter months in the grocery stores in small cellophane packages. Indeed, lefse has even hit the World Wide Web, with eleven online distribution sites the last time I looked. For those far-flung Norwegian Americans in Arizona, Florida, or California, web lefse must be a blessing.

LEFSE'S INGREDIENTS AND BASIC METHODS

"Lefse" is an umbrella term; lefse itself is not simple either in ingredients or method of cookery. The most popular form of lefse has potatoes as the main ingredient, but beyond that, the ingredients vary. There needs to be a binder, which might be butter, whipping cream, margarine, lard, or shortening. Salt and sugar are also generally called for. Beyond this basic template, many variations abound. And while lefse may be a culinary artifact that Norwegian Americans savor, it is in the details that divisions and battle lines are drawn. Each variation on the theme has its own evangelists and detractors.

Mashed Potatoes versus Riced Potatoes

Any "real" lefse maker has her own preference for her potatoes. Generally, the russets have to be peeled first, then boiled to softness, but definite lines are drawn as to whether the next step involves ricing the potatoes or not. Whoever is giving the recipe insists that her method produces a more desirable lefse.

Real Potatoes versus Instant Potatoes

Any true-to-form lefse maker would prefer to use russets that are not instant. There is pride in not taking short cuts when preparing holiday foods. However, with the aging population of lefse makers and the simultaneous instant-gratification tendencies of the newer generations of lefse makers, more and more instant potatoes are being regarded as a nice way to take some of the work out of the project. The slight difference in taste is often noted. The potatoes then need to be cooled, either in a refrigerator or on the counter (some argue that overnight cooling is best). If instant potatoes are used, there is still a debate pending: flakes or buds. As with all things lefse, these two forms of dried potato also have their distinct sets of fans.

Butter, Margarine, Shortening, Cream, or Lard

After the potatoes have been cooked and mashed and/or riced, the binder needs to be added. Some recipes call for adding it while the potatoes are still warm, arguing that the flavors mix more thoroughly. Some recipes ask for just one of the binders, some ask for a combination of them. The ratio of binder to potato varies greatly from recipe to recipe because of personal tastes. An attempt at mathematical simplification of this ratio would be insulting to the craft itself.

Sugar and Salt

These are both often-seen ingredients in lefse recipes, but not all recipes call for sugar. Some cooks have told me that powdered sugar makes for a smoother, softer lefse. Other cooks have told me that sugar is to never touch lefse, either in the making or the dressing. Salt is standard for every recipe that I have read.

Cooking Lefse

Once the ingredients have been assembled and flour added, the mixture is kneaded by hand into a dough consistency. Next, after chilling, the dough is rolled to a thinness of just millimeters, which takes muscle, skill, a floured sock over your rolling pin, and a well-floured pastry cloth. The lefse round is then carefully turned and rolled onto a lefse stick (often a smooth yardstick, but lefse sticks can be purchased) for carrying to the preheated, ungreased griddle, where it is then unrolled and toasted on both sides. The desired affect is a lefse round that is white, slightly speckled with brown spots, and pliant.

Eating Lefse

Lefse is eaten is a variety of ways, and the different manners of serving it provides for some lively conversation. The first time I tried lefse, I didn't know what I was doing. The person I was sitting with at the diner, a hardy North Dakota boy, said, "Put butter on it." And so I did. "No, more." And I did. "No, more. Act like you mean it." I began to think that lefse was an excuse for butter. He then showed me how to fold it up into a pie-slice shape and eat it. But this fellow never mentioned sugar on the lefse.

For Norwegian Americans, lefse is often a traditional accompaniment to lutefisk, but it also can stand independently as part of a larger meal setting. Generally, the round is buttered, folded, and eaten. Other factions insist that rolling the lefse after dressing it is the proper method. Some families prefer it with sugar sprinkled on, and extravagant folks even use cinnamon sugar. There are serious divisions in lefse-eating communities about the "proper" way to eat your lefse. My friend Liz (Morken) Tollefson said that nobody under her father's roof would *ever* be allowed to sugar a lefse. "You'd be seen to the door," she told me.

Tasting Lefse

The sensory reaction to lefse is quite varied. Plain, it is rather bland and unassuming. With melted butter and sugar and/or cinnamon, it certainly is a bit tastier. The charm of lefse escapes some people, even some Norwegians. For example, Susan Taylor, a Norwegian American, wrote a cookbook memoir, in which she describes a visit with a neighbor named Kari: "Even when Kari offered me that staple of peasant fare, lefse, a kind of limp, tepid, floury pancake that tasted exactly like boiled flannel, I managed to choke it down."[13]

Other Lefses

Some lefse (which falls under the more inclusive label of "flatbread" or "flotbrod") does not have potatoes at all. These more rare versions are concoctions of various ingredients including sour cream, corn syrup, lemon rind, and milk. In my personal collection of regional cookbooks, I have a little book named "Scandinavian Recipes: Norse-Svensk," made entirely of mimeod blue construction paper, created by the Scandinavian Heritage Group in Grafton, North Dakota.[14] There are nine recipes for lefse—potato lefse, low cholesterol lefse, and *milk* lefse. In a nonpotato lefse, flour is the main ingredient. Mrs. Helmer Haug contributed her version of milk lefse for the project:

Milk Lefse

5 cups whole milk
5 cups flour
3 tbsp. sugar
2 tbsp. salt
1 cup lard
1 cup shortening

Put shortening in pan and melt, then add milk, let come to a boil, for 5–10 minutes. Pour this while boiling, over flour, sugar, and salt, a little at a time, stir in well and quickly while milk is hot. Cool well. Add 2 or 3 egg yolks, beaten and about a cup of cream. This will make a much richer and better lefse. If dough is too soft add more flour. Roll out thin as possible. Bake on lefse griddle. This makes about 29 lefse, 10 to 12 inches in diameter. (This is a favorite recipe of Mrs. Ole T. Haug Family).

—Mrs. Helmer Haug

In *The Last Word on Lefse*, Greg Legwold reports a recipe from Bitten Nor-voll called "krinalefse" that also uses flour along with buttermilk, soda, whip-ping cream, lemon rind, sugar, and even cardamom. This particular version of lefse is the only time that I have seen a hint for decorating lefse. Bitten Nor-voll suggests "Design can be made on top with fork."[15]

LEFSE AS TRADITION AND IDENTITY MARKER

Lefse is a cultural production; it is recreated because of a deep sense of loss by the Scandinavian homesteaders and the following generations. It is not a German dish. It is not a Swedish dish. It is not, normally, made by Baptists or Catholics. It belongs primarily to the Norwegian Lutheran population of the upper Midwest.

Every decent Lutheran church cookbook has at least one matriarch's recipe for lefse in it. Every person who makes lefse, and they are becoming the hon-ored few, has her or his recipe that is the best around, by all accounts. While people who barbeque guard their sauce recipes with their lives and chili mak-ers will never reveal their secret ingredients, lefse makers are always more than happy to share a recipe. A yellowed scrap I found gives reference to this prac-tice; it was tucked in a cookbook that I purchased at an auction sale, titled "Bethesda Lefse," and it reads "It wasn't hard tracking down a recipe for lefse this week. The women from United Lutheran Church have their recipe boxes open as they prepare for their lutefisk dinner Sunday at their Camp Shalom on Maple Lake." When I began discussing my interest in lefse, more than ten colleagues jumped to my aid, offering recipes galore. I hadn't even asked for recipes, just a conversation. Another colleague where I currently work prides himself on initiating the newcomers to northwest Minnesota by inviting them to a lefse-making party at his house.

I have theories about this willingness by lefse makers to share their in-gredient lists. First, lefse makers are most often women, and women cooks have a long tradition of recipe sharing in most cultures. Second, and more importantly, it does not matter what the recipe might be; the trick to lefse is perseverance in learning the craft. You could have the best recipe in all of the upper Midwest, but if you cannot roll without tearing the lefse or use the lefse stick properly to carry the paper-thin concoction to the griddle, it won't matter. There are vocal factions about what are "proper" lefse ingredi-ents, but technique is the harder element to isolate. The secret to lefse is the ability to discern, by hard-won experience, whether there is too much flour or too little, whether the griddle is hot enough, or if the mixture is of the right temperature. One must also have the dexterity to roll it thin, turn it onto the stick, carry it, turn it out, and cook the lefse without it falling apart. Skill is the badge of a good lefse maker.

But what about those varied ingredients and the multitude of recipes for lefse? As I mentioned before, there are definite opinions about what goes in lefse: riced/mashed potatoes; regular potatoes/instant potatoes; sugar/no sugar; cream/lard; margarine/butter; shortening/no shortening; cinnamon/no cinnamon; pepper/no pepper; white flour/wheat flour. Carrie Young, in her prairie-influenced culinary memoir titled *Prairie Cooks: Glorified Rice, Three Day Buns, and Other Reminiscences*, recalls how unique lefse could be: "The women in our small farm community each made such distinctive lefse that you could almost close your eyes, take a bite, and tell who had baked it. My mother's lefse was very rich with butter and cream, and it came off the range still rather moist inside. Some of the women liked theirs thicker or thinner or drier or browner. One or two even put sugar in, which my mother thought was a sin."[16] The ability to identify a cook by her lefse speaks to the intimacy of the community, but it also speaks to the power traditional foods hold. The women cooks are the keepers of the traditions, whether they want to be or not. They contribute to the very fiber of community by providing lefse for the holiday table. Carrie Young describes a town so intimate with the talents of its citizens that town members knew different lefses by taste alone. And while one might be able to appreciate other people's lefse, only the lefse from *your* family tradition was truly good. "You have to hate everyone else's lefse," says Liz Tollefson. Solidarity.

Lefse making is hard, messy work. Flour floats all about the room, ingredients abound, griddles must be kept hot, and cooling racks, lefse turning sticks, pastry cloths, and rolling pins crowd the work surface. When I have talked about lefse making with acquaintances and friends who are of the grandmother generation, I get the distinct feeling that some of these women liked the product but not the process. Some of them enjoyed the attention received from adoring, ravenous family members. Others just made the lefse out of a sense of obligation. And when this happens, when people do work because it is simply expected of them without gaining joy from that activity, it is then that the maker and the product begin to be folded into one another by the observers and consumers, unfortunately.

Like the Little Lefse Maker in the Fisher graveyard, the women became their food. In *The Last Word on Lefse*, Legwold writes "Grandma was a lot like lefse, I suppose: There was nothing about either to dislike, and plenty to love. Just as potatoes and lefse seemed to be always on the table and always warm, so was Grandma: always there and always warm to every member of the family."[17] While I can appreciate the comparison and nostalgic sentiment that Legwold is trying to evoke, I also find it alarming that he can equate a woman and a dish so easily. Lefse is a food that is consumed. And if Grandma is lefse, then she, too, is consumed. We do not know from Legwold's book if Grandma Legwold liked making lefse; we simply know that she did so. Legwold's equation between a woman and her dish is not uncommon. Interestingly enough, Legwold himself, in anguish over his inability to turn out a perfect lefse round, longs to hear the reassuring words, "You are not your lefse."[18] While this is humorous enough, it is noteworthy that the thought that he clings to himself he does not transfer to his own grandmother. I would argue that she is not her lefse, either.

Antonia Till asserts in her Introduction to *Loaves and Wishes* that women "are burdened with the necessity of providing food for their families, day after day, week after week, year after year . . . any failure to do this with good grace is readily equated with a failure of love."[19] Legwold sees the lefse, he sees his grandmother, and he equates love with both. A few of the women lefse makers that I have spoken to feel also that sometimes their families at holiday times appreciate the lefse more than them as members of the family. Lefse making is hard work, and some makers feel resentment at the expectation that they will produce, year after year. One woman, who wished that I not use her name, said to me, "If they love me so much, why don't they ask me to put down my rolling pin and join them in the front room?"

On the other hand, if a woman's responsibilities are the work of the kitchen, as was for these older generations, it can also be in the kitchen that a sense of self is developed, an identity with production is created, and a contribution to the community fostered. In anthropological and sociological studies, the assertion has been made that belonging to a community is enhanced by the sharing of food. Anna Meigs notes that "food and eating are intimately connected with cultural conceptions of self. Food as object and eating as act resonate with attitudes and emotions related to the individual's understandings and feelings about self and other and the relationship between."[20] Making food for others and sharing a table crosses cultures generates good will and engagement in a community. A majority of the time, the women that I have spoken to take pride in their lefse skills and don't begrudge the work.

Anthropologists and sociologists have repeatedly noted that the work of daily food production has been the domain of women.[21] Mary Douglas, a noted anthropologist, has argued in several forums for the close examination of the social and cultural aspects of daily food beyond the obvious studies of holiday feasting and public gatherings.[22] In America, the field of folklore studies was one of the first to attempt a serious look at foodways, but this movement has only developed in the last two decades. While studying food as a biologically necessary element for survival may be "undeserving" of deep analysis, the "social imperatives that accompany it [food]" can be fruitful areas of research.[23]

RITUAL LEFSE

Food produced for holiday fare, like lefse, can also have a ritual element. The phenomenon of lefse is indicative of patterns associated with many other cultures and many other foods. Beliefs and values can be perpetuated by foods associated with particular communities. Pamela R. Frese proposes that these "beliefs and practices can be divided into two related aspects: the gender qualities associated with particular types of food and the importance attached to food because it is associated with the private sphere of women and the family."[24] She goes on to note that because food and its preparation for special events is acknowledged in some cultures as "sacred female knowledge," ritual foods have come to mirror intricate and culturally bound associations with reproduction and social life. I am not proposing that we regard lefse as sacred or that lefse making is a knowledge imparted only to women; however, as a repository of cultural knowledge, lefse holds a staunch place in a world that is rapidly losing its sense of community, place, and connectedness. Lefse makers are still sought out by their communities when traditions are most dear.

Lefse is an indicator of a larger socially constructed framework: meaning generated by generations. The ingredients and methods of lefse making are passed down through the layers of family, much like photographs, names, and other traditions. Gwen Kennedy Neville, author of *Kinship and Pilgrimage: Rituals of Reunion in American Protestant Culture*, asserts from her observations at family reunions that food obtains its meaning because it is created by multiple generations of women: "While these [holiday or ritual foods] may have originally been functional foods, popular items in the country, or easily affordable foods in Depression times, they are in the 1980s not necessarily easy, popular, or affordable. They are instead, symbolic. They are carefully prepared by each mother and presented as her contribution to the whole. They are consumed primarily by others. . . . The sharing of food prepared by others is highly symbolic in the expression of oneness as the family."[25] Feeding one's family by evoking heritage and tradition has also been called "kin work" by some scholars who have studied the power of the invisible work that women often contribute to a family structure.[26]

The contribution of special foods, such as lutefisk and lefse for Norwegian Americans, links women inextricably to the task of maintaining historical and generational ties by producing food and presenting it to the community/family. Such ritual or ceremony gives women a specific ritual function that is visible and appreciated by those who partake of it. Sidney Mintz asserts that the traditional, ritual food is "always conditioned by meaning. These meanings are symbolic, and communicated symbolically; they also have histories."[27] Because lefse is a winter holiday food, and because lefse has its artisans and historians, and because lefse recipes are passed from generation to generation as part of larger family traditions, lefse has meaning. When we recognize that this food is a product of many hundreds of laboring "little lefse makers," we begin to realize the influence and importance that these Norwegian American Lutheran women have in their communities and families.

As the producers of special food, these women perform the task of maintaining and preserving some of the social customs for these towns and parishes. Society creates itself, in part, by its food rituals. Lefse is accepted as "good food" by many people in and outside of the Norwegian community in the upper Midwest, but it has not crossed over into mainstream cooking habits like the Mexican tortilla.[28] Lefse remains Norwegian, Lutheran, and from the upper Midwest. In general, the recognition of foods and their acceptability is what defines a culture: "Food—what is chosen from the possibilities available, how it is presented, how it is eaten, with whom and when, and how much time is allotted to cooking and eating it—is one of the means by which a society creates itself. . . . Food shapes us and expresses us even more than our furniture or houses or utensils do," claims Visser. [29]

My first introduction to the idea of lefse, in the bar in Twin Falls, Idaho, is a testament to this reality. The man who initiated me into the basics of Norwegian American habits decided that the *first thing* that I should know about the extreme upper Midwest was lutefisk and lefse. I had never heard the words before, and I certainly had never tasted them before. If I had joined the North Dakota/Minnesota community and revealed that I had no idea what these important foods were, I would have surely marked myself even more glaringly as an outsider. But because I knew the words and could talk about the food and ask about the traditions respectfully, despite never having tasted them at the time, I could engage many people in a way that otherwise would have eluded me. The elders actually welcomed my questions; they told me that they were impressed that I even knew those foods existed at all.

PUBLIC AND PRIVATE LEFSE

Men do not traditionally participate in the making of the lefse. Overwhelmingly, this is the work of women. Sometimes, a man is a lefse artisan, but not often. More often, I have been told, the man's job is to praise the work of his wife, bragging about the taste, quantity, and lacy-thinness of her work. Occasionally, a man will help rather than be left out of the flurry of activity in the kitchen at holiday time, but men in many cultures often help with festival foods because the work is more glamorous in those settings.

Mary Weismantel, in her essay "Commentary: A Well-Cooked Sauce," asserts that cooking can be a "gendered paradigm in which male work is seen as contributing to the larger public good: when men cook, they do so for the wealthy and powerful, or even for the gods. Men make public ceremony: the emphasis is upon the visible, the show. Female work in such analyses belongs to the domestic sphere and is intended for daily consumption: it is the invisible, the taken-for-granted."[30] This idea of lefse as an invisible domestic task taken for granted was discussed earlier in this essay. Lefse made for private family affairs is generally produced by women.

A perfect example of "public lefse" occurred in Starbuck, Minnesota, in 1983. A group of nine men calling themselves "The Boys of Starbuck" took on the challenge of making the world's largest lefse. They accomplished their goal, making a lefse nine feet eight inches by nine feet one inch. Mixed from thirty pounds of instant potatoes, thirty-five pounds of flour, one pound of sugar, one pound of powdered milk, and four pounds of shortening, it was rolled by a pin made of twelve-foot pipe with a circumference of 3.14 feet. It was then grilled on steel sheets ten feet by twenty feet. About 1,000 spectators turned out to see these men have fun, roll and cook lefse, and partake of the results.[31]

What did the women think of the largest lefse? When asked this question, June Olson, also of Starbuck, simply said, "Imagine a nine-foot lefse made by men who never make lefse."[32]

Another kind of public lefse is that which is produced en masse for smorgasbords, church feasts, and other ethnic/heritage festivals. Generally, I have observed that because of the magnitude of the events and the hundreds upon hundreds of lefse needed, everyone pitches in to help. At these events, however, there is generally a lefse matriarch "in charge," who keeps everyone moving and rolling and baking.

SCRIPTED LEFSE

We have the recipes, stored away on tattered cards, in church cookbooks, or in messy drawers full of other scraps of paper. This part of the artifact is the "how-to" for the cultural production. Like music that is printed on the sheet, the interpretation of the written cues is what makes an artist. Like a play written on parchment, it is only when the play comes alive through interpretation and execution that we recognize the genius.

When we encounter scraps of recipes, we begin to realize that the recipe writer assumes a cultural base (indeed, an entire ethnic and culinary training) from her readership. For example, in the cookbook called *Our Recipes*[33] produced by the Bethel Women's Missionary Fellowship of Grand Forks, North Dakota, the lefse recipe is simply this:

Potato Lefse

3 cups mashed potatoes
1 cup flour
1/2 cup shortening (margarine)
1 tsp. sugar
1/2 tsp. baking powder
1 tsp. salt.

Potatoes must be cold before flour is added.

—Mrs. R. Teige

This recipe is similarly bereft of details; it is taken out of *Scandinavian Recipes*, courtesy Ruth C. Holt:[34]

Lefse

4 cups mashed potatoes
1/3 cup melted shortening (Crisco)
1/2 cup whipping cream (heated)
2 tsp. salt
1 tsp. sugar
2 cups flour (after potatoes are cooled)

—Ruth C. Holt

We may not think, at first glance, that these recipes tell us much of anything. The order of mixing ingredients is missing. We don't even know if the potatoes should be peeled. We are not instructed at all what to do with this mixture. There is no mention of a pastry cloth, a rolling pin, lefse stick, or the griddle and its temperature. Despite the lack of detail, these recipes speak to us in volumes. Indeed, the assumptions made by Mrs. R. Teige and Ruth C. Holt about who will use this recipe and what that cook should already know reveal the deeply held belief that any worthy home cook could take it from here. If you need lefse lessons, these cookbooks are not the place. Go fetch an apprenticeship with a lefse maker if you don't know how to make lefse. The cue cards are in place here, but the action on the stage has been left from the script. The actors should know their parts already. But the lack of instructions is not meant to be cruel or unthoughtful. Lefse makers need to learn from each other, generation to generation, standing next to each other in the kitchen with floured arms and hands, hot griddles, and melted butter.

Again and again, recipes that aren't "complete" denote the cook's bias about the cookbook buyer. The cook's voice implies that the reader should already know the method; her contribution here is a variation. For example, Mrs. Lloyd Slatten contributed a lefse recipe to the cookbook efforts of the Mountain Ladies Aid of Adams Lutheran Church of Adams, North Dakota.

Lefse

4 cups mashed potatoes
1/3 cup shortening
1/2 cup heated cream
1 tsp. salt
1 tsp. sugar
2 1/2 cups flour

Mix and cool first 5 ingredients before adding 1/2 to 3/4 cup flour. Use rest of flour for rolling.

Like the recipes above, in order to cook this dish, we must have already mastered lefse. This is not a recipe for beginners because no detailed explanations or instructions are given. What does this mean? It indicates that the writers of the cookbook did not expect the cookbook to travel beyond their own culinary community, a community that already understood the intricacies of lefse making. These recipes are made for an internal audience of other cooks who are already competent lefse makers, such bare recipes also imply that the cook reading the recipes can see and interpret the unwritten elements. In this recipe exchange, as with so many other church cookbooks from small communities, the unspoken and unwritten takes up volumes.

No matter how humble or slick these church/community cookbooks appear, their very existence demands self-revelation by the individual to support the needs of a community. The premise behind the genre is that each person voluntarily contributes one or more recipes for a publication that will have, most likely, a limited distribution (mainly in the immediate geographic area) with the possibility that the recipes will be purchased by people outside of that community as well. As such, these cookbooks reveal the standards and habits of food habits for a particular group in a decidedly public forum, making them depositories of social and historical information. In her essay about compiled cookbooks, Lynne Ireland labels them as "autobiography."[35] The compiled cookbook is a revelation to the public about one aspect of family and community life as meditated by the sharing of recipes. The recipes' texts, then, are a reflection of their own cookery styles and preferences.

The only place that I have ever seen the entire process for making lefse documented from beginning to end is in Greg Legwold's book. His mission is clear: to make lefse learning available to those who do not have a mentor to learn from. It takes him fifteen pages of detailed instructions, analysis, photos, and conversation about various methods before the process is adequately detailed. His book documents his struggle to conquer the lefse, and he means to pass on the elusive details. At the end of his work, he passes on lefse variations from eighteen different cooks—some are individuals and some are groups. Each recipe is a marker of years of experience, participation in a community, or perhaps a relationship with another woman who has passed on her recipe.

Would these women have been recognized for their cultural contributions had Legwold not written his book? Of course. The only reason Legwold was able to find lefse tales was because those people had been previously identified as the gurus by other community members. When he researched his topic by having conversations with various town members, he was pointed to the noteworthy lefse makers without hesitation.

GALLERY LEFSE

When a cultural production is as ultimately temporary as food is, a consuming audience is essential to pass on the tradition and its stories. It is important to recognize that the women are most often responsible for maintaining traditions within families by recreating foodstuffs, but it is also those foodstuffs that disappear as soon as the meal is served, and therefore must be constantly recreated. Folk food, ethnic food, regional food—these are all cultural productions that need to be heeded as art, just as other folk arts are.

We cannot frame a round of lefse. We cannot piece it into a quilt. It cannot be displayed on the shelf. It is not a piece of furniture that can be passed down. It will not hang in an art gallery. The best we can do is to write it down. Lefse is transitory in its very nature, but it makes its mark in the mind. Traditional food is a temporary, tactile memory that is directly connected to particular people or groups. Lefse is a complicated food with a long history. Those who make it are carefully trained, and the field itself has noted practitioners and artisans. Artisans? Is lefse making an art?

It is not unfamiliar to hear the phrase "the art of cooking," whether listening to a radio cooking show, watching a cooking segment on a morning talk program, reading an article, or perusing a cookbook. The phrase has become a cliché. If cooking is truly an art, however, why are not the artists lauded and recognized for their daily work? Over the last few years, artisan breads have created a niche market in the supermarket aisles. Why not other traditional breads? Interestingly enough, Martha Stewart, the maven of homemaking, received a lesson in Norwegian cooking from Beatrice Ojakangas for a televised episode of *Martha Stewart Living* in the winter of 1999. Perhaps lefse will become chic, not just folksy.

But when is it art and when is it regional food or folk material? Don Yoder, folklorist, wrote a chapter in *Folklore and Folklife: An Introduction* entitled "Folk Cookery" wherein he defines folk cookery as "traditional domestic cookery marked by regional variations."[36] He also addresses the function of folk cookery and describes that function: "Like all aspects of folk culture it [folk cookery] was related, integrally and functionally, to all other phases of the culture, and in its elaboration became, like dress and architecture, a work of art."[37] Folk cookery, the food preparation habits and practices of cooks, is also artistically bounded by rules of structure and form, but it also must reflect and/or enhance the social setting.[38] Lefse is most definitely bounded by rules and forms because it is considered a winter food, a holiday food, a family food, and an ethnic food. Structure and form for production and consumption formulate the very basis for lefse making and eating.

Another folklorist, Charles Camp, speculates that if cooking is, indeed, an art, it is not counted among the national treasures because it "is not an elective art to which one may feel a calling" like the making of lace or composing literature or music. Rather, it is "a compulsory domestic skill . . . based on the unforgiving premise that one who cooks is consistently and quietly good at it."[39] The culinary artist, then, driven by community and family tradition, performs her art daily without recognition and to an audience that, generally, demands production and ignores artistry. Every now and again, culinary artisans of lefse are recognized by a trip to the Smithsonian for an ethnic celebration, or by important visiting politicians of Norway, or by a small TV spot. But lefse making is a dying art, when it comes right down to it.

The people who make the foods of memories are the perpetuators of tradition. The hundreds of lefse makers are keeping regional food, folk art, and the ethnic heritage alive. Those around them value them for their specialized culinary skills because those talents keep customs alive. Lefse is exile food that ties immigrant families back to the past and the old country, simultaneously looking to the future by carrying forth a cultural marker. By a taste alone, the lefse artist can be recognized by her followers, and lefse makers have their interns. They pass on their skills, secrets, and recipes, hoping that the next generation will keep the tradition alive. In the end, lefse is a cultural indicator of a set of larger social phenomena that defines the Norwegian American Lutheran tradition of the upper Midwest.

As an Idahoan of Irish heritage that wandered into the Norwegian ethnic enclave of northern Minnesota and North Dakota, I have become very aware of how lefse, as a regional food, defines communities, parishes, and families. I would never make the claim that I am a lefse connoisseur or artisan. But I do know how to listen and observe others when they speak of their lefse. I have come to recognize how much foodstuffs can mean when people are struggling to keep their culture. While I am still in a quandary as whether to sugar my lefse or not, I have discovered that it is just best to watch the people around me as they eat their lefse, and I try to follow suit. My personal preference? Pass the sugar and cinnamon, please.

NOTES

1. Sidney W. Mintz, *Tasting Food, Tasting Freedom: Excursions into Eating, Culture, and the Past* (Boston: Beacon, 1996), 103.

2. Lutefisk is cod steeped in lye, then well rinsed for serving. It is white, slightly gelatinous, and has a strong scent. It is traditional Norwegian holiday fare, but I have met only a few who actually enjoy it. However, there is enough of a population who eat it still that various groups continue to have fund-raising dinners with lutefisk and lefse as the main draw. In some restaurants, it is offered as a Sunday special during the winter months.

3. Greg Legwold, *The Last Word on Lefse* (Cambridge, Minn.: Adventure, 1992), 56–57.

4. Joan Nathan, *An American Folklife Cookbook* (New York: Schocken, 1984), 299.

5. Lefse itself remains constant. However, uses for lefse are affected by other culinary influences. For example, in community compiled cookbooks are recipes for "lefse tacos," wherein the lefse is filled with lettuce, browned hamburger, tomatoes, onions, cheese, and the mildest of mild taco sauces. (Norwegians don't like spicy foods, and the taco sauce is often "cut" with catsup.) Lefse can also be filled with eggs and sausage for breakfast, egg salad, or other concoctions.

6. Nathan, *An American Folklife Cookbook*, 299.

7. P. G. Kittler and Kathleen Sucher, *Food and Culture in America: A Nutrition Handbook* (New York: VanNostrand Reinhold, 1989).

8. Elaine N. McIntosh, *American Food Habits in Historical Perspective* (Westport, Conn.: Praeger, 1995), 186.

9. Harriet Light and Peggy Houge, eds., *A Tribute to North Dakota Families* (Fargo, N.D.: Richtman's Printing, 1990), 33.

10. Light and Houge, *A Tribute to North Dakota Families*, 34.

11. Legwold, *The Last Word on Lefse*, 62.

12. Cathy Luchetti, *Home on the Range: A Culinary History of the American West* (New York: Villard, 1993), 112.

13. Susan Taylor, *Young and Hungry: A Cookbook in the Form of a Memoir* (Boston: Houghton Mifflin, 1971), 58.

14. Scandinavian Heritage Society, *Scandinavian Recipes: Norse-Svensk* (1984).

15. Legwold, *The Last Word on Lefse*, 157.

16. Carrie Young and Felicia Young, *Prairie Cooks: Glorified Rice, Three-Day Buns, and Other Reminiscences* (Iowa City: University of Iowa Press, 1993), 5. For an in-depth look at women's culinary memoirs, see Traci Marie Kelly, "If I Were a Voodoo Priestess," *Kitchen Culture in America: Popular Representations of Food, Gender, and Race*, ed. Sherrie A. Inness (Philadelphia: University of Pennsylvania Press, 2001).

17. Legwold, *The Last Word on Lefse*, 8–9.

18. Legwold, *The Last Word on Lefse*, 9.

19. Antonia Till, Introduction, *Loves and Wishes: Writers Writing on Food*, ed. Antonia Till (London: Virago, 1992), ix–xi.

20. Anna Miegs, "Food as a Cultural Construction," *Food and Foodways* 2 (1988): 352.

21. See Bettina Aptheker, *Tapestries of Life: Women's Works, Women's Consciousness, and the Meaning of Daily Experience* (Amherst: University of Massachusetts Press, 1989) and D. E. Smith, *The Everyday World as Problematic: A Feminist Sociology* (Boston: Northeastern University Press, 1987).

22. Meigs, "Food as a Cultural Construction," 352.

23. Charles Camp, *American Foodways: What, When, Why and How We Eat in America*, ed. W. K. McNeil (Little Rock, Ark.: Little Rock August House, 1989). Camp defines "foodways" as the "intersection of food and culture; all aspects of food which are culture-based, as well as all aspects of culture which use or refer to food." People who are involved in "foodways studies" are "people who balance a comprehension of food as a system of symbols and sustenance with an abiding curiosity about and respect for the cultures that structure its meanings." I accept his definitions for my purposes.

24. Pamela R. Frese, "Food and Gender in America: A Review Essay," *Food and Foodways* 5.2 (1992): 205–11.

25. Gwen Kennedy Neville, *Kinship and Pilgrimage: Rituals of Reunion in American Protestant Culture* (New York: Oxford University Press, 1987), 72.

26. Michaela de Leonardo, *The Varieties of Ethnic Experience: Kinship, Class and Gender among California Italian Americans* (Ithaca, N.Y.: Cornell University Press, 1984).

27. Mintz, *Tasting Food, Tasting Freedom*, 7.

28. McIntosh, *American Food Habits*, 185. The other markedly regional food, lutefisk, has not been embraced outside this tight enclave; indeed, the claim has been made that lutefisk is the most *rejected* traditional food from Scandinavia.

29. Margaret Visser, *Much Depends on Dinner: The Extraordinary History and Mythology, Allure and Obsessions, Perils and Taboos of an Ordinary Meal* (Toronto: McClelland and Steward, 1986), 12.

30. Mary Weismantel, "Commentary: A Well-Cooked Sauce," *CommuNicAtor* 20.1 (1996): 15.

31. Legwold, *The Last Word on Lefse*, 35–47.

32. Legwold, *The Last Word on Lefse*, 84.

33. Bethel Women's Missionary Fellowship, *Our Recipes* (Grand Forks, N.D.: 1977).

34. Scandinavian Heritage Society, *Scandinavian Recipes: Norse-Svensk* (Grafton, N.D.: 1984).

35. Lynne Ireland, "The Compiled Cookbook as Foodways Autobiography," *Western Folklore* 40.2 (1981).

36. Don Yoder, "Folk Cookery," *Folklore and Folklife: An Introduction*, ed. Richard M. Dorson (Chicago: University of Chicago Press, 1972), 325.

37. Yoder, "Folk Cookery," 338.

38. William Woys Weaver, *America Eats: Forms of Edible Folk Art* (New York: Harper-Collins, 1989), 40–41.

39. Camp, *American Foodways*, 49.

• 3 •

"I Am an Act of Kneading": Food and the Making of Chicana Identity

Benay Blend

During the 1960s and 1970s, Chicana feminists began to question the portrait of the so-called Ideal Chicana drawn by Chicano cultural nationalists.[1] This stereotype reflected an ideology that equated Chicano cultural survival with the glorification of traditional gender roles for Chicanas. As a result, emerging Chicana feminists challenged this narrow concept of the family, with its traditional role of women as producers and reproducers of the race.[2] While Chicana feminists challenged domesticity as a space that demeans or diminishes women, others, when confronted with women's traditional art, found that their sympathies were torn. Wanting at the same time to honor and lament, Chicana feminists continue their struggle to change cultural definitions by using mundane activities as metaphors for an agenda of larger social issues. "I am an act of kneading," writes Gloria Anzaldúa,[3] calling attention not only to her *mestiza* heritage but also the power of certain foodways, in this case the grinding of corn for such dishes as tortillas and tamales, to act as sites of resistance to the dominant culture through which Chicanas can affirm and strengthen cultural identity. Moreover, because foodways are never static, but are constantly changing, much like culture, both activities offer an important venue in which to examine how tamale- and tortilla-making can act as a site of resistance to cultural hegemony. At the same time, the food-making process itself is in a constant state of change, creating new forms of tortilla/tamale hybrids.

This chapter explores how tortilla- and tamale-making provides an arena of performance in which statements about race, class, and gender issues can be made. It addresses how each author claims or reclaims culinary rituals, some by transforming them or creating new ones out of personal and collective rituals, others by generating themes that are essentially domestic, yet nevertheless convey controversial ideas about women's experiences. Not only has preparation of this food been traditionally associated with women's domain, it also connotes a sense of art, aesthetics, creativity, symbolism, communication, social propriety, and celebration within the Chicana(o) community. That being the case, it follows that evoking images of preparing and eating tortillas/tamales might serve various ends, including political ones, as in sociologist Teresa Martinez's memories of her mother's kitchen. In "Tortilla-Making as Feminist Action," Martinez writes: "She was truly a master of this fine art. . . . For me, these were her most delicious creations, and they came to symbolize my culture, my family, and especially my mother."[4] Because of her recognition of the artistic dimensions of foodways, Martinez enlarges the so-called fine arts to include the traditional, collective, domestic crafts that are usually associated with women. By focusing on how preparing, serving, and eating food provides a basis for interaction, this chapter reveals much about Chicana's position within a communal context while at the same time maintaining individuality.

As a basic necessity of survival and therefore a central aspect of everyday life, food plays a prominent role in the manipulation of the Southwestern environment and serves as an entry into the history, culture and identity of not only women tied to that environment but those who carry its traditions elsewhere. In *Cocina de la Familia*, a cookbook that honors Mexican-descended people continuing to celebrate their traditions in the diaspora, Marilyn Tausend notes that tamales represent most distinctly a direct generational link to Mexico, an attempt to duplicate as much as possible rituals that assert women's duty—and authority—to nourish their families.[5] As Jeffrey Pilcher notes, traditional Mesoamerican cooking, which required kneeling for hours to grind up corn and shape tortillas, probably originated in the central highlands of Mexico. Serving as eating utensils and also plates, tortillas wrapped around meat or vegetable fillings to form a taco resulted in a variety of regional cuisines that provided basic sustenance but also aesthetic nourishment in a merciless environment. Too often devalued by modern nutritionists as merely as source of carbohydrates, as Jeffrey Pilcher notes, these maize griddle cakes manifested remarkable epicurean qualities as women toasted their ingredients first on a *comal* (griddle). While tortillas served as a daily staple, tamales, which probably originated in the central valley of Mexico (c.250 B.C.–A.D. 750), offered women an opportunity to indulge their gastronomic imagination at festive gatherings. Cooks created them by spreading corn dough within a husk, adding chile sauce along with meat or beans, then shaping the sealed package into ovals, canoes, animals or stellar constellations to be steamed in an *olla*.[6] Perhaps the most fundamental work of women, the one most obviously tied to maintenance, centered around processing corn into tortillas and tamales. The effort and time involved in processing and the love of the land which produced it imbued this staple with a symbolic significance that is reflected today in Chicana writing.

In her study of Hispanic village women throughout the Southwest during the early twentieth century, Sarah Deutsch has described the raising of food and providing for families as a female responsibility. In their productive work, she continues, women achieved an autonomous base and, simultaneously, integration into the village as producers of food. As in religion and in the family, both mutuality and symmetry characterized the sexual division of labor.[7] Moreover, wherever Mexicans settled in the United States, the *tamalada* that, as Pilcher notes, originated in nineteenth-century Mexico as a picnic expressly for eating tamales,[8] continues to create an opportunity for women to express and reinforce values regarding food and food making. In San Antonio, Donna Gabaccia notes that groups of female kin annually prepare several dozen of the corn husk–wrapped steamed masa for the Christmas season. Because they choose to use traditional methods the work often takes all day: rinsing of the corn husks without cracking them, grinding corn for the masa, cooking either chicken or pork, smearing the husks with cornmeal, adding meat, and finally binding each folded corn wrapper to steam in a pot that is filled with water.[9]

In *"Una Tamalada*: The Special Event," educator M. H. de la Peña Brown focuses on a brief experience to explore how tamale-making fosters a spirit of unity and community that enriches also the individual's sense of self-worth and dignity.[10] Brown demonstrates that food conveys meaning as well as nourishment. Thus not only the tamales, but the preparation, the rituals, the smells, and the seasonal association are forms of cultural expression and identity. In Santa Fe, New Mexico, where blue corn tamales are stuffed with green chiles or served with a green chile sauce, they are often served on New Year's Eve around a huge bonfire offset by the lights of *farolito* (paper bags containing candles held in sand).[11] Intricately tied up with Southwest cuisine, then, especially for those of Mexican descent, like Gloria Anzaldúa, are meanings of culture and self-identity: "For me," Anzaldúa writes, "food and certain smells are tied to my identity, to my homeland. . . . Homemade white cheese sizzling in a pan, melting outside a folded *tortilla*. . . . My mouth salivates at the thought of the hot steaming *tamales* I would be eating if I were home."[12] In answer to Roger Abrahams' query: "Is there any question that the currencies of primary importance in our culture are three—food, sex, talk,"[13] this chapter highlights those three categories. Specifically, I explore what might be termed tortilla/tamale discourse. While replete with contradictions, it acts as a symbol of cultural resiliency that enables self-assertion at the same time it celebrates tortilla/tamale-making as a woman-centered, role-affirming communal ritual that empowers women as the carriers of tradition.

This chapter will address not so much the way Chicanas prepare their food as the ways in which writers such as Ana Castillo, Sheila Ortiz Taylor, and Gloria Anzaldúa use literary images of tortillas and tamales to interrogate and challenge certain stereotypes both within and without the culture. The Chicana writer, who is in a double bind, restrained within her own and the dominant culture's patriarchal stereotype, must reformulate her heritage to claim a new relationship between herself and the Chicana(o) community. On the one hand, for example, as Brett Williams observes, tamales represent an important oral tradition involving women's personal identity and position within the family.[14] Cookbook author Marilyn Tausend agrees. Not only are tamales fiesta food, Tausend asserts, but because of the work involved, *la tamalada* nearly always calls for communal effort that results in camaraderie. As friends and family gather they pass on, along with the latest gossip, certain cultural values and traditions.[15]

In the same vein, M. H. de la Peña recalls in *"Una Tamalada"* that a woman's ability to make good *"masa para embarrar"* (dough with the correct consistency for spreading) is a skill to be imitated. Though the woman who was honored with the position of beating the masa at this *tamalada* had been a homemaker noted for her own tamales for over twenty-five years, she still relinquishes this job to her mother, "the perfectionist," when she comes to visit. Such cultural practices are a means of locating the individual with respect to a sense of community and ethnic traditions, as evidenced in the comments of another participant at this event. "When we are together, we are like equals," she asserts. "No one is better. Making tamales is a good time to show children how good it is to be in union with each other." Such a recuperation of a female legacy enables self-worth to those elders most skilled in tamale-making while at the same time obligating all "to help each other. Even if one is poor, one is obligated to help a less fortunate person at this family's *tamaladas*."[16]

In *Food and the Making of Mexican Identity*, Jeffrey Pilcher notes that such culinary skills were recognized by men who "complemented women by praising their tortillas and some claimed to be able to identify the unique taste and texture of their wives' corn grinding and tortilla making"[17] Here the domestic sphere is a space where women dwell, excel, and create. On the other hand, for Jennie Chávez, who articulates the sentiment of some contemporary feminists, such a "traditional role" reflects "women as tortilla-making baby producers, to be touched but not heard," within the household.[18] In particular, women who participated in the Chicano Rights Movement felt annoyed at being relegated to the kitchen, while men talked, as Lorna Dee Cervantes relates in a poem.[19]

In "You Cramp My Style, Baby," Cervantes turns such a Movement woman into "un taco, dripping grease," a food to be literally consumed by men who "tell [her], / 'Esa I LOVE / this revolution!'" Not recognizing the personal as political, they continue outdated stereotypes by yelling, "Come on Malinche, / gimme more!" (101). No longer the idealized symbol of selflessness, as was Malinche—considered a sellout, as are some Chicana feminists, both because they are seen as assimilated into the dominant culture—Cervantes' narrator breaks away from traditional values of caring for family and standing by her man without abandoning ethnic solidarity or her culture.

Kitchens epitomize a space where cultural and bodily sustenance takes place, but these interior spaces are often enclosing and narrowing. In "The Corn Tortilla," poet Teresa Paloma Acosta redefines the cultural boundaries associated with tortillas that for centuries have constrained its makers. "The corn tortilla," she affirms, "has nothing to do / with a man finding himself a tortillera to marry" who will "agree to fill in the space between / tortillera feedings with / her body laid out upon the floor mat / for him to step over."[20] Refuting the custom that no woman in some Mexican villages was eligible for marriage until she had demonstrated this skill,[21] Acosta also rebels against cultural values that require women to be reproducers rather than shapers of tradition. Tortilla-making has more to do, she says, with the pleasure that "picking / the right hour, comal, mixing bowl" gives her self. A culture that lies within wherever "she calls home at the moment," it nevertheless requires community, time to "leisurely exchange tips / over café."[22] Her invocation of a specific food also speaks against such "fake recipes" as "Diana Kennedy's expensive cookbook" (2) because, Acosta implies, such writers explore the foods of a particular region while severing both from the traditions that they have altered for their own taste. For Acosta, reproducing a recipe, like retelling a story, privileges an "oral tradition cookbook (authors / *mujers;* circa—you name it)" (3). In this way, she recuperates the power to authenticate those voices who have often been anonymous and prohibits further extra cultural access to their knowledge. Caught between the contradictions inherent in her culture, that of tortilla-making as a valuable oral tradition that signifies generational solidarity among women who nevertheless are encouraged to sacrifice their own nourishment for that of others, Acosta seizes authority of this domestic space to provide for her own pleasure and independence.

Despite Acosta's admonition of food writers such as Diana Kennedy, whose *My Mexico*[23] continues American incursions into foreign ground, albeit cultural rather than geographical, not too long ago others considered Mexican food inedible. Moreover, the upper class in nineteenth-century Mexico, historian Jeffrey Pilcher notes, considered tamales, enchiladas, and quesadillas "the food of the lower orders." Class divisions revealed themselves in foods chosen for special occasions. Just as certain Southwestern foods have now been incorporated into mainstream cuisine, so the prevalence of diverse regional dishes, accented by elaborate festival foods seasoned by pungent chiles, ultimately became features of Mexico's national cuisine. But before this happened, it was mostly for the masses that important occasions meant tamales.[24] Chicana "coming of age literature" records that traditional foods valued in the home are even now sometimes a source for ridicule by racially intolerant classmates. As Tiffany Ann Lopez notes, "something as simple as taking a piece of meat wrapped up in a tortilla set me apart. I read of children taking their sandwiches to school," but, perhaps inspiring Lopez' collection, *Growing Up Chicana*, "never in my childhood reading experiences did I read about a child taking a tortilla."[25] In the world of words, Lopez says, Chicanas like herself and others in her anthology found "salvation. [Literature] taught us about ourselves and told us what others would not. It was the permission we needed to realize our dreams."[26] In writing, Lopez finds a haven from reality while describing it, a place where rebellion against traditional domestic order produces neither guilt nor anxiety, but instead creates a different space and the self-expression to go with it.

By inscribing her own meaning, remembering a past that was a basis for the meaning, Lopez formulates a new perspective of what the Chicana perceives herself to be. Others construct such a creative space in defiance of limits imposed by society, thereby finding freedom through their creative imagination. Yet each reflects a central paradox of the domestic space. On the one hand, it defines a territory in which women are honored as the carriers of tradition. On the other, it encloses women within a female space defined by external assumptions. Nevertheless, many women writers, including those covered in this chapter, speak from the peripheries of culture to define a woman-centered identity within a self-described zone of their imaginations.

SELF AND OTHERS: COOKING UP TRADITION

The kitchen can embody such a space of articulation when inhabited by a community that supports, maintains, but also participates in the innovation of tradition. If Chicana writers focus on the diversity of individual experience, they are also women creating and affirming identity through connections. Describing food traditions not only fosters such connections; it also suggests new ways to configure community and family. To remember a recipe is to honor the woman it comes from, how it was passed on to her, and where she situates herself within a culinary female lineage that defies patriarchal notions of genealogy. Food and its preparation is often what is remembered when communities come together.

Food exerts a powerful force in defining a specific Latin milieu. Moreover, tortilla-making, in addition to its creative potential, also connects Chicanas to a world closely associated with the *abuelita*, a grandmother figure who carries on old Mexican customs and cooking. In Alma Villaneuva's autobiographical *Mother, May I?* (section 3), references to tortillas are associated with her recreation of a nostalgic childhood world. Raised by a maternal grandmother until she was eleven years old, a biographical fact that accounts for her close identification with Mexican culture,[27] Villaneuva learns the positive values of her culture at home where the *mamacita* "defines their customs." Together they "pray and dunk *pan dulce* in coffee" and make tortillas,[28] testifying to the connections between tortilla-making and the maternal, nurturing aspects of this private utopian world. In this way, the elder woman passes on tradition that comforts children, but as Marta Sánchez notes, contrasts with the public world that devalues women who are solely nurturers and mothers.[29] Significantly, it is the grandmother who escorts her to school, where "everyone speaks so fast"[30] in English, and Spanish is not tolerated in the classroom. But she realizes her grandmother's was a world in which women of her class were limited to the tortilla-making sphere rather than transforming it into a symbol for ethnic resiliency in their poems. However, Villaneuva knows, too, that the more public, active world no better suits her needs. To obtain the desired vision, to remain part of "the story / [that] connects between . . . grandmothers, mothers, daughters"[31] yet retain the autonomy needed for her work, Villaneuva transforms those lessons learned while helping the grandmother make tortillas into material for her poems. "Dreams of our ancestors," Villaneuva says, gives her the "irrational courage" to write. So neither the grandmother's tortilla-making world, associated with communal, nurturing values, nor the dominant society that she knows has traditionally devalued those aspects of her culture, offer a fulfilling image. By using her sense of "poetry as transformation,"[32] Villaneuva calls on her poetic voice that requires autonomy to remember a collective past that provides a refuge.

In Villaneuva's poem, the writer's identification with her grandmother's tortilla-making connects her to women who came before her. As noted in *"Una Tamalada,"* this event also offers an opportunity for family and friends to share local gossip as well as long-held customs. Moreover, according to chef Josefina Howard, Mexicans have more than 150 different ways of making tamales";[33] whether wrapped in dried cornhusks or banana leaves, filled with chile-infused meat or black beans, recipes for it can be easily adapted to new circumstances, much like the culture surrounding it. By mixing a variety of things—ingredients, technology, and code-switching language—Cordelia that in "Haciendo Tamales," certain ingredients might be replaced with ingredients more easily obtained, but the product/cultural values remain essentially the same. "Mi mamá wouldn't compromise," she says, "no mftr chile, no u.s.d.a carne," but the daughter's choice to code switch indicates how not just her mother's tamale-making but the culture that embodies it changes over time.[34] Although the ingredients stay the same, "oregano . . . wildly grown / tamale wrappers . . . dried from last year's corn," and both "nurtured by sweat—¿cómo no?" the poet gives notice by her inclusion of English words that the final dish will also be a cultural gumbo. "To change her country / she couldn't sacrifice her heritage," Candelaria affirms, but the tamales that her mother made "from memory" were "cooked with gas under G.E. lights" (115), thereby honoring the oral tradition surrounding tamale-making but allowing for the addition of modern, timesaving living into the traditional mixture. Acknowledging that American-made technology complicates the purity of tamales, Candelaria nevertheless proclaims her mother's cooking "bien original to the max!" (115). In this way, she proclaims that despite compromises tamale-making remains one of the most viable aspects of Chicana(o) culture and a significant way of celebrating group identity. By implying that group identity is a process rather than a static marker, and by demanding an internal definition of ethnicity, Candelaria celebrates the elasticity of culture instead of the more common mode of mourning its decline.

SELF AND IDENTITY: "MEMOIRS OF A DUTIFUL DAUGHTER"

As Cordelia Candelaria's description of "Haciendo Tamales" shows, a recipe is never completely new; it is based on recipes and procedures of the past, reflecting the communal sense of cooking and long tradition behind it. As evidenced too in this poem, reading/writing about recipes is an interpretive act as well; cooks/writers change a recipe/self-identity at will, leaving out ingredients that they lack or that they find distasteful, but also adding elements to create a different dish. Perhaps because sharing recipes in Mexico has been predominantly oral, as Cecilia Lawless notes,[35] Mexican cooking has encouraged experimentation by producing a dish that, like its creator, reflects this material hybridity. Is the above recipe for tamales an "original," as the poem suggests, or the product of a long lineage of women sharing their ideas about food? Most stories of cooking and of recipes lie on a continuum of cultural and personal beliefs.

Recently, critics of literature have begun to look at how the exchange of recipes in texts expresses an identity politics in which the idea of cooking and authorship are connected. According to Anne Goldman, "reproducing a recipe, like telling a story, may be at once cultural practice and autobiographical assertion";[36] therefore, self-articulation takes place always within a familial space. In *Mother Tongue*, for example, Demetria Martínez focuses on identity politics that are elsewhere associated with tortilla-making— cooking as a way to represent tradition, the breaking of tradition, and inscribing oneself into the collective representation of women's work. In this way, Martínez makes clear the intersections of the narrator's developing political awareness and the domestic but no less political messages that she hears from Soledad. An older woman who helps Mary, a young woman adrift in Albuquerque, New Mexico, find her voice, Soledad ties food closely to a woman's ability to stay connected to her inner feelings, and so helps Mary understand that sharing a recipe and cooking produce more than a communal subject. "You'd be amazed at how learning to cook takes your mind off men," she tells Mary, thus echoing the sentiment in Acosta's use of tortilla-making as a metaphor for self-nourishment. "Every woman should have a special place inside where she can think," continues Soledad, "a place that will, you know, endure."[37] While Soledad emphasizes the importance of an ethnic heritage she encourages Mary to provide for her "own pleasure,"[38] which means revising symbols such as tortilla-making to provide for self-nourishment rather than deprivation.

The cook's/writer's creative impulses bring endless plurality to these texts, a plurality described by Gloria Anzaldúa as "indigenous like corn" but at the same time crossbred for survival under a diversity of conditions.[39] A plurality derived too from the collective nature of tortilla/tamale-making and the specificity of a particular woman's life, such a multiplicity is a quality both satisfying and frustrating to many Chicanas, especially those who negotiate a balance between the dominant culture and their own. A central theme of this literature, then, is exploration of cultural hybridity, or in Anzaldúa's terms, "the borderlands," an artificially determined political boundary, called by some the "Tortilla Curtain." A "thin edge of / barbed wire" (3) that artificially divides, it also helps to create a border culture, a merging of two worlds to form a "third country." A literal and figurative terrain, by its very nature such a transitory state encourages the integration of ancient and modern cultural beliefs, but also allows for the interrogation of internalized icons that have historically oppressed women. "Indigenous like corn," Anzaldúa writes, the *mestiza* endures, enmeshed in the "husks" (81) of her culture. Her freedom to rebel comes from being so secure in her culture that she can honor her tortilla/tamale-making foremothers while leaving behind those socially imposed expectations associated with the domestic sphere that would limit her.

Like the "Tortilla Curtain," which functions to divide but also produces a new culture, Ana Castillo's *Peel My Love Like an Onion* crosses many boundaries. Reviewed variously on the jacket cover as a "union between *One Hundred Days of Solitude* and General Hospital," "a refreshing wedding of Chicagoan humor to Mexican American spunk," Castillo veers constantly between humor and pathos in her story of a love triangle between Carmen "La Coja" (the Cripple) Santos, "one-legged dancing queen," afflicted with a childhood case of polio, and two members of her dancing troupe, Augustín and his godson Monolo.[40] However sentimental the storyline may be, it calls upon the Hispanic woman to love herself before committing to a partner. By exploring the limitations of a woman's role as tortilla-maker while stressing the reproduction of a distinct Mexican cultural cooking practice, it portrays Carmen as an independent spirit who is nevertheless very much aware of her Chicana(o) roots. In this novel of a strong resilient woman, Castillo presents a firmly centered female protagonist who acts, not as the Other of a male protagonist but, rather, as a subject who debunks the stereotypical view of passive, submissive Chicana whose sole role is to make tortillas for her men.

Rewriting borders is a primary focus of Castillo's text, as it explores what José David Saldívar calls the "ethno-racialized cultures of displacement" in America.[41] In this vein, Castillo's character uses wit and irony as a tool to deal with ambivalence she tries to resolve as she is caught between two cultures. According to Diana Rebolledo, through humor, Chicana writers strive to break the restrictive stereotypes of their culture.[42] In her novel, Castillo explores how Chicanas struggle to bond with others while, at the same time, recast images of traditional icons, family members, and friends. An integral part of her heroine's definition of herself is made up of how others see her, as nurturer, caretaker, rebel. "A teenage girl spell[s] trouble with a capital T," her aunts complain," as they predict her future. "You can't get them to cook . . . none of the things we learned as *señoritas*."[43]

This novel stresses the labor involved in producing various recipes, particularly tortillas. As punishment for not marrying, Carmen fulfills her penance by making tortillas each Saturday for her father (32). Debra Castillo points out this aspect of cooking in the preface of her book on Latin American women writers, *Talking Back*: "the recipe serves as an index of creative power, it also describes a giving of self to appease another's hunger, leaving the cook weakened, starved."[44] The question remains: does Carmen sell out by continuing to seek self-definition? Or does she sell herself out by seeking "a man of her own" to define her? Eventually she escapes cultural norms by recognizing that traditional male sexuality and independence are also hers. But the parallel that the author draws between the proper serving of tortillas and culture implies that Carmen will also equate cooking authentically with resistance to assimilation.

Carmen's sole objective is to control her own life. She is able to do so without assuming male characteristics. Possessing a keen intuition and receptivity to others, all qualities associated with the feminine, she nevertheless feels no nostalgia for Mexico and its tortilla-making traditions. Instead, her life is neither black nor white but embraces shades of grey. For example, her boyfriend Monolo cooks when she refuses. But her deviation from traditionally feminine characteristics imposed by men, including the making of perfect tortillas, does not preclude ethnic self-acceptance at the same time that she acknowledges feelings that society deems illicit about female sexual behavior.

Carmen's ability to enjoy bodily sensations depends partly on the functions she assigns to food and dancing, both of which are instrumental in connecting her inner and outer worlds. "Flamenco is not just a dance," Carmen explains. "It is how you step, eat, dream, think."[45] By establishing a connection between her mental work and the manual work of daily living, she gives voice to corporeal feelings that transcend those binaries inherent in the dominant culture. Moreover, by claiming that "you just have to feel what you are doing" (39), she opens up a sense of difference between herself and the only Anglo member of the troupe. Courtney, who "came in with a stack of show costumes over her arms . . . look[ing] like a one-woman float in an ethnic parade" (46), cares only about competing, she says, an ethic associated with male heroes who dominate the world they conquer. While Carmen rejects those aspects of her culture associated with female self-sacrifice, she retains those features that nourish her and give her cause for pride. Because Courtney seeks superiority and dominance, not parity and equality of stature often associated with women who share their skills at tamale-making events, she will never succeed, as Carmen does, at this particular performance art.

If, as Susan Kalcik states, "foodways provide a whole area of performance in which identity can be made,"[46] it follows that Ana Castillo also uses foodways to communicate about the self. For Chicana writers, according to Diana Rebolledo, an integral part of self-identity is defined by others and so, to break free of what she calls a "reflection on circular mirrors," creators like Castillo must "give birth to themselves."[47] In *Peel My Love Like an Onion*, Castillo's literary persona plays a multiplicity of roles. Eventually she gives up dancing to express her *mestiza* self as a crossroads music star. Her kitchen, too, reflects this diaspora consciousness as she learns lessons about ethnicity by making shrimp fricassee. A dish she traces back to preconquest Mexico, Carmen makes it in a blender, the "modern equivalent," she notes, "for the *molcajete* the Aztecs used to grind."[48] As she mixes modern technology with indigenous Mexican ingredients, Carmen personalizes and individualizes traditional culinary dishes.

"There was a lot more to the Conquest of Mexico," Carmen says, that she was learning, than "extracting Indian recipes" (210). Coming full circle, first as vilified, victimized, and finally vindicated as a crossroads music superstar, Carmen quite naturally would identify with another "story of love and betrayal, like all those paperback romances [read her own] sold in grocery stores promise" (209). Here she is referring to the historical/mythical figure of La Malinche, Indian consort of Cortés and mother of his illegitimate children, said to symbolize the Spanish conquest. "One very great although misunderstood woman," as Carmen also sees herself to be, Malinche now helps to explain the self-hatred felt by some Chicanas, including Carmen. Cutting to the core of this "high drama" (209) to reveal the truth about this woman previously maligned in Mexican history, Carmen arrives at a certain truth about herself. Before, Carmen's attitude toward her own sexuality was clouded by that original rape via European culture. By restoring Malinche's good name, at the novel's end, she restores her own as well.

As Carmen finds answers in her cooking, she enfolds the lives of friends, lovers, and historical figures into one another in a very different manner from her mother's construction of domesticity. The very title of this novel insists that to write about food is to write about the self as well, but its culinary equation suggests a woman's suffering in love. As Carmen learns to appreciate the art of cooking through her openness to experimentation with innovative ingredients, she also manipulates the accepted image of passive female nature. Significantly, she is peeling not an onion but a shrimp when the "love of her life [Manolo] returns" (209). Though, by reminding her of his "future mother-in-law's" expectation that she "make the tortillas for [her] father" (210), he attempts to resurrect a discourse of commands, Carmen takes control. Having transformed her kitchen into positive space of culinary/cultural knowledge, she redefines, too, her life. "Sometimes when Manolo calls," she says "okay, you can come see me" (212). And she says "sure, come on!" to Augustín, who now knows to call ahead or "he stays outside" when she refuses to "buzz him up" (213). As did La Malinche, who many Chicana writers now view as having made her own choices in order to survive,[49] Carmen decides what ingredients from her heritage to accept. "And when I don't want to see anyone I don't answer the phone at all."[50] Secure in "a room of her own," not necessarily defined by either lover or by Virginia Woolf, this performer no longer plays roles others give her, but creates her own. In this novel, Carmen's association of identity politics, food, and sexuality serve as a medium whereby she achieves a voice.

Peel My Love Like an Onion demonstrates the author's use of culinary metaphor to transform traditional feminine values into radical messages by revising myths that constrain Mexican popular culture. The evolution represented in Carmen's search for self-fulfillment is paralleled by her mythic identification as Malinche. Carmen appears initially as the suffering victim of male-inflicted abuse. Nevertheless, at the close of the novel she is no longer the idealized symbol of selflessness; she is now a whole person who rejects self-sacrifice, signified by dutifully making tortillas weekly for her father, but substitutes not control or dominance but instead respect and parity exemplified elsewhere by the cooperative nature of communal tamale-making parties. In this way, Ana Castillo grapples with Mexican icons of sexuality and motherhood that, internalized, have imposed on women a limited, often negative, definition of their selves. Her novel dramatizes the positive aspect of border consciousness—the possibilities it offers for transformation. By negotiating with cultural icons that are both inalienable parts of oneself and limitations to one's potential as a woman, Carmen tries out different modes of being a woman. Finally, her obligation to make tortillas for the father form both a contrast and a focus on Carmen's emotional life; rebellion against traditional domestic order produces pain, guilt, and sorrow. Until she learns that domesticity, not unlike her distorted body that still revels in dancing, can be a productive medium for writing the self within a distinctly female space, she is as doomed as her tortillas that always come out oblong.

Read as a discursive whole, this novel opens up a way of writing the self and writing about women from a specifically female space. Domesticity is the author's creative springboard, a vehicle which she uses to discuss more subversive issues. In Castillo's writing, the prevalence of feminine imagery coupled with domestic metaphor, particularly that of tortillas, may also be viewed as a means to preserve the domestic within the realm of women's art—a way of making the familiar into something less mundane.

There are still other readings of the domestic component of Castillo's writing. In traditional Mexican society, woman is equated with the sphere of marriage, children, and socially acceptable position of wife, the duties that she performs in the home. For Carmen, too, obedience and conformity are stressed by her female relatives as the recipe for a successful marriage. It is therefore a deceptive space from which to say more subversive things about woman's place because the messages can be said in traditionally feminine codes. Thus, using the domestic metaphors surrounding tortilla-making is a subtle way of criticizing the basic institutions surrounding this practice in a socially acceptable way. In other words, by using a deceptively "safe" medium, that of a romance novel, Ana Castillo delivers what in fact turns out to be a radical message, that of her heroine's refusal to conform to her role as dutiful daughter much less as dutiful wife. Her cooking lessons produce only oblong tortillas, as much a critique of conventional marital responsibilities as evidence of Carmen's cooking disasters in her mother's kitchen. The domestic textuality of tortilla-making does not equate with the sexual or intellectual needs of this modern woman: both the tortilla and the rites surrounding it turn out to be unpalatable.

RESISTANCE/AFFIRMATION/TRANSFORMATION

In Ana Castillo's texts, cooking lessons are often survival lessons, explored through feminine metaphors. As the following section shows, when these images are displaced from their original domestic situations, they acquire new interpretations which often revolve around repression or liberation of women. This new function of transmitting a message is exactly the opposite of the original one, in other words, the displacement of what is expected in favor of a more radical message, informs the remaining works considered in this chapter. By deconstructing conventional patterns of thought and social practice, and reconstructing women's experience previously hidden or overlooked, these writers and artists transform domestic space into one that protects and nurtures women.

The response to culinary tradition by Chicana writers is a complex one that often is shaped by individual history, culture, and emotions. The struggle for Chicana(o) rights during the late 1960s through the 1980s placed Chicanas in a tenuous double bind between fighting sexual oppression within the mainstream women's movement and joining their Chicano colleagues in a struggle for racial equality. As Diana Rebolledo notes, this dilemma was even move complex for Chicana lesbians, who felt excluded by their heterosexual sisters.[51] As a poet who struggles with issues of unity and separation, Alicia Gaspar de Alba, whose aforementioned "Making Tortillas" uses culinary imagery to depict a split identity, equates "tortilleras" (a slang word for lesbians[52]) to "slow lovers of women," for both are sensual moves that her "body remembers" as it starts "from scratch."[53] Here Gaspar de Alba bridges not two worlds but three. Whether within a double or triple bind, however, Chicana writers inscribe their sexuality within a specific cultural terrain.

In her distinctive South Texas paintings, Carmen Lomas Garza also articulates what Amalia Mesa-Bains calls a "combination of resistance and affirmation, a kind of Chicano self-recovery."[54] As do writers in this paper, Lomas Garza traces her artistic inspiration to her experience in the Chicano movement and her family, both of which taught her that painting which exposes social ills leads to a healing process. Specifically, she seeks to overcome childhood trauma that she experienced by encountering language difference for the first time. In her introduction to *A Piece of My Heart*, she explains how her art overcomes this self-division by transforming her "heart and humanity"[55] into a visual narrative of cultural reclamation for children. In *Family Pictures/Cuadros de familia*, food acts to bind the family, though, as José David Saldívar notes, her spatial arrangements vary. On the one hand, she depicts what Saldívar describes as "unalienated sexual division of labor,"[56] for in *Tamalada* (tamale-making gatherings), the painter says, everybody helps.[57] On the other, in *Conejo (Rabbit)* (18), the child Carmen is absent but clearly looking on as the grandfather delivers fresh rabbit for his wife to cook after she prepares tortillas.

In the final painting, *Comas para soñar (Beds for Dreaming)* (18), Lomas Garza distances herself from such gendered social spaces in yet another way. This canvas makes clear that she knows her mother's tamale/tortilla-making activities are not to be her future, but nevertheless she will return to them imaginatively through her paintings. Encouraged by her mother to lie on the roof and dream, as she does here while looking inside at her mother working, Lomas Garza acknowledges that her mother "made up our beds . . . [to] have regular dreams, but she also laid out the bed for our dreams of the future" (30). Because her mother's life is too confining for the daughter, she eventually does leave home but carries it inside through her creative imagination.

Moving from Lomas Garza's rural spaces into urban kitchens, Sheila Ortiz Taylor's memoir, *Imaginary Parents*, reclaims a childhood vision. In common with new works in cultural anthropology, feminism, literary studies, and other border studies, *Imaginary Parents* is structurally innovative and highly personal. Part autobiography, memoir, poetry, fiction, and, like *Family Pictures*, a chronicle, it fuses dream and reality, life and death, present and past, in addition to mixing genres. Throughout, the author informs her writing with a deep-rooted belief in the life of the dead, as she "crouch[es] over the bones of [her] parents, remembering and transforming memories.[58] In this vein, as Amalia Mesa-Baines comments on the *ofrendas* (home altars) in Lomas Garza's work, *Dia de Los Muertos* (Day of the Dead celebration) was resurrected by the Chicano Movement as a "vehicle for continuity," a means to make manifest the historic past by honoring personal and communal *antepasadoes* (ancestors).[59] For Taylor, who collaborated with her sister, an artist whose "small objects with big means" disrupt this literary text with visual presentations of such altars, death and its relationship to life are significant dualities that operate at many textual levels. An act of resistance, like Lomas Garza's cultural chronicle, this "rescue work"[60] empowers the author to claim individual and collective history as her own; by "accept[ing] what comes and the order in which it comes," she claims "all the ghosts that rise up" (xiii) are her's. In this way, she joins others who, according to Mesa-Baines, replace a culture of "poverty and exploitation" with what is "true and real."[61]

The central focus of *Imaginary Parents*, as the title suggests, is the daughter's nostalgic though not always idyllic, relationships with her father, mother, grandparents, and other family members. In sometimes utopian but more often ambivalent culinary images, Taylor documents her "layer[ed]" understanding of "family history"[62] and its domestic economy. As Taylor traces her development as a writer, she notes how "the past continues to influence the present time of both my sister and myself," inspiring each as they "cooked together or dreamed our way through boxes of family photographs" (xv). As a self-conscious form of storytelling combined with visual representation, this text, like Lomas Garza's paintings, closely associates domestic spaces with cultural values related to Spanish language and traditions. "To sit in my mamma's [Grandmother Ortiz] kitchen" was to hear stories being told in both English and the "song-like cadence of . . . Spanish" (xvi). As she recalls "the staccato sounds of my mamma's brown soft hands as she slapped the tortillas into shape for the griddle" (xv), food and women's bodies, writing and cooking are fused into ethnographic discourse that is built upon maternal lineage. Just as Alice Walker, among others, has looked to the domestic arts crafted by African American foremothers as both the result of enforced labor and as the creations of skillful craftswomen who are also often artists, so Taylor looks to her grandmother's tortilla-making as the "origin of [her] strong narrative proclivities" (xvi). "I certainly was drawing then, and my grandmother was my archivist" (xvi) not just of her artistic ambitions, she implies, but of a culture, the maintenance of which is often a woman's duty.

Her grandmother's kitchen is a nurturing space where Taylor metaphorically returns for inspiration. While communal values can be a source of resistance against assimilative forces, she also understands her mother's knowledge that a relational model of self often means in practice that the interests of others come before one's own. Faced with the preparation of endless meals, her mother preferred cigarettes and coffee, rejecting her more health-conscious husband's belief that her "essential self" (147) depended entirely on what foods she took into her body. By asking her family to respect her individuality ("I am *not* what I eat" [147]), the mother draws her daughter's attention to sexual division of labor not noted above in the tortilla-making activities of the grandmother. In Grandmother Ortiz's kitchen, Taylor might have felt that she was participating in a living family history, but listening to her parents she begins to understand that family ties can be oppressive at the same time that they offer solace. Seen in terms of ambivalent images of kitchen and food, Taylor's house may not be the one she wants with its unsolved family problems. But it is also the imaginary space that protects and nurtures her creative self, one in which growth continues to take place.

"THE WRITER'S KITCHEN"

Writing within the confining space of home, Chicana writers have created their own territory. They have combined women's experience, in this case tortilla- and tamale-making, with imagination. According to Cordelia Candelaria, many of them underscore home and geography in order to highlight how personal surroundings and homeland shape psychological and cultural perceptions. Candelaria refers to this place as the "Wild Zone," a separate space also serving as a metaphor for ethnic and racial experience in America. A central paradox of this writing, she continues, is that it depicts, on the one hand, an unrestricted zone free of imposed definitions of identity. On the other, it encloses women within a female space circumscribed by external assumptions.[63]

This dialectic constitutes one of the most difficult contradictions encountered by women writers in this chapter. Denied access to "high art," they are now making a place for expression, either singly or as part of a group. Domestic literature provides such a space in which women can assert their values. Daring to write subjectively, as women, from their experiences, they yearn, at the same time, to be included in literary history written by men. Moreover, another concern informs much of the above writing. No matter how much Chicanas have written about tortilla/tamale-making and culture, they also imagine transforming things of the kitchen into a world in which there are no politics of oppression.

In her essay "The Writer's Kitchen," Rosario Ferré, a Puerto Rican author, sums up many of the themes interwoven in this paper. Just as Ferré writes, she says, to create a space for unbalancing conventional expectations,[64] so Ana Castillo achieves a public voice by transforming the mundane into a vehicle to critique larger issues. In *Peel My Love Like an Onion*, for example, Castillo redefines the term "hero" in order to encompass both female and male traits within its meaning. As two complex cultures intersect in Castillo's text, conflicting cultural gender definitions and icons of femininity clash—becoming either more flexible or more persistent. While the male protagonist of the traditional genre acquires wisdom, maturity, his *compañera*, and reintegrates into society as a result of his arduous trials, Castillo's female hero gains control of her life, achieving independence from male-imposed expectations without sacrificing the positive traits of tortilla/tamale-making discourse honored by women in her culture. Finally able to realize her goals by becoming a popular music star, Carmen retains those values of creativity, mutuality and the passing on of tradition, all associated with tortilla/tamale-making, while recognizing that the self-sacrifice implied by the act itself imposed limitations on her mother's generation.

A room of her own, a space in which to write for an unrestricted time, is often used as a metaphor for creative space. If Virginia Woolf proposed a room of one's own, such a place for women often is the kitchen, a site honored as a place for exchanging recipes and gossip not unlike the communal focus of their work. Nevertheless, while a woman might look to her grandmother's tortilla-making as skilled practice, she often finds that the kitchen has been the locus of oppression, thereby privatizing and marginalizing the experience of many women. Recognizing this tension and its source in the context of women's culinary metaphors facilitates a greater understanding of the texts.

Another dominant theme is breaking out of silence, "reinventing myself,"[65] as Ferré writes, by recording memories within a historical and cultural context. Part of her power, as it is for other writers, comes from a framework deeply rooted in ethnic beliefs and practices. Interwoven in all the voices included here are typically domestic events that serve as a springboard for larger social issues. As did the *madres* of Argentina, who, as Myriam Jehensen notes, used their protective "maternal status" to overturn a dictatorship in 1983 by exposing torture and disappearances to the world,[66] so these writers compose from the safe refuge of the kitchen. From that space they call attention to what Ferré calls the secret of good writing. Comparing that art to cooking, she notes that both require skillful mixing of ingredients. Tortilla/tamale discourse illustrates this theme, for not only are there many varieties of both in Mexican cooking, the preparation of each food generates both positive and disabling icons of femininity that are connected to Chicanas' self-images and self-esteem. Where cultures overlap, however, definitions become fluid, so that stirring together different cultural paradigms can engender a new space in which to subvert feminine gender roles. Locating tortilla/tamale discourse within a network of continuity and relationship with other women, Chicana writers honor their foremothers who serve as mediators by offering a cultural context within which to pursue individuality and independence that are traditionally associated with men.

NOTES

1. Although there are different connotations for the term "Chicano(a)," I use the label to mean people of Mexican descent inhabiting the United States. The term "Latina" in this chapter connotes members or elements of the larger Latin American culture. Similarly, while conscious that citizens of Canada, Mexico, and Latin America are also "Americans," I employ this nomenclature when referring to non-Chicano(a) United States citizens because it seems appropriate when discussing mainstream eating habits and culture in the United States.

2. Alma García, ed., *Chicana Feminist Thought: The Basic Historical Writing* (New York: Routledge, 1997), 6.

3. Gloria Anzaldúa, *Borderlands/La Frontera* (San Francisco: Aunt Lute, 1987), 81.

4. Theresa Martinez, "Tortilla-Making as Feminist Action," *Network* (May 11–14, 1996): 14.

5. Marilyn Tausend, *Cocina de la Familia* (New York: Simon and Schuster, 1997), 290.

6. Jeffrey Pilcher, *Que Vivan los Tamales! Food and the Making of Mexican Identity* (Albuquerque: University of New Mexico Press, 1998), 6, 11.

7. Sarah Deutsch, *No Separate Refuge: Culture, Class, and Gender on an Anglo-Hispanic Frontier in the American Southwest, 1880–1940* (New York: Oxford University Press, 1987), 52–53.

8. Pilcher, *Que Vivan Los Tamales!* 55.

9. Donna Gabaccia, *We Are What We Eat: Ethnic Food and the Making of Americans* (Cambridge: Harvard University Press, 1998), 44.

10. M. H. de la Peña Brown, "Una Tamalada: The Special Event," *Western Folklore* 40 (1981): 64–71.

11. Mark Miller, *Coyote Café: Foods from the Great Southwest* (Berkeley: Ten Speed Press, 1989), 57.

12. Anzaldúa, *Borderlands/La Frontera*, 81.

13. Roger Abrahams, "Equal Opportunity Eating: A Structural Excursus on Things of the Mouth," *Ethnic and Regional Foodways in the United States: The Performance of Group Identity*, ed. Linda Keller Brown and Kay Mussell (Knoxville: University of Tennessee Press, 1984), 21.

14. Brett Williams, "Why Migrant Women Feed Their Husband's Tamales: Foodways as a Basis for a Revisionist View of Tejano Family Life," *Ethnic Foodways in the United States: The Performance of Group Identity*, ed. Linda Keller Brown and Kay Mussell (Knoxville: University of Tennessee Press, 1984), 122.

15. Tausend, *Cocina de la Familia*, 289.

16. de la Peña Brown, "Una Tamalada," 70.

17. Pilcher, *Que Vivan Los Tamales!* 106.

18. Jennie Chávez, "Women of the Mexican American Movement," *Chicana Feminist Thought: The Basic Historical Writing*, ed. Alma Garcia (New York: Routledge, 1997), 37.

19. Lorna Dee Cervantes, "You Cramp My Style, Baby," quoted in Tey Diana Rebolledo, "Walking the Thin Line: Humor in Chicana Literature," *Beyond Stereotypes: The Critical Analysis of Chicana Literature*, ed. María Herrera-Sobek (New York: Bilingual Press, 1985), 101.

20. Teresa Paloma Acosta, "The Corn Tortilla," *Floricanto Sí: A Collection of Latina Poetry*, ed. Bryce Milligan, Mary Guerrero Milligan, and Angela de Hoyos (New York: Penguin, 1998), 1.

21. Pilcher, *Que Vivan Los Tamales!* 106.

22. Acosta, "The Corn Tortilla," 1.

23. Diana Kennedy, *My Mexico: A Culinary Odyssey with More than 300 Recipes* (New York: Clarkson Potter, 1998).

24. Pilcher, *Que Vivan Los Tamales!* 21, 46, 54.

25. Tiffany Ann Lopez, *Growing Up Chicana* (New York: Avon Books, 1995), 18.

26. Lopez, *Growing Up Chicano*, 20.

27. Alma Luz Villanueva, "Abundance," *Máscaras*, ed. Lucha Corpi (Berkeley: Third Woman Press, 1997), 39.

28. Alma Luz Villanueva, *Mother, May I?* (section 3), *Infinite Divisions: An Anthology of Chicana Literature*, ed. Tey Diana Rebolledo and Eliana S. Rivera (Tucson: University of Arizona Press, 1993), 123.

29. Marta Sanchez, "The Birthing of the Poetic 'I' in Alma Villanueva's *Mother, May I? The Search for Feminine Identity*," *Beyond Stereotypes: The Critical Analysis of Chicana Literature*, ed. María Herrera-Sobek (New York: Bilingual Press, 1993), 140.

30. Villanueva, *Mother, May I?* (section 3), 123.

31. Villanueva, *Mother, May I?* (epilogue), quoted in Sanchez, "The Birthing of the Poetic 'I,'" 145.

32. Villanueva, "Abundance," 52–54.

33. Josefina Howard, *Rosa Mexicana: A Culinary Autobiography with 69 Recipes* (New York: Viking, 1998), 40.

34. Cordelia Candelaria, "Haciendo Tamales," *Infinite Divisions: An Anthology of Chicana Literature*, ed. Tey Diana Rebolledo and Eliana Rivera (Tucson: University of Arizona Press, 1993), 115.

35. Cecelia Lawless, "Cooking, Community, Culture: A Reading of *Like Water for Chocolate*," *Recipes for Reading: Community Cookbooks, Stories, History*, ed. Ann Bower (Amherst: University of Massachusetts Press, 1997), 218.

36. Anne Goldman, "'I Yam What I Yam': Cooking, Culture, and Colonialism," *De/Colonizing the Subject: The Politics of Gender in Women's Autobiography*, ed. Sidonie Smith and Julia Watson (Minneapolis: University of Minnesota Press, 1992), 172.

37. Demetria Martínez, *MotherTongue* (New York: Ballantine, 1994), 117.

38. Martínez, *Mother Tongue*, 117.

39. Anzaldúa, *Borderlands*, 81.

40. Ana Castillo, *Peel My Love Like an Onion* (New York: Doubleday, 1989), 10.

41. José David Saldívar, *Border Matters: Remapping American Cultural Studies* (Berkeley: University of California Press, 1997), 7.

42. Tey Diana Rebolledo, "Walking the Thin Line: Humor in Chicana Literature," *Beyond Stereotypes: The Critical Analysis of Chicana Literature*, ed. María Herrera-Sobek (New York: Bilingual Press, 1985), 91.

43. A. Castillo, *Peel My Love*, 17.

44. Debra Castillo, *Talking Back: Toward a Latin American Feminist Literary Criticism* (Ithaca, N.Y.: Cornell University Press, 1992), xiv.

45. A. Castillo, *Peel My Love*, 39.

46. Susan Kalcik, "Ethnic Foodways in America: Symbol and Performance of Identity," *Ethnic and Regional Foodways in the United States: The Performance of Group Identity*, ed. Linda Keller Brown and Kay Mussell (Knoxville: University of Tennessee Press, 1984), 54.

47. Tey Diana Rebolledo, *Women Singing in the Snow: A Cultural Analysis of Chicana Literature* (Tucson: University of Arizona Press, 1995), 75–77.

48. A. Castillo, *Peel My Love*, 210.

49. Rebolledo, *Women Singing in the Snow*, 193.

50. A. Castillo, *Peel My Love*, 213.

51. Tey Diana Rebolledo and Eliana Rivera, eds., *Infinite Divisions: An Anthology of Chicana Literature* (Tucson: University of Arizona Press, 1993), 24.

52. Rebolledo, *Women Singing in the Snow*, 143.

53. Alicia B. Gaspar de Alba, "Making Tortillas," *Infinite Divisions: An Anthology of Chicana Literature*, ed. Tey Diana Rebolledo and Eliana S. Rivera (Tucson: University of Arizona Press, 1993), 355.

54. Amalia Mesa-Bains, "Chicano Chronicle and Cosmology: The Works of Carmen Lomas Garza," introduction to Carmen Lomas Garza, *A Piece of My Heart/Pedacito de mi Corazón: The Art of Carmen Lomas Garza* (New York: New Press, 1991), 20.

55. Carmen Lomas Garza, *A Piece of My Heart/Pedacito de mi Corazón: The Art of Carmen Lomas Garza* (New York: New Press, 1991), 12.

56. Saldívar, *Border Matters*, 86.

57. Carmen Lomas Garza, *Family Pictures/Cuadros de familia* (San Francisco: Children's Book, 1990), 22.

58. Sheila Ortiz Taylor, *Imaginary Parents* (Albuquerque: University of New Mexico Press, 1996), xiii.

59. Mesa-Bains, "Chicano Chronicle and Cosmology," 28–29.

60. Taylor, *Imaginary Parents*, xv.

61. Mesa-Bains, "Chicano Chronicle and Cosmology," 31.

62. Taylor, *Imaginary Parents*, xv.

63. Cordelia Candelaria, "The Wild Zone," *Chicana Critical Issues*, ed. Norma Alarcon et al. (Berkeley: Third Woman Press, 1993), 22.

64. Rosario Ferré, "The Writer's Kitchen," trans. Diana L. Vélez, *Feminist Studies* 12 (1986): 228.

65. Ferré, "The Writer's Kitchen," 227.

66. Myriam Jehensen, *Latin American Women Writers: Class, Race, and Gender* (Albany: State University of New York Press, 1995), 9.

4

Taking the Cake: Power Politics in Southern Life and Fiction

Patricia M. Gantt

$\mathcal{I}$n the cultural rituals that unofficially signal the holding, withholding, and transmission of social power, gatherings where food plays a part are central to people in any locale. In fact, most recent studies of American culture—whether done by anthropologists, folklorists, literary scholars, or those who simply like to observe the passing scene—note that food comprises one of the most telling links between people. It forms, as Dillon Bustin observes, an important part of a culture's "conceptual knot of ideas."[1] Simply put, food gives us far more than calories: It tells us who we are. The identification of self with food is especially well entrenched for women, whose traditional roles have required them to plan, shop for, prepare, serve, and clean up after its consumption. Even for modern women, this connection remains strong.

Seldom is food more culturally encoded for women than in the South, where, according to Peggy Prenshaw, "images and practices of food preparation, service, and consumption define women's lives."[2] She draws specific attention to the connection between food and southern culture—most notably the culture of women, observing that "the kitchen and the garden have served as arenas where many southern women, Black and White, have exercised power and creativity."[3] For such women in particular, the personal truly signifies politically. To understand the roles of women in a culture, then, one cannot ignore the foods they prepare and serve. These foods reveal what signals a culture is sending, as well as what use women make of those signals. Of notable importance is whether women accept these cultural codes at face value, internalizing messages sent as guides for their behavior, or reconfigure them to their own design.

Regardless of the variety of foods that play an essential cultural role in women's lives, there is one delectable item that has become established as a social *sine qua non*—the cake. Cakes are an important part of individual, family, and community celebrations all across America and make their appearance with most definite frequency at social gatherings in the South. According to Mildred Council, "At family reunions it sometimes seems that half the buffet table is filled with cakes, pies, and cobblers."[4] Council—known as "Mama Dip" to the customers in her Chapel Hill, North Carolina, restaurant—has devoted over sixty years to southern food and its preparation. Her fame has led her to national talk shows, the publication of a cookbook, and a restaurant of her own, frequented by southerners and just plain lovers of southern food alike, including celebrities Michael Jordan and food editor Craig Claiborne. She readily acknowledges the importance of cake in a woman's cooking repertoire, vowing, "Nothing is as memorable, or enhances a cook's reputation so much, as a spectacular cake."[5] Whether those cakes are served in a restaurant, in a home, or at a gathering such as Mama Dip's reunion, the cultural expectation is that women will make them. The overwhelming presence of cake recipes in publications, web sites, and other media whose expected audience is women amply demonstrates this view.

Baking cakes is not just something women were expected to do a long time ago. The contemporary connection between women and cake is unmistakable as well. A recent search on America Online, asking for both "cake" and "women," resulted in 4,054 sites for possible exploration; one site alone contained 254 more specific listings on cake.[6] Going beyond this simple search, a sweep of the entire Internet garnered 205,163 links, many suggesting "relationships" and "society" as interrelated areas to "cakes" and "women."[7] Cakes occupy a central position in items marketed to a female audience, from print to the multiple sites found on the Internet, including home pages like the one maintained by the high priestess of what is considered appropriate for women, Martha Stewart. There is even a web site for displaced southerners and their friends, enabling them to subscribe to a cake-of-the-month service that can speed southern desserts anywhere. This service offers both elegant packaging and delectability, with selections described as follows: "Very Vera's freshly baked triple-layer cakes zoom in from Augusta, Georgia, by FedEx, elegantly ensconced in white tins, resting on satin ribbons that help even butterfingers to safely extricate the delicate gift within."[8] Recipients are promised not only that each cake will be delicious or that it will look beautiful when it arrives, but that it comes from the South—and from the warm oven of a southern woman, Vera.

A look at a single popular publication aimed at women, *Family Circle* magazine, further indicates how strong this tie continues to be. The current issue, for example, features dozens and dozens of recipes—many of them for cakes. The banner "Party Cakes Made Easy" is displayed above the magazine title on its cover. A color photograph of a cake, accompanied by the injunction to the reader to "make our rosebud cake," comprises the visual background of the issue.[9] The language of the recipe sections, in addition to claiming how simple the cakes are to make, is full of extravagance: These cakes and their presentation are described as "gorgeous," "scrumptious," "showy," "delightful," "festive"—even "glorious."[10] The implication is unmistakable that those who use magazine directions to make or decorate their cakes can be delightful, too. At the very least, they are guaranteed, "the results will be memorable."[11] *Family Circle* is not unique in its emphasis on cakes. Advertisers around the country know that where there are American women, there will inevitably be cakes.

Emblems of southern life, especially, are replete with toothsome cakes, from Knoxville, Tennessee's cable television hit, the Home and Garden channel,[12] to the pages of that grande dame of southern cookery, *Southern Living*, where cakes have appeared on the covers of sixteen of its twenty-one annual collections of recipes. The New Orleans King Cake, a part of traditional Mardi Gras celebrations, exemplifies the cake as a southern cultural symbol. Born in religious custom, the King Cake was originally known only for its part in Catholic Lenten ceremonies. When cut, it reveals small tokens, symbols of the fortune those who eat the cake may expect in days to come. Icing on the King Cake is always purple and gold, the colors of the Mardi Gras. Today, with the Mardi Gras separated from much of its religious function and transposed into an international party, the function of the King Cake has also changed. It does still contribute to the larger cultural and economic life of the South. No longer made at home for sacred or secular ceremonies, King Cake has become the feature of several web sites, where it is sold around the world to people who may know about New Orleans—or Lent—only from their evening news.

In the capital-*S* South, no food so clearly *belongs* to the woman at the top of the social hierarchy as does a cake, especially a pound cake or a fresh coconut cake. Taking a cake to a social occasion anywhere in the region has traditionally been the culinary equivalent of flaunting a Star-tac phone in an airport waiting line—a symbol of cultural power and with-it-ness. When a cake is present, one simply *must* comprehend the implicit cultural gravity not only of the occasion, but also of the subliminal cultural statements that are being made there. Finding out who has brought that cake is a way for one to discern which woman holds indisputable social power in the situation at hand. The relationship between women and cake, then, is one that is both complex and firmly entrenched in southern society.

Perhaps this connection between women and cake is particularly strong in the South because women's traditional domestic roles are so clearly defined there. Lucinda H. MacKethan, Elizabeth Fox-Genovese, Minrose C. Gwin, and other social or literary critics have noted the continuing primacy of relational identities—that is, the use of terms such as "daughter," "wife," or "mother" as indicators of who one is personally and socially—in the cultural language of the South. MacKethan further argues that, because of the widespread acceptance of the definitions these relational identities provide in determining who southern women are, the "growth into autonomous selfhood" is "delayed even more strenuously in the South than in other regions."[13] Victoria E. Bynum holds that patriarchal self-interest, in conjunction with the lack of factories in the nineteenth-century South and the weakness of the abolitionist movement there, worked together to promote "women's production in the home."[14] For the most part, southern women stayed in the kitchen, stewing, boiling, roasting—and baking.

More than just dessert, the cakes that make their obligatory appearance at southern gatherings are emblems of female power politics. Whether sacred or secular, real or fictional, social events where cakes appear are defining ones for a community, provoking questions that delineate its central structure and remain after the last delicious crumbs are swept away: What is the importance of that gathering to the community in which it is held? Which social occasions call for cakes, rather than other sweet finales? What type of cake is served? Is it eggless (hard times), chocolate (unsuitable for the most formal occasions), coconut (created by one who has attained the upper rungs of the social ladder), or that ultimate power statement, the perfect pound cake? Whose recipe is established in a community as "the best"? Who dares to flaunt social confidence and cultural control enough to take a cake to a gathering, rather than a more plebian offering like ham, potato salad, or even another favorite, a pie?

In fiction, cakes have been a frequent part of depictions of southern life early and late, ranging from the writings of the local colorists to the parties of Rebecca Wells' outrageous Ya-Yas. Scenes of family and community gatherings, without which southern fiction seemingly could not exist, are typically laden with cakes. Their presence is conspicuous, too, not just in mainstream southern writers, but in the full range of fiction by and about southern women. Whether in novels by widely recognized writers like Eudora Welty, by those associated with a particular southern subregion like Wilma Dykeman, or by young adult novelists like Mildred D. Taylor, when we read about the South, we read about cakes.

Eudora Welty, who skillfully delineates the "hidden reaches of human hearts" and the exterior worlds of the communities that form them, makes extensive use of social customs relating to food.[15] Her short stories and novels are replete with communal gatherings: births, weddings, family reunions, funerals—every traditional occasion to "bind a local people together . . . by offering images that awaken the heart to recognitions of commonality."[16] From these experiences, it becomes possible for Welty's people to reassess their lives, often drawing from their shared customs a sense of what is appropriate for their daily actions—at times, they even gather from these customs a strength that helps them to endure. Since her work focuses on southern communities and southern women, naturally Welty makes considerable use of gatherings where cakes appear. She includes them not only where one might expect to see a cake, such as at a wedding, but in the range of communal ingatherings that occur in her writing.

In the tightly knit stories that make up *The Golden Apples* (1949), Welty twice employs cakes to contribute to the definitions the women of Morgana, Mississippi, formulate of themselves and of each other. In each case, intense social competition is involved in their interactions. When asked to compare women to men, Welty once expressed her opinion that women are "more competitive; less passive . . . as strong, violent" as men are.[17] Drawing on her sense of females as strong competitors, she makes the forces at work between women evident in "June Recital" and "The Wanderers."

It does not take the reader of "June Recital" long to sense the resentment the Morgana community feels toward its resident artist, Miss Eckhart. To these women, the music teacher is just too much—mostly too much *unlike* themselves. They dwell on a catalog of difference, summed up in what they refer to as Miss Eckhart's "Yankeeness," a term conveying their widespread feelings of disregard.[18] Miss Eckhart's ancestry alone puts her outside the Morgana circle. She is resented all through World War I and even after it, when "people said Miss Eckhart was a German and still wanted the Kaiser to win."[19] The night of the piano recital is, according to Danielle Pitvay-Souques, the "one night in the year the ladies of Morgana cooperate with Miss Eckhart to celebrate themselves, in the end, under the pretense of honoring their daughters. Staged by a narcissistic town enamored of its own image, the brilliantly colorful recital derives its deceptive splendor from success and power. It represents the supreme illusion of the town contemplating its social achievement therein."[20] The difference between these two factions is emblemized in the cake Miss Eckhart serves on her dainty Bavarian china. It is an ordinary *Kuchen*, a cake whose name local women cannot even pronounce. Her cake, "sweet, light, and warm" is simple, not the contrived confections Morgana's ladies prefer, such as the cream puff swan with "whipped cream feathers, a pastry neck, green icing eyes" that one of their own serves at her tea party.[21] Like their maker, Miss Eckhart's little cake has a natural elegance impossible for the women of Morgana to comprehend, and they ostracize her for it.

The last story in the collection, "The Wanderers," depicts the people of Morgana as they gather to observe the passing of Miss Katie Rainey. As soon as they hear of her death, the entire community reverts to enacting well-practiced roles, familiar ones they have been rehearsing all their lives. The Morgana community is directed by a strict sense of appropriateness that governs everything they eat, wear, say, and do. The community thus offers the physical expression of support tradition calls for. People who "never had cause to set foot in the Rainey house for over five minutes" soon inundate the place with their presence and their culinary offerings.[22]

Tradition demands food at a Southern funeral. When word of Miss Katie's death gets out, the arrival of huge amounts of food at the Rainey door begins. Welty enumerates the items sent to the home; cakes lead the list: "Food—two banana cakes and a baked ham, a platter of darkly deviled eggs, new rolls—and flowers kept arriving at the back, and the kitchen filled with women as the parlor now filled with men."[23] Far more than a practical consideration to accommodate the many mourners, these dishes have symbolic value. For Morgana society, propriety reigns in everything.

First, these banana cakes are a form of female competition. Mrs. Stark, who feels her elevated position in society very keenly, tells her maid to "start cooking for the funeral, if others didn't beat you to it yesterday."[24] Later, when Virgie Rainey goes into her own mother's kitchen and turns over "a piece or two" of frying chicken, the women who have marked the kitchen as their territory look at her "in a kind of wonder and belligerence."[25] They halt their conversation and stare, "as though something—not only today—should prevent her from knowing at all how to cook—the thing they knew."[26] The women in the kitchen feel that Virgie's energies should be given over to grieving; she is not supposed to be functioning practically there, but is an intruder in the domestic rites of mourning tradition has assigned to them. Virgie is confused; she wants a quiet moment, simple fare. Yet the women in her mother's kitchen, strangers/not strangers to her, insist on displaying their mastery. Again they remind her of the variety that has been presented, not only the picnic foods that always show up at southern gatherings, but the more elaborate ones that exemplify their skill and status, the special cakes.

Why do they cling so steadfastly to regulating minute community customs like the sending of cakes? Morgana must assert what to them is appropriate. If the community loses autonomy over the small things it can control, larger social supports will surely go next. Soon, they feel, the foundations of the entire community may fall. In these simple matters, people "have their own peculiar ways to say at once: I am capable, we are right."[27] Whether in the kitchen, where cakes are delivered and sliced up for serving, or in the living room, where the slices are consumed, the scenes involving Morgana's women are more of a social tug of war than a demonstration of grief. Their behavior enacts a lifelong dance for ascendancy over one another, and comes from an evolved sense of decorum they cling to firmly. At the table a community educates its intimate members in the details of its social constructs.

In Welty's *Delta Wedding* (1945), cakes are at the center of an intricate investigation of the ways communities and individuals clash with one another. The story line of the novel revolves around the wedding of Dabney Fairchild to Troy Flavin. From the day that the narrator, Laura McRaven, arrives on the Yellow Dog, it is evident that the Fairchilds are the leading family in this part of the Delta. The town itself is named for them. Because the Fairchild plantation, Shellmound, is the focus of all social activity in the area, it logically follows that the wedding of Shellmound's only daughter will be a broad display of Mississippi style and privilege. The fact that she is marrying an outsider does not diminish the responsibility of the Fairchilds to declare who they are in every wedding detail. Rather, it intensifies this need. Despite the weight of heavy Fairchild disapproval about this marriage, custom requires the family to act as a unit, to put on a show for the community—and especially for their future in-laws, who are beneath them by every measure that counts in Delta society.

As soon as the novel begins, we see cake after cake. Cake is served beginning with Laura's first dinner at Shellmound, where we learn that the family disapproves of the bridegroom. This evening's cake signals the family pecking order—it is the favorite cake of the "best loved" of the Fairchild men, George.[28] Even though he is absent and is known not to be arriving until the next day, George is the Fairchild whose preferences Aunt Ellen caters to. At the mention of George's name, the relatives and guests gathered around the table fall silent, and sit "sighing, eating cake, drinking coffee," waiting for the favored son to come.[29] The next cake that is made, too, will be for George. Just as Aunt Ellen is about to go into the kitchen to get her baking underway, she notices Laura. Knowing Laura's mother has died recently—so recently that protocol will not allow her to be a member of the wedding party—Ellen decides to reach out to the little girl by letting her help in the preparation of this special cake: "She's the poor little old thing, she thought. When a man alone has to look after a little girl, how in even eight months she will get longlegged and skinny. She will like as not need to have glasses when school starts. He doesn't cut her hair, or he will cut it too short. How sharp her elbows are . . ."; in a spontaneous gesture of compassion and inclusion, Ellen says, "Come help me make a cake before bedtime, Laura."[30] Hand in hand, they enter the kitchen.

The importance of this cake is soon made clear: it is to be a coconut cake, not a plain cake they might have on any ordinary day. For this one Ellen has gathered "fourteen guinea eggs . . . and that's a sign I ought to make it."[31] Soon Laura and the Fairchild cook, Roxie, are given their working orders: "'Well,' Ellen says to Roxie, 'you get the oven hot.' Ellen tied her apron back on. 'You can grate me the coconut, and a lemon while you're at it, and blanch me the almonds. I'm going to let Laura pound me the almonds in the mortar and pestle'"[32] At first Laura is worried that the task may be too challenging for her, but soon she is busy, happy to be included in this special family moment. Her aunt "beat the egg whites and began creaming the sugar and butter, saying a word from time to time to Laura who hung on the table and watched her."[33] Just making the cake makes Ellen feel "busily consoled for the loss of Dabney to Troy Flavin by the happiness of George lost to Robbie"— for George, too, has "married 'beneath' him."[34] Ellen becomes almost dizzy as she mixes the nutmeg and grated lemon rind into the batter, caught up in her certainty of the pleasure the cake will give her beloved brother. She adds milk and egg whites, then precious drops of rose water for flavor, carefully following the recipe that has been handed down through generations of Fairchild women.

Finally she pours the batter "out in four layer pans and set the first two in the oven, gently shutting the door" and telling Laura to "save me twenty-four perfect halves—to go on top."[35] Next she turns to the filling. "[S]he would just trust that Laura's paste would do, and make the icing thick on top with perfect almonds over it close enough to touch."[36] Caught in a troublesome reverie about everything that she thinks is not quite right for George and Dabney, Ellen seems caught off guard when Dabney appears at the door, begging her mother's approval. Rather than reassuring her daughter, Ellen responds in a puzzling way: "'Smell my cake?' she challenged."[37] Suddenly the four females stand silent together, caught in the tense nexus of inclusion, affection, pity, defiance, and rejection that characterizes their family relationships and has met in the baking of this cake.

Later, on the evening before the wedding, another cake is served, and again it signals the ebb and flow of Fairchild connections. The serving of this one, the bridesmaids' cake Delta tradition calls for after the wedding rehearsal, is like an intricately choreographed ballet, in which family members register and respond to one another's emotional needs as they pass plates of cake and move about the room. The narrator comments: "Here they sat—all dreamily now, each with a piece of cake to spoil his supper—their truest selves, like their truest aberrations and truest virtues, not tampered with. Here in the closest intimacy the greatest anonymity lay, and a kind of basking, a kind of special pleasure, was in it."[38] Cake in hand, they are unified, yet isolated from one another.

The most significant cake in the novel is Dabney's wedding cake, a unique confection ordered all the way from Memphis. This cake gives the Fairchilds bragging rights all around the Delta. At a cost of thirty-five dollars, it is easily the most expensive one anyone in the area has ever seen. Great strategy is applied even getting it out of the wagon, where it rests in "the tallest box yet from Memphis"; they have to slide it out on a cutting board "big as the head of a bed."[39] When they see the cake itself, one of them immediately exclaims, "Talk about spun sugar!" and wonders, "Now did they forget the ring and thimble and all inside?"[40] These little baked-in favors promise good fortune to those lucky enough to receive slices containing them. Positioned as they are in society, the Fairchilds have no choice but to offer such an elaborate display.

The cake is transported into the dining room, where it rests in state "in the center of that lace rose that's the middle of Mashula's cloth," a family heirloom.[41] Children are cautioned not to "shake the house, from now on," lest something happen to spoil this grand symbol.[42] As soon as Dabney awakens on her wedding day, she, her sisters, and her aunts go and sit around her cake, checking to make certain that it is all right. At the reception, the cake does its duty, standing proudly as a conspicuous display of Fairchild wealth and social eminence. Thus Welty exemplifies her conviction that "the most profound thoughts can be expressed in the simplest ways."[43] In her novels, cakes are powerful metaphors of class and community.

Food or even its unexpected absence can illustrate an author's point, as Wilma Dykeman reveals in two interrelated novels set in the Appalachian Mountains. *The Tall Woman* (1962) and its sequel, *The Far Family* (1966), tell the stories of Lydia McQueen, a strong mountain woman of the Reconstruction period, and her modern descendants, the fictional Thurston family. In each book, cakes carry messages from the women who prepare them.

Dykeman initially presents her heroine in her roles as wife and daughter. McQueen is in many ways a woman of her time who will continue to view her responsibilities in traditional terms. However, her sense of self expands rapidly as she becomes a voice for issues in the public mind, working to build a school for Thickety Creek and to keep mountain streams pure. Dykeman, in presenting the daughter-mother-wife-activist McQueen, seeks "an integration of mind and place that both celebrates and transcends gender."[44] Lydia's traditional domesticity provides only a base from which to chart her emergence as an innovator in community social reform. Her involvement with the preparation and serving of food is key to this portrayal.

Thickety Creek marks most of its rites of passage—births, marriages, religious meetings, and deaths especially—by bringing food to share, and by telling stories while they prepare or eat what they have brought. Aware of the connection between sharing food and storytelling, Dykeman frequently writes scenes that take place in kitchens or around dining tables. She believes that people gather in this way to share "memories—not just food."[45] Often cakes play a central part in those gatherings.

Depicting women baking not only provides the author with a way to portray traditional mountain culture in accurate detail, it gives her fictional women silent opportunities to express themselves. They show hospitality, reinforce the connections between family and community, distract themselves from their worries, or think their private thoughts as they mix batter and wait for it to bake. Because the novel takes place in the nineteenth-century Appalachian South, a time when the hardship experienced throughout the region was particularly felt in the mountains, on many occasions the form of baking they serve is simple. It may be a cake of cornbread, a fresh blackberry cobbler, or a stacked apple cake, a mountain treat made of "plain sweet layers with applesauce between each."[46] Their plain fare reflects the hard times they endure.

Cakes in Dykeman's fiction can demonstrate women's attempts to connect or mend their families, torn apart by war or estranged from one another by the normal pressures of living. The Civil War, which serves as background for early portions of *The Tall Woman*, is a time of extreme privation for this mountain community. Even so, when a "bearded, weary young soldier" stops by, Lydia's mother reaches into her meager stores, offering him a cake of cornbread "to carry as he went, thinking of her husband and her son and her daughter's husband as she fixed the food and gave it."[47] In sharing with a stranger, she affirms her connection with her missing family. At another point, Lydia also seeks to draw her family closer by baking a cake. Her husband, his frustrations with poverty and emotional scars from the war festering inside, flings out at his family. Turning to her little daughter, Martha, who is frightened by her father's outburst, Lydia says: "Now why don't you and David put on your coats and go out to the barn and see if you can find a nest some old hen's hid out? Bring me an egg and I might make us a little sweetbread cake for supper."[48] Lydia sees that the children are startled; she wishes to comfort them as well as her husband, and tries to do so by making a cake.

When Lydia's mother dies, the community gathers for her funeral. Entering the house, Lydia sees the table piled with food, offerings of compassion and solidarity from their mountain neighbors: "She looked at the groaning table again. Everyone in the valley was pinched for food at the close of a long winter after a slim harvest, but they had brought dried-fruit pies and one-layer cakes, puddings, dishes of cooked vegetables, pots of stewed chicken with flaky dumplings, slices of ham. How many times had Lydia watched her mother fix a basket to take on just such an occasion to someone in the valley?"[49] Despite the barrenness of their own cupboards, the women of Thickety Creek scrape together a meal that will be a tribute. They even include a cake: although it has only one layer, it is made with precious sugar, one of the few resources people would have to pay cash to obtain. Their customs are "components of a power system . . . that protects the culture from the worst of all failures, the loss of the people's confidence in their way of life."[50] Like people across the fictional or the actual South, these mourners gather around a table laden with their gifts of food, homage to the life lost and affirmation of their own vitality. As the novel proceeds, cakes continue to appear—at barn raisings, church dinners, and other private or community events. When Lydia herself dies, Dykeman uses the tradition of bringing food to a funeral to new effect—she writes it out of the novel. Dykeman omits this entrenched community custom as a marker of respect for what her heroine has tried to accomplish, to show that this death is unlike any other.

The Far Family's Ivy Cortland, like her grandmother Lydia, uses food in an attempt to bring her spiritually disconnected family together. Growing up, they have grown apart. Ivy decides to see what she can do to bring them into harmony, goes to the kitchen, and ties on her apron. Later that day, she calls her family to a buffet dinner she has prepared. Seeing the dishes Ivy has spread before them, her brothers and sisters are inundated by memories that suggest how much they still share. Ivy concludes this huge meal with a sumptuous cake—not one contrived from meager ingredients—but "wedges of coconut cake, light and rich with the moisture of freshly grated coconut between each layer."[51] Her sister declares, "Ivy, Papa would have traded his interest in heaven for a piece of cake like this."[52] Ivy uses favorite dishes to remind her family that, in spite of the emotional distances that separate them, they are allied by a common past. Soon the Thurstons are relaxed and easy with one another: "They sat at the table and pealed forth laughter as they remembered . . . their overall allegiance to each other remained. And Ivy had used their common memory of big meals together to remind them of the old strong bonds."[53] At least for a while, food and memory combine to smooth out family differences and soothe Thurston pain.

In Lydia McQueen and Ivy Cortland, Dykeman has fashioned a literary construct to serve as a powerful rejoinder to generations of stereotypes—new heroes from a reconstructed and gendered mythos. Joseph Campbell explains the stature of characters invested with such mythic power. He says they are "fixed stars" who give their societies "a known horizon."[54] Adding that "myths offer life models," Campbell says they are "metaphorical of potentiality in the human being. . . . The courage to face trials and bring a whole new body of possibilities into the field of interpreted experience for others to experience— that is the hero's deed."[55] Dykeman's protagonists are literary women who fit this design. They may be wives or mothers, but they are also family historians, keepers of the culture, scholars (in books or in the lore of the woods), dispensers of folk wisdom, healers of body and spirit, or bringers of real community progress. Dykeman's portraits of women with strong ties to the domestic sphere derive from her impetus "to try to deal with life, internal and external, in all its complexity" and to avoid "the tendency to compartmentalize thought and feeling, home and work, self and other."[56] Lydia and Ivy create connections, not just cakes, as they stand at their kitchen stoves.

Young adult books about southern life, too, may contain scenes that denote the cultural importance of baked goods at communal gatherings. One of the most celebrated works of young adult fiction, Mildred D. Taylor's *Roll of Thunder, Hear My Cry* (1976), includes such scenes. The book tells the moving story of a middle-class African American family living in Mississippi in 1933. The central character is fourteen-year-old Cassie Logan, whose literary experiences reflect the racial and economic oppression of the time. Taylor's central themes are serious ones: growing up, racism, class conflict, and the true meaning of courage. For its profound treatment of these and other important issues, Taylor's novel won the 1977 Newbery Medal as the most outstanding novel written for children and young adults. To allow her strong fictional family the opportunity to pass on values that are crucial for their full knowledge and survival, Taylor creates various situations in which the Logans come together at the table, whether in pairs or as a multigenerational unit. In these gatherings they laugh, tell stories that illustrate life's deepest lessons, and draw comfort from one another's strength. Cake plays a part in those moments, signaling that the occasion in which it appears will be anything but ordinary and will also bring lessons to be learned or renewed.

On the day before Christmas, Cassie's mother, Mary, and grandmother, Big Ma, fill the house with aromas that "smell of Sunday: chicken frying, bacon sizzling, and smoke sausages baking. By evening, it reeked of Christmas. In the kitchen sweet potato pies, egg-custard pies, and rich butter pound cakes cooled."[57] When the Logans join in this special family meal, "the warm sound of husky voices and rising laughter mingle[s] in tales of sorrow and happiness of days past but not forgotten."[58] The pies and cakes Logan women have worked so lovingly to prepare for their family have set the stage for the key event to follow, as the adults teach their cultural history through a series of instructional family memories.

David Scofield Wilson and Angus Kress Gillespie point out that meanings invested in food come from the contexts into which we place them.[59] Certainly the context of those buttery pound cakes Mama and Big Ma serve is crucial to Taylor's narrative. To begin with, the entire novel is set in the Depression Era, when the ingredients for rich cakes were hard to acquire, and eggless (much less butterless) cakes were the order of the day. Taylor signals the reader that whatever follows the consumption of these cakes is also precious. By having the Logans eat the cakes in an intimate setting—in their own home, on a holiday, at the conclusion of a festive meal—Taylor not only pictures innumerable family gatherings, but invests this gathering with even more significance. It is the preface to the family storytelling session in which the adults will delineate the history of Blacks in this country, as revealed through a series of family memories. Their recollections not only draw the Logans closer to one another, they offer instructive memories to the children.

The stories they share span African American history from its beginnings in slavery up to the Depression, when the novel is set. They give a balanced portrayal of long injustices, exemplified primarily in the sufferings of members of the Logan family. The history they teach is found nowhere in the children's school textbooks, castoffs that paint positive stories of Whites-only history. The Logans' memories sometimes involve horrific incidents passed on through oral histories from past relatives or their own eyewitness accounts. Custom does not exclude even the harshest stories. Once, a family friend forces himself to remember the murders of Black women and children by a KKK-like group of night riders, witnessed when he was only a child. Though painful to relate, these stories remind Cassie and her brothers of their family's role in a heritage of courage and pride and signal the other adults not to give up their fight for justice.

Everything in this family gathering has been leading to a crescendo for the Logans—a call to further action, not only to protect their own land, but to begin a plan of economic resistance for the whole Black community. As the evening ends, Mary Logan takes the strength furnished from their meal, its rich conclusion, and the stories of courage shared around their family fire to form a new resolve. She will spearhead an economic boycott of the Wallace store, the local establishment that is the source of covert and overt racist attacks, ranging from bill-padding and serving liquor to Black teenagers to the more sinister and life-threatening visits of the night riders. Everyone knows, too, that the Wallaces are at the root of the brutal murder of John Henry Berry—tortured, burned, and left to die. "It may not be real justice," Mary tells her family, "but it'll hurt them and we'll have done something."[60]

The gatherings at the table, particularly the Christmas Eve one during which the cake is served, are almost a sacrament for the Logans. Lessons imparted there will prove essential to them in knowing who they are as an individual family, as members of the larger community, and as a people. After that holiday evening in which they share the butter pound cakes, the Logans must find the strength to organize a resistance movement among the members of the local African American community. As the only Black landowners in the area, they are the ones people turn to for responsible leadership.

It is critical to Taylor's thematic development that this scene comes near the center of the novel, preceded by escalating acts of open brutality on the part of racist whites and followed by increased civil action on the part of their victims. The author devotes a full eight pages to setting up and delineating the intimate scene of Logan family and friends together, sharing food, fellowship, stories, and civic resolve. However, she gives the Christmas feast that comes the next day a mere mention, saying only: "The meal lasted for over two hours through firsts, seconds, thirds, talk and laughter, and finally dessert."[61]

The thunder Taylor embeds in the title increases as the book builds to its conclusion. There is no other incidence of a quiet family evening in *Roll of Thunder, Hear My Cry*, and there is only one more scene in which cake appears. This time cakes are served at a revival at the Great Faith Church. By now Mary Logan has made good on her resolve to back a boycott of the Wallace store. An air of tension is omnipresent in the novel, because the Wallaces and their crowd know who is behind the boycott, and will not stop until they have taken the Logan land and destroyed the family. The Black community is well aware that they risk death in defying Wallace and the night riders, and several of them have backed out of the boycott. Because the community needs the public declaration of solidarity that is inherent in the yearly meeting and its accompanying feast, Taylor once more writes a scene of abundant sharing around the table. Again, cakes are in evidence.

Cassie, as narrator, describes the scene, a classic southern meal: "After the first of three services was dismissed . . . the women proudly set out their dinners in the backs of wagons and on the long tables circling the church. It was a feast to remember. Brimming bowls of turnip greens and black-eyed peas with ham hocks, thick slices of last winter's sugar-cured ham and strips of broiled ribs, crisply fried chicken and morsels of golden squirrel and rabbit, flaky buttermilk biscuits and crusty cornbread, fat slabs of sweet potato pie and butter pound cakes, and so much more were all for the taking. No matter how low the pantry supplies, each family always managed to contribute something, and as the churchgoers made the rounds from table to table, hard times were forgotten at least for the day."[62] Once more, the sharing of cake and other foods carries heavy symbolic weight for this community.

It is at its base a practical thing to do—their day is a long one, with three complete church services to be held. Further, this feast is the gift of proud women to their neighbors; they deprive themselves to scrape together the ingredients for creating a meal so sumptuous that it can make the community temporarily forget their extreme political and economic hardships. In addition, the meal comes at a moment when their mutual resistance is low. Having weathered so much, and being in harm's way of losing so much more, they need spiritual refreshment more than even they realize. This meal, with its rich finale of butter pound cake, gives it to them. Note the foods they eat: turnip greens, black-eyed peas, ham hocks, sweet potato pie, and more. This food is not just any groceries. It is soul food. It is tradition. When the church-goers gathered together to eat it communally, they are being reminded of their history. Just as surely as the stories told around the Logan hearth do, these foods encourage them to remember the struggles they have endured to get this far and reassure them that they are one. Once again, Taylor has written a meal that functions as a kind of sacrament for her characters. These two brief scenes of family and community feasts serve Taylor's purpose—bringing, with their plentiful harvest of food and memory—solid reminders of tradition, of pride, of unity, and of shared determination.

In *Little Altars Everywhere* (1992) and *Divine Secrets of the Ya-Ya Sisterhood* (1996), her contemporary novels about female bonding and defiance of cus-tom, Rebecca Wells presents a very different picture of women from the ones given in earlier fiction discussed here. Both works center on the families of four women known as the Ya-Yas, childhood friends who have lived their en-tire lives in actual and psychic proximity to one another. They exemplify the female connection Rosemary M. Magee describes as "a set of intertwining cir-cles . . . that spiral into the present."[63] Vivi Walker and her pals, Necie, Caro, and Teensy, are the members of this "gang of girlfriends," a close-knit group whose apparent *raison d'etre* is mutual support and having fun.[64] Wells' initial Ya-Ya characterizations suggest that there is little more to them than their motto, "Smoke, Drink, Never Think," would indicate.[65] Clearly, their princi-pal occupations are to "drink bourbon and branch water and go shopping to-gether" or to sing, dance, and play bourrée, "a kind of cutthroat Louisiana poker."[66] The Ya-Ya idol is Tallulah Bankhead, whom they identify with as a southern woman who has achieved her fame through a combination of talent, outrage, and notable excesses. Their children, the "Petites Ya-Yas," travel in their wake.[67] All the Ya-Yas are married, but for the most part, their husbands operate on the periphery of their universe, with few evident options other than going along with whatever excessive schemes the Ya-Yas devise.

The Ya-Ya connection to one another is unbreakable. Their shared credo is "the gospel of popularity," a doctrine they are intent on ingraining into their offspring, assuring that their children cannot "be left out on the fringes" of life around Thornton, the principal setting of both novels.[68] The social leadership the Ya-Yas provide the community *does* often find them on the fringes of pro-priety, however, as their free-spirited antics win both admiration and ardent community disapproval. They follow what most locals regard as a highly un-usual set of behaviors. Despite external pressures, however, Vivi and her friends adhere strictly to well defined—although very Ya-Ya specific—taboos and obsessions, mostly based on their devotion to good times and high personal style.

To be sure, the Ya-Yas do not bake: they would rather "Shake a tail feather, Dahlins! . . . Cut a rug!"[69] The dessert preparation most memorable to their children is when the Ya-Yas "get out the Hershey bars and jumbo marshmallows and graham crackers and we make s'mores."[70] This treat is invariably a preface to one of Vivi's storytelling sessions, times when she really shines at a skill that means more to her than cooking. Ya-Yas consciously avoid domestic chores—especially baking—preferring to jump into a convertible and go tearing off at top speed, in a blatant effort to outrage their neighbors and escape the demands of the "jealous pissants" whose social pressure the Ya-Yas find so constricting.[71] When occasions arise that traditionally call for cakes—like the birthday of Vivi's daughter Sidda—they order them from the local bakery. Sidda recalls, "Vivi ordered not one but two birthday cakes from the bakery. . . . One for their morning orgy, and another for the birthday party later in the day."[72] Iconoclast in every respect, Vivi wakes Sidda with a "rose-bedecked cake at dawn," inviting her and the other children to breakfast on cake: "As they licked sugar roses Vivi would make them promise not to tell their father. Big Shep claimed eating cake like that so early in the morning was a 'whore's breakfast.' The rest of them didn't care. They were happy little whores who didn't worry about saving a morsel."[73] This unusual birthday breakfast holds multiple social currencies for Vivi: It allows her to indulge her children according to her uniquely outrageous sense of style, as well as to thumb her nose surreptitiously at her husband's set of rules for proper females.

The Ya-Yas can be extremely creative cooks if they decide to do so. That is the key principle—it must be their choice to go into the kitchen. But on the rare occasions when they choose to cook, they always make dishes that are more essential than cake, consisting of equal portions of butter, audacity, and pure Louisiana bayou. Then they can turn out delectable fare like the crawfish *étouffée* that sends an unmistakable message: "With each bite, Sidda tasted her homeland and her mother's love."[74] The Ya-Yas' avoidance of the kitchen except on their own terms, along with the verbal snipes they take at women who do stay in the kitchen and create cakes, is one of their extensive assortment of techniques for shaking off community expectations.

The marriage between southern women and cakes is also well defined in the writing of Dori Sanders, a novelist who has taken her knowledge of southern life to the street. Following the publication of two immensely successful works of fiction—*Clover* (1990) and *Her Own Place* (1993)—Sanders wrote *Country Cooking* (1995), a cookbook that combines stories she recalls from growing up in South Carolina peach country with Sanders' own treasured recipes. Like those of most southern families, Sanders' recipe collection is a mixture of the plain fare served daily and special dishes for Sundays or important occasions. She calls the first group "basic, simple survival foods, dishes that brought us through the Great Depression and the hard times of failed crops and lean harvests"; the second aspect of the collection evokes "a world of old-fashioned family cooking and southern country warmth and hospitality."[75] Each category contains cakes.

One of Sanders' earliest memories is of the arrival of her Aunt Vestula, a dignified lady who cooked for a wealthy Charleston family and always brought treats when she came to visit the upcountry. "Of course, in Aunt Vestula's wicker hamper there was always a great big fruitcake wrapped in heavy, brandy-soaked brown paper and stored in a decorative airtight tin."[76] Sanders explains how her aunt was able to obtain the rich ingredients for such a cake, giving insight into southern cultural practices as she does so. "You must also know that Aunt Vestula worked at a time when the 'pay and tote' system was in effect. It was just a little southern thing. 'Pay' was the amount of money you received for your services, 'tote' was the extra food you carried home to your own family. Cooks during that time always prepared a little bit more food than necessary for the family they worked for. That way they were guaranteed to have some food to tote home. They simply added a little more sugar to the pound than necessary. It wasn't considered stealing; it was understood as part of their wages."[77]

For the women in Sanders' family "food—and the joy it brought when shared with family and friends—was truly the center of their lives."[78] Its preparation and consumption alone could mark the occasions of a family year. Certainly the cakes they made were a form of social commerce, especially at reunions: "Yes, family reunion cooking can be intense. The competition is keen, the demand for originality high. We all want to outdo each other."[79] Any Sanders reunion would definitely bring forth a celery cake, a secret recipe from a cousin who just called it a "vegetable cake" and "refused to tell what was in" it.[80] This cake was her special province, and to give up the recipe would be to relinquish some of her personal power. In fact, for the cookbook Sanders still could not get the recipe; she, her sister, and their female cousins practiced until they devised a reasonable facsimile of the cake they remember.

Another recipe Sanders passes on is for a "Neighbor Cake," so named because it requires simple ingredients a woman might borrow from a neighbor if she found herself without them. This sense of extended community is typical of the rural South, less so now than when Sanders was a child. Several cakes call for items that could be found close at hand, in the natural world around them rather than purchased at a store, like wild persimmon roll and sweet potato pound cake with peach glaze. Families had to make the most of what was available, and enjoyed the fresh ingredients the cycles of the seasons furnished for their baking. At times cakes could even help a woman to play a joke on her friends or neighbors. One such confection is chocolate zucchini cake, prepared at the height of the harvest season, when zucchini is so plentiful that everyone is sick of it. Sanders cautions, "I recommend that you not reveal what this cake contains, and please don't crack a smile when somebody says, 'It's great not to eat zucchini again.'"[81] For Sanders' relations Christmas brought the year to a close with its "thick slices of cake and sassafras tea" served only to grownups, marking a rite of passage to adulthood.[82] In her family, one can herald the passage of the seasons just by noting what cakes are baked and offered for mutual enjoyment.

What is the significance of all these connections or conscious disconnections between women and cake, then? Are they something simply to note and dismiss, nothing more? Is making a cake just that—making a cake, creating food—or does it assume greater importance in women's lives? Is it further indication of the power of the many cultural prescriptions society writes for women? Surely, we may ask, if women simply comply with a cultural expectation that grounds them once again in familiar domestic routines, are they not inscribing the same designs that have traditionally halted their progress?

Domesticity, threaded through situation and metaphor, recurrently figures in female narratives. Some critics interpret this domestic orientation as lessening the significance of characters depicted in such settings. Carol Christ does not share that critical view, and feels that domestic spheres are not inherently limiting to female characters—or, by extension, to actual women—but can constitute a new territory for symbolic heroic action. Heroic quest narratives have typically disallowed female domestic experience, since those who could not travel far from home (that is to say, go on a standard quest) were routinely barred from being known as heroes.[83] Considering the limitations of traditional concepts of heroes, Christ does acknowledge the problem critics find in reconciling a heroic character's impact with the lack of power typical of many domestic narratives. But Christ, along with an increasing number of critics such as Carol Pearson and Katherine Pope, sees concepts of the heroic plane as extending to any spot where a character is involved in self-definition or redefinition of roles. This fresh image of the female hero is one Pearson and Pope argue for—one who enjoys mastery that comes from understanding the world and coping, not from "dominating, controlling, or owning [it]," as is true in the majority of instances for traditional male models of heroism.[84]

An extension of the usual (male) heroic paradigm is significant for a consideration of work by numerous writers treating women's experience, so commonly based in the world of home and family. Lee Smith, who prefers a domestic setting for her fiction, argues that the subjects "women have often written about, which are deep kinds of rituals or families or relationships . . . are just as important as some traditionally male thing. I don't think there's a degree that makes it lesser."[85] If women take those same domestic patterns that have long been relegated to them and reinscribe them as methods of asserting their own power, they are performing what Michel de Certeau calls "an oppositional practice," "a guerrilla warfare of everyday life."[86] By such means women are able to redefine their lives in accordance with newer, less restrictive paradigms. The smaller the amount of power that is granted to a woman by her society or community, the more such tactics are called for.

Women who take the cake, then, must be doing more than embracing a totally domestic orientation, as has so often been assumed. On occasion they *are* simply expressing affection for their families and friends by presenting them with a special dish on a festive occasion. But they can—and frequently do—use cakes to assert their authority, as Welty's Mississippi women do, or even to provoke their own political activism, as the Logans do in Taylor's novel about the Civil Rights Movement. They can use cakes to bind people together, as Dykeman's Ivy Cortland does in *The Far Family*, or to reject traditional roles ascribed to them, as the Ya-Yas do in Wells' contemporary classics. They can even use them to keep secrets from other women or to play jokes, as the recipes in Sanders' *Country Cooking* indicate.

It must be acknowledged, though, that whatever ascendancy women achieve by means of the cakes they create and serve can be problematic. Like a variety of symbols of women's domestic productivity, their achievements consist of social pressures, rather than publicly recognized economic or political control. The authority their domestic products give women is also likely to be limited. Special attention should continue to be paid to assessing such limitations. Crucial, too, is a consideration of who the combatants are in women's culture wars: though no less dramatic than those fought on larger playing fields, these battles take place in arenas peopled mostly by other women. That an appreciable number of those women may already be marginalized because of their class or race makes their treatment by their sisters even more tangled with complications. As Minrose C. Gwin observes, "[I]n our own kitchens, we may be reenacting the processes of our own disempowerment as women."[87] Whether in life or in fiction, one woman's gain can regrettably engender another's loss. Thus the relationship between women and cake remains a complex one—at times, reaffirming; at times, injurious.

Clearly, however, when a woman whips up a cake or takes one to a family or community event, she is making a cultural statement holding complexities that extend beyond those the most intricate recipe can contain. Through her contribution to the communal plate, she states her importance in a society that has frequently cut women out of its traditional access to power. In so doing, she works to bring about her own social transformation. As Bailey White has pointed out in her musings about life in rural Georgia, cakes are at the top of a food hierarchy that begins with jams and jellies, then progresses through pickles and preserves, biscuits and pastry, bread, sauces and marinades, shellfish, game, and soufflés before climaxing in desserts.[88] The cultural parallels are obvious. If a woman wishes to attain the top rung of her community's social ladder, she must be able to create the dish that signifies her elevated status.

Matters that are important in southern culture are passed on in subtle ways—are, in fact, more caught than taught. They are the sorts of things that "Everybody knows," despite whether they are actually true. The connections between women and cakes and between cakes and cultural power exemplify this kind of social osmosis. Everybody knows that really good cakes are hard to make. Everybody knows that a cake is a statement of social authority. Everybody knows that the leading women in a community make the best cakes. Everybody knows that there is as wide a cultural void between a cake made from a box and a fresh coconut cake as there is between the *Jerry Springer Show* and *Masterpiece Theatre*. If this were not true, why would a typical southern cookbook that contains fourteen cake recipes have half of them be for pound cake or coconut cake alone?[89] Does a woman want to take a shortcut to social power in the South? Does she wish to be unobtrusive, yet unmistakable, in pursuing this power? A sure way for her to do so is to master that most intricate delicacy, a light and fluffy, rich and memorable cake. Like its creator, in a southern social gathering a cake invariably "takes center stage."[90]

More than simply a rich confection, a homemade cake can be far sweeter than its ingredients. Part sweet treat, part offering, it can also become her personal instrument for asserting cultural control. When a woman bakes a cake, she may be seeking a way to pass on important family or community stories, a means of meting out social retribution, an avenue for achieving dominion over her world, or a method for reaching out toward a growing personal autonomy. These signals are part of the symbolic nature of food, particularly when we share it in communal gatherings, where cultures knowingly or unknowingly utilize what they eat to convey messages they wish to be made plain. Taking the cake, then, is a telling inclusion in any real or literary event involving those complex women of the South.

NOTES

1. Dillon Bustin, "New England Prologue: Thoreau, Antimodernism, and Folk Culture," in Jane S. Becker and Barbara Franco, *Folk Roots, New Roots: Folklore in American Life* (Lexington, Mass.: Museum of Our National Heritage, 1988), 1.

2. Peggy Prenshaw, "Introduction," *Southern Quarterly* 30.2–3 (1992): 8.

3. Prenshaw, "Introduction," 6.

4. Mildred Council, *Mama Dip's Kitchen* (Chapel Hill: University of North Carolina Press, 1999), 171.

5. Council, *Mama Dip's Kitchen*, 171.

6. America Online, version 5.0, 12 February 2000.

7. America Online, version 5.0, 24 January 2000.

8. "Just Desserts," *American Home Style and Gardening* (May 2000): 23.

9. Susan Ungaro, ed., *Family Circle* 113.4 (7 March 2000): front cover.

10. Michael Tyrrell, "Party Cakes Made Easy," *Family Circle* 113.4 (7 March 2000): 118–19, 136.

11. Tyrrell, "Party Cakes," 118.

12. The hostess of HGTV's "Start to Finish," a how-to program about craft projects that may be completed in one sitting, recently reinscribed the importance of having even the *image* of a cake appear at a women's social gathering. Using thirty-two newborn-sized diapers, she gave directions for making a "diaper cake" to function as the centerpiece for one of the most culturally important female enclaves, a baby shower.

13. Lucinda H. MacKethan, *Daughters of Time: Creating Woman's Voice in Southern Story* (Athens: University of Georgia Press, 1990), 5.

14. Victoria E. Bynum, *Unruly Women: The Politics of Social and Sexual Control in the Old South* (Chapel Hill: University of North Carolina Press, 1992), 51.

15. Bessie Chronaki, "Eudora Welty's Theory of Place and Human Relationships," *South Atlantic Bulletin* 33 (2 May 1978): 36.

16. Joseph Campbell, *The Inner Reaches of Outer Space: Metaphor as Myth and as Religion* (New York: Alfred Van Der Marck, 1986), 22.

17. Barbaralee Diamondstein, "Eudora Welty," in *Conversations with Eudora Welty*, ed. Peggy Whitman Prenshaw (Jackson: University of Mississippi Press, 1984), 36.

18. Eudora Welty, *The Collected Stories of Eudora Welty* (New York: Harcourt Brace Jovanovich, 1980), 297.

19. Welty, *Collected Stories*, 305.

20. Danielle Pitvay-Souques, "Technique as Myth: The Structure of *The Golden Apples*," in *Eudora Welty: Thirteen Essays*, ed. Peggy Whitman Prenshaw (Jackson: University of Mississippi Press, 1983), 154–55.

21. Welty, *Collected Stories*, 314, 328.

22. Welty, *Collected Stories*, 427.

23. Welty, *Collected Stories*, 434.

24. Welty, *Collected Stories*, 427.

25. Welty, *Collected Stories*, 434.

26. Welty, *Collected Stories*, 434.

27. Henry Glassie, "The Idea of Folk Art," in John Michael Vlach and Simon J. Bronner, *Folk Art and Art Worlds* (Ann Arbor, Mich.: UMI Research, 1986), 271.

28. Eudora Welty, *Delta Wedding* (New York: Harcourt Brace Jovanovich, 1945), 15.

29. Welty, *Delta Wedding*, 17.

30. Welty, *Delta Wedding*, 24.

31. Welty, *Delta Wedding*, 24.

32. Welty, *Delta Wedding*, 24.

33. Welty, *Delta Wedding*, 24–25.

34. Welty, *Delta Wedding*, 24–25.

35. Welty, *Delta Wedding*, 26.

36. Welty, *Delta Wedding*, 26.

37. Welty, *Delta Wedding*, 27.

38. Welty, *Delta Wedding*, 188.

39. Welty, *Delta Wedding*, 200.

40. Welty, *Delta Wedding*, 200.

41. Welty, *Delta Wedding*, 201.

42. Welty, *Delta Wedding*, 201.

43. George W. Boyd et al., "The Artist and the Critic," in *Conversations with Eudora Welty*, ed. Peggy Whitman Prenshaw (Jackson: University of Mississippi Press, 1984), 16.

44. MacKethan, *Daughters of Time*, 11.

45. Wilma Dykeman, interview with the author, 14 March 1992.

46. Wilma Dykeman, *The Tall Woman* (New York: Holt, Rinehart and Winston, 1962; Avon, 1967; Newport, Tenn.: Wakestone, 1962), 183.

47. Dykeman, *The Tall Woman*, 23.

48. Dykeman, *The Tall Woman*, 122.

49. Dykeman, *The Tall Woman*, 139.

50. Thomas J. Steele, *Santos and Saints: The Religious Folk Art of Hispanic New Mexico* (Santa Fe, N.Mex.: Ancient City, 1982), 95.

51. Wilma Dykeman, *The Far Family* (New York: Holt, Rinehart and Winston, 1966; Avon, 1967), 99.

52. Dykeman, *The Far Family*, 99.

53. Dykeman, *The Far Family*, 84–85.

54. Joseph Campbell and Bill Moyers, *The Power of Myth* (New York: Doubleday, 1988), 12.

55. Campbell and Moyers, *The Power of Myth*, 12 passim.

56. Mary Field Belensky et al., *Women's Ways of Knowing: The Development of Self, Voice, and Mind* (New York: Basic, 1986), 137.

57. Mildred D. Taylor, *Roll of Thunder, Hear My Cry* (New York: Puffin, 1976), 145.

58. Taylor, *Roll of Thunder*, 146.

59. David Scofield Wilson and Angus Kress Gillespie, *Rooted in America: Foodlore of Popular Fruits and Vegetables* (Knoxville: University of Tennessee Press, 1999), xii.

60. Taylor, *Roll of Thunder*, 151.

61. Taylor, *Roll of Thunder*, 154.

62. Taylor, *Roll of Thunder*, 234.

63. Rosemary Magee, ed., *Friendship and Sympathy: Communities of Southern Women Writers* (Jackson: University of Mississippi Press, 1992), xvi.

64. Rebecca Wells, *Little Altars Everywhere* (New York: HarperCollins, 1992), xi.

65. Rebecca Wells, *Divine Secrets of the Ya-Ya Sisterhood* (New York: HarperCollins, 1996), ix.

66. Wells, *Little Altars*, 4.

67. Wells, *Divine Secrets*, ix.

68. Wells, *Little Altars*, 5.

69. Wells, *Divine Secrets*, 355.

70. Wells, *Little Altars*, 9.

71. Wells, *Little Altars*, 326.

72. Wells, *Little Altars*, 176.

73. Wells, *Little Altars*, 177.

74. Wells, *Little Altars*, 285.

75. Dori Sanders, *Dori Sanders' Country Cooking: Recipes and Stories from the Family Farm Stand* (Chapel Hill, N.C.: Algonquin Books of Chapel Hill, 1995), xv.

76. Sanders, *Country Cooking*, 2.

77. Sanders, *Country Cooking*, 3.

78. Sanders, *Country Cooking*, 3.

79. Sanders, *Country Cooking*, 164.

80. Sanders, *Country Cooking*, 175.

81. Sanders, *Country Cooking*, 141.

82. Sanders, *Country Cooking*, 17.

83. Carol P. Christ, *Diving Deep and Surfacing: Women Writers on Spiritual Quest*, 2nd ed. (Boston: Beacon, 1986), 9.

84. Carol Pearson and Katherine Pope, *The Female Hero in American and British Literature* (New York: R. R. Bowker, 1981), 5.

85. Dorothy Hill, "'Every Kind of Ritual': A Conversation," *Iron Mountain Review* 3.1 (winter 1986): 27.

86. Michel de Certeau, "On the Oppositional Practices of Everyday Life," trans. Steven F. Rendall, in *Pratiques Quotidiennes: Pour une Semiotique de la Culture Ordinaire* (Berkeley: University of California Press, 1988), 6.

87. Minrose C. Gwin, "Sweeping the Kitchen: Revelation and Revolution in Contemporary Southern Women's Writing," *Southern Quarterly* 30.2–3 (1992): 61.

88. Bailey White, *Mama Makes Up Her Mind and Other Dangers of Southern Living* (New York: Addison-Wesley, 1993), 153–55.

89. Council, *Mama Dip's Kitchen*, 171–83.

90. Council, *Mama Dip's Kitchen*, 171.

Is Meatloaf for Men? Gender and Meatloaf Recipes, 1920–1960

Jessamyn Neuhaus

$\mathcal{T}$he *Boston Cooking School Cook Book*, one of the best selling cookery books in the late nineteenth century, featured a unique meatloaf recipe. The author, Mrs. Lincoln (head of the Boston Cooking School and predecessor to the famous Fannie Farmer), offered a recipe for "Meat Porcupines": a ground beef loaf decorated with bacon "quills" (figure 5.1). A few years later, *The Settlement Cook Book*, a popular cookbook compiled by settlement house workers to help immigrant women learn American cooking, included a simple "beef loaf" recipe: ground round steak seasoned with onions, salt, and pepper, and bound together with bread crumbs.[1] Like this beef loaf, every meatloaf recipe includes ground meat, seasoning, and a filler. However, as Mrs. Lincoln's whimsical meat porcupine demonstrated, meatloaves lend themselves to variation. They may be seasoned with ketchup, dehydrated onion soup mix, horseradish, onion, mustard, or Worcestershire sauce. They hold their shape with the help of breadcrumbs, cracker crumbs, crumbled potato chips, oatmeal, crushed corn flakes, tapioca, or gelatin. They may be topped with bacon strips, a brown sugar and pineapple glaze, tomato sauce, mashed potato "frosting," mushrooms, or blue cheese. And they may be made of beef, pork, veal, Spam, liver, sausage, chicken, lamb, ham, or a combination thereof. But although endless modifications of the basic meatloaf recipe appeared in cookbooks and popular domestic magazines throughout the twentieth century, meatloaf's *image* never really changed.

Cookbook authors and editors characterized meatloaf as a meal a woman could easily prepare for her loved ones, a simple main dish best suited for the family dinner table. In fact, perhaps no other American dish so evokes images of work-a-day, Midwestern, hearty home meals as meatloaf. Since at least 1920, cookery instruction described meatloaf as a way for homemakers

Meat Porcupine.

Chop fine some *lean cooked veal*, *chicken*, or *lamb*; add one *fourth* its amount of *cracker* or *bread crumbs*, or *mashed potato*, and a small quantity of *chopped bacon*; season highly with *salt*, *pepper*, *cayenne*, and *lemon juice*; moisten with *beaten egg* and *stock* or *water* enough to shape it.

Fig. 37   Meat Porcupine.

Mould it into an oval loaf, and put into a shallow pan well greased. Cut strips of *fat bacon*, one fourth of an inch wide and one inch long. Make holes in the loaf with a small skewer, insert the strips of bacon, leaving the ends out half an inch, and push the meat up firmly round the

Meat Porcupine from Mrs. D.A. Lincoln, *Boston Cooking School Cook Book: A Reprint of the 1884 Classic* (Mineola, New York: Dover Publications, 1996) 272.

Figure 5.1. Mrs. Lincoln's "Meat Porcupine" recipe from her 1884 Boston Cooking School Cook Book. Its quills were made out of strips of bacon.

to stretch the meat budget or to use up leftovers. Meatloaf enjoyed the status of a humble but tasty dish, suitable for fathers and children to eat and not difficult for mothers to prepare. And recipe writers made it clear that Mother would indeed be the one to mix, bake, and serve the meatloaf. From 1920 until the end of the century, meatloaf recipes appeared regularly in books and articles addressed to the white, middle-class wife and mother. In contrast, cookery instruction for men rarely included meatloaf recipes and when it did, man-made meatloaf differed in significant ways from meatloaves in general cookbooks. Recipes intended for the "man in the kitchen" represented men's cookery as a fundamentally different activity than women's cooking. Women cooked humdrum everyday meals, but men cooked for fun and to exercise their creativity at the stove.

In meatloaf recipes, authors and editors underscored gender norms in the kitchen: they assumed women bore total responsibility for the family's daily meals and meatloaf, believed to be simple family fare, seemed to belong in women's recipe books and magazines. Though deemed a filling dish suited to family appetites, meatloaf did not often appear in cookery instruction intended for male readers. Men could eat, but rarely cooked, meatloaf in twentieth-century cooking literature. Cookery instruction gendered the dull but dependable meatloaf as a feminine recipe. Comparing how cookery instruction for men and cookery instruction for women offered different versions of meatloaf illuminates the way cookbook authors and recipe purveyors represented women as solely responsible for the family's daily meals. Cookery books for men encouraged them to take up cooking as a hobby but only a hobby—as the story of meatloaf reveals. Examining recipes for "Mom's meatloaf" offers an instructive way to explore the gendering of "home cooking."

THE JOY OF COOKING MEATLOAF, 1920–1940

In 1920, students dining in the tearoom at Vassar College might well have lunched on cold veal loaf. And those interested in replicating the loaf at home could consult a cookbook authored by the tearoom matron. Her recipe called for veal, fat salt pork, cracker crumbs, eggs, and salt and pepper baked into a perfectly lady-like dish suitable for the feminine appetites at Vassar.[2] Croquettes, timbales, and other foods that neatly held their shape on the plate found much favor among the cooking school instructors and tearoom proprietresses of the late nineteenth and early twentieth century. They favored "dainty" dishes, and enjoyed making tidy balls of fish, cream cheese, or potatoes and bedecking the results in a white sauce or a sprinkling of parsley. During the late 1800s, cooking school cuisine wielded enormous power over the American palate and helped to establish the long-lived popularity of meatloaf. The Vassar veal loaf exemplified the meatloaves of the late nineteenth and early twentieth century: usually served cold, these loaves called for meats we do not associate with meatloaf today, such as veal and tongue, and usually appeared as a luncheon main dish or a sandwich filling. Meatloaf recipes like the 1903 beef loaf recipe published in *The Settlement Cook Book*, however, exemplified the meatloaves of the twentieth century after 1920: served hot and nicely browned, it called for a minimum of preparation time and consisted mainly of beef.

As commercial published cookery instruction took its twentieth-century shape, so did meatloaf. After World War I, cookery instruction in a variety of guises—food product advertisements, radio shows, domestic magazines and cookbooks—increasingly offered advice and directions to middle-class white women about learning how to cook and assured these women that cooking could be an artistic and creative joy. Significantly, the post–World War I boom in cookbook publication coincided with a marked decline in the number of household servants in middle-class homes. As more married middle-class women faced the kitchen for the first time, often without the support of an extended family structure, more women turned to published cookery advice. The most famous cookbook published during this era, *The Joy of Cooking* (self-published by author Irma Rombauer in 1931 and commercially published in 1936), achieved its remarkable success by offering soothing advice and simple but showy recipes for the hostess/cook. Rombauer's title perfectly reflected the changing nature of cookery instruction: after World War I, with consumerism on the rise and servant labor on the decline, recipe writers in cookbooks, advertisements, and promotional literature set about convincing middle-class women that daily cooking could be a daily creative joy. In the 1920s and 1930s, cookbook authors and recipe purveyors strove to come up with foods that demanded little real cooking skill but would produce wholesome meals for the whole family, and, at the same time, allow women a little creative leeway. Meatloaf fit the bill.

Meatloaf recipes required a minimum of cookery knowledge—simply measuring and mixing the ingredients and putting them into a loaf pan—but resulted in a neatly formed, nicely browned main dish. And meatloaf lent itself to easy adaptations and additions of whatever leftovers or premade ingredients the housewife had on hand. A 1928 cookbook counseled that leftover baked potato, spaghetti, baked beans, or peas could all be added to a basic hamburger loaf. Processed, canned, or bottled ingredients like ketchup and canned vegetables began to show up with increasing regularity in 1920s and 1930s meatloaf recipes. In 1937, in *To the Queen's Taste*, author Helen Hilles offered a recipe for Campbell's Soup Loaf, made with canned tomato soup and chopped round steak. Post Toasties, a breakfast cereal, ran an advertisement that featured a meatloaf recipe (made, of course, with a cup of crushed Post Toasties). In 1939, *The Canned Foods Cook Book* included meatloaf recipes that called for a variety of canned foods, such as chili sauce, canned mushrooms, evaporated milk, corned beef, and canned pears. The "Veal Loaf à la King in Rice Ring" called for "1 medium can veal loaf."[3] Numerous meatloaf recipes in the 1920s and 1930s contained such convenience foods, reflecting the de-skilling process happening in American middle-class kitchens.

While meatloaf recipes provided simple main dishes for the novice cook, they also offered her the opportunity to safely experiment a little in the kitchen, and to add her personal touch to the meal. Recipe writers throughout the 1920s and 1930s tinkered with the basic combination of ground meat, filler, and seasoning and urged readers to approach the loaf creatively. Veal loaf still enjoyed popularity during this period, and ham loaf (sometimes served "upside down" with a brown sugar–pineapple glaze) appeared more often than beef loaves, but authors experimented with a variety of meats, sauces, and cooking techniques. Some gave directions for pan frying meat loaves, rather than baking them. The 1922 cookbook published by *Good Housekeep-*

ing suggested adding olives, green peppers, and canned tomatoes to meatloaf. The editors of a 1939 cookbook published by a lesser-known domestic magazine included a recipe for "Chili Loaf," which took its name from the addition of chili powder to a basic meatloaf. *America's Cook Book*, a 1938 collection of recipes edited by the Home Institute of the *New York Herald Tribune*, included over fourteen meatloaf recipes, ranging from sausage loaf seasoned with sage to jellied chicken loaf to a pork loaf stretched with minced apples.[4]

In 1934, Nell B. Nichols, food editor for *Women's Home Companion*, raved about a new way of making meatloaf. The recipe called for baking a meatloaf within a loaf of bread. Like most authors, Nichols praised meatloaf as a thrifty value for the cost-conscious housewife: "A square of moist flavorsome meatloaf bounded on all sides by a crisp layer of buttered and toasted bread. This is one definition for the new dish which is ascending to popularity like a skyrocket. The smartest meat service discovered in months is another way of describing this thrifty and versatile creation."[5] The article included recipes for beef, veal, pork, lamb, and dried beef meat loaf and used ingredients such as canned tomato soup, bottled chili sauce, and white sauce. Meatloaf baked in bread and topped with ketchup sauce epitomized, in many ways, meatloaf recipes in the post–World War I era. "Smart," but easily made with a minimum of kitchen work and with the assistance of premade ingredients.

The meat itself, however, demanded a bit more labor. Many meatloaf recipes in the 1920s and 1930s began with directions for hand-grinding the meat or with instructions about obtaining such meat from the butcher. Well into the 1950s, most Americans bought their meat from a butcher's shop or at a meat counter in the grocery store. Meat cutters prepared and wrapped meat to order, unlike today when we can easily purchase prewrapped, preweighed hamburger at any supermarket.[6] Meatloaf recipes often called specifically for leftover meats in the 1920s and 1930s—a housewife would have been more likely to grind up the odds and ends of leftover roasts and hams than to purchase specially ground meat. Meatloaf's reputation for thriftiness grew from its ability to incorporate a variety of leftover ground or chopped meat, as well as nonmeat "stretchers." During the Great Depression of the 1930s, publishers continued to produce cookbooks in ever-increasing numbers, but most cookery books totally ignored issues of economy. However, several recipe writers did recommend meatloaf as a way to extend the meat budget in the 1920s and 1930s. Ida Bailey Allen, a prolific cookbook author in the first half of the century, included numerous recipes in her cost-conscious 1940 cookbook *Ida Bailey Allen's Money Saving Cookbook*. Allen offered a wide range of hints on eking out a main dish from just a little beef. She suggested using cereals, tomatoes, baked bananas, rice, hominy, or chopped peppers to fill out a loaf.[7]

Another penny-pinching cookbook published that same year, *Better Meals for Less Money* by Hazel Young, explained that using a variety of meats actually enhanced the flavor of meatloaf, and suggested combining leftover bacon in a beef loaf or a leftover pork chop in a veal loaf. "Even three or four leftover cooked sausage links add flavor to the loaf," Young asserted. She also urged housewives to experiment with the basic meatloaf theme: "One day, be dramatic and serve the meatloaf on a plank with a border of mashed potatoes and mounds of peas and carrots as a really professional garnish. Another day, button the loaf up in a biscuit blanket and serve it sliced with mushroom sauce."[8] Young depicted meatloaf as a flexible food that offered women a chance to be both thrifty and creative. In 1940, the editors at the Culinary Arts Institute, a food and kitchen product clearinghouse, also depicted meatloaf as both a thrifty and creative way to serve meat. Its booklet *250 Ways to Prepare Meat* included fourteen different meatloaf recipes, ranging from simple "Savory Meat Loaf" (made of ground beef, egg, vegetable soup, and cereal flakes) to "Two-Tone Meat Loaf" (two layers of contrasting meatloaf, veal and pork, baked together). The recipe for "Fruited Meat Roll" called for a filling of raisins, sage, parsley, and onion, garnished with bacon, broiled pineapple and baked sweet potatoes, and reminded the reader that a wide selection of meats (sausage, ham, beef, ground pork) could be used to add variety to this meatloaf. And, like Taylor, the editors of *250 Ways to Prepare Meat* recommended a "biscuit blanket" to give ham loaf pizzazz.[9]

Cookbook authors lauded meatloaf's adaptability, its effortless incorporation of leftover mashed potatoes or stale cereal flakes, its amenability to biscuit topping or raisin stuffing. But for recipe writers in the 1920s and 1930s, meatloaf also underscored the general message about gender roles found in much commercially published cookery instruction: middle-class white women facing new responsibilities in the kitchen should view daily meals not as a chore, but as a chance for creative expression, a chance to nurture the family with wholesome but simply prepared meals. Young introduced her remarks on meatloaf by pointing out the importance of the meatloaf maker's attitude and emphasized how meatloaf could be helpful in fostering a sense of culinary competence and pleasure:

> In exploring the possibilities for thrifty meals, we find meat loaf high in favor. There are several types of meat loaf and the woman who goes into this job of meal-planning with enthusiasm and interest will master more than one kind. She will have half a dozen different recipes at her finger tips—or at least in her recipe cabinet.

She concluded that "The point we are trying to make is this: Good foods need not be expensive foods. Ingenuity and really liking one's job can work wonders."[10] Young used meatloaf to illustrate a broader point, one readily found in most post–World War I cookery instruction: women needed to approach daily cooking "with enthusiasm and interest," and to make every effort to "really like one's job." From sturdy beef loaves seasoned only with a little salt and pepper, to individual lamb loaves baked in ramekins, to the European "German Loaf" (seasoned with curry powder, sage, cream, and ham fat, and cooked by tying the loaf in cheesecloth and immersing in boiling water and vinegar) in the 1933 edition of Fannie Farmer's cookbook, meatloaves offered a woman an easy way to use leftovers and to exercise creativity without overly taxing her culinary skills. Meatloaf recipes offered a woman a chance to place "half a dozen recipes at her finger tips," and to better exercise her daily cooking duties.

Cookbook publishers, magazine writers, food processing companies, grocery stores, and kitchen appliance manufacturers devoted most of their attention—and their recipes—to the married middle-class female consumer, presumably the person in charge of the family's daily meals. But during the 1920s and 1930s, popular household magazines also regularly discussed and depicted male culinary adventures. A significant number of cookbooks authored by men appeared on the market in the 1920s and 1930s as well. These recipes for men emphasized that although men possessed natural cooking skills, they cooked only for fun. Unlike cookery instruction for women, men's recipes did not offer ideas for practical, daily, family meals, but concentrated on special occasion cooking, such as frying freshly caught fish or concocting potent spaghetti sauce for late-night guests. Unlike cookery instruction for women, recipe books and articles intended for the male reader did not urge husbands to cheerfully take up, and learn to enjoy, the task of cooking everyday meals. Instead they portrayed men as naturally skilled in the kitchen, more adventurous and willing to experiment at the stove than women, and less inclined to slavishly follow a cookbook recipe.

Meatloaf recipes exemplified this difference between men's recipes and women's recipes. Meatloaf recipes for "the man in the kitchen" certainly did not represent a simple, thrifty family dinner, or a tasty way to use up odds and ends. The meatloaf's creative possibilities, as described by cookbooks for women, rarely exceeded a simple stuffing or layer of biscuit dough. But in cookery instruction for men, meatloaf usually called for somewhat exotic ingredients, fine grades of meat, and required far more work than meatloaves in cookery instruction for women. For instance, George Rector, a well-known restaurateur in the 1920s, recommended decorating the bottom of jellied veal loaf with an intricate design of cooked egg and pimento in his 1939 cookbook. In William Rhodes's 1938 memoir and recipe book, *Of Cabbages and Kings*, the author claimed his meatloaf recipe came straight from Russia. It demanded that the meatloaf maker carefully place long strips of boiled carrot in the center of a meatloaf so that "when the loaf is ready and sliced each slice will have a few carrot slices piercing out like 'eyes.'" The recipe also required new bread soaked in milk and "real or fake Cumberland sauce."

The Stag Cookbook, a 1922 collection of recipes by and for men, included a recipe for campfire meatloaf. It consisted of ground sirloin steak (the author advised grinding the meat yourself and not entrusting this delicate task to the butcher) fried in melted butter over a fire and doused in cream.[11] But perhaps the most elaborate male meatloaf recipe came from John MacPherson's cookbook. MacPherson hosted a popular radio show called "The Mystery Chef" during the 1930s (when the show first aired, he concealed his identity to protect his mother, who found the idea of her son doing such a feminine thing as cooking disturbing). Though MacPherson prided himself on providing expert assistance to inexperienced housewives, his recipes often called for complicated procedures or ingredients. His meatloaf recipe called for four different kinds of meat, carefully minced twice by the butcher, a variety of seasonings, and cooked under no circumstances in a loaf pan but patted into a loaf shape and baked in a flat pan. His meatloaf also had to "stand in ice box for at least one hour" in order to let the meat absorb its seasoning.[12]

Meatloaves rarely appeared in the pages of cookbooks and popular magazine articles addressed to the male amateur chef. And when they did, man-made meatloaves often called for campfires or enormous amounts of cream and ground sirloin. Simply mixing up a pound of ground meat with some cracker crumbs, an egg, and salt and pepper and packing it into a loaf pan could not be constituted as manly cooking. In keeping with most of the recipes found in cookbooks for women, meatloaves (even fancied up with bacon strips or chili sauce) offered a simple main dish, easily prepared for the family with ingredients readily available in the kitchen. Most of the men's recipes, in contrast, often called for unadulterated cuts of meat like steak or roasts, and paid virtually no attention to the problem of daily family meals. Men's recipes suggested, again and again, that men only cooked as a hobby or on hunting trips. A meatloaf suited the meals prepared every day by the woman of the house far better: meals that were occasionally creative but limited by time, financial constraints, and lack of natural flair in the kitchen (according to most cookery instruction for men, women suffered from an inability to experiment in the kitchen).

In the 1920s and 1930s, meatloaf's image as a family dish prepared by Mother's loving hands flourished. Cookery books, increasingly focusing on the new bride or the inexperienced housewife, offered meatloaf recipes as the ideal novice meal—and a dish amendable to extra touches made by more experienced cooks. Single career girls with little time or inclination, like the intended audience of Marjorie Hills and Bertina Foltz's 1937 *Corned Beef and Caviar*, could whip together a beef, veal, pork, and sausage loaf with a little catsup or tomato soup, baked in a bacon-lined loaf pan. *The Kitchenette Cook Book*, published in 1936, also recommended meatloaf as a tasty and economical company dish for the busy working girl. Even a child could make a meatloaf, especially when the loaf was a miniature one, just the right size for a young appetite. Cookery books for young girls (a growing field in a time when fewer and fewer women learned how to cook from mothers or grandmothers), often included meatloaf recipes in the 1920s and 1930s. Twelve-year-old Sue, the fictional protagonist in the 1924 cookbook for girls *When Sue Began to Cook*, enjoyed great success with her first meatloaf: "When we took the meat out, it was crusty and brown and looked dee-licious!"[13] Dee-licious meatloaf appeared again and again in cookery books for women, and girls, and only occasionally in men's recipes. These recipes both reflected and helped to shape Americans' perceptions of meatloaf as a typical dish from women's home kitchens. When the United States entered World War II, however, women's home kitchens took on a whole new level of symbolic importance. During wartime, meatloaf, and Mother's home cooking, took on heightened, patriotic meaning.

MEATLOAF GOES TO WAR ON THE HOME FRONT, 1941–1945

After the United States entered the war, discussions about male culinary prowess in cookbooks and popular magazines virtually disappeared, at least in comparison to the multitude of such references in 1920s and 1930s cookery instruction. A man might occasionally appear in a Swan's Down cake flour advertisement, demonstrating that the flour made cake baking so easy that even men could do it. But the men who had boasted about their bread sticks, barbecues, and beef stews in 1941 fell silent in 1942. Dad did not have time during the war to help his daughter learn how to cook chicken paprika, as he had in a 1941 article in *Parents' Magazine*.[14] Cookery instruction turned full attention to women, to the cooking responsibilities of white, married, middle-class women with children, and presented home cooking as the key to Victory. Just as cookbooks in the 1920s and 1930s had stressed that middle-class white women should view cooking a pleasurable and creative task, cookery books published during the war years depicted food preparation in the home as a woman's most important wartime job: a job critical to the defense of the nation and to winning the war.[15]

The preparation of meat, in particular, concerned American recipe writers.

Long associated with hearty appetites and healthy families, fresh meat had played the starring role in American meals for decades. A typical American meal, if such a thing existed, consisted primarily of a meat main course accompanied by vegetable and starch side dishes. The adjustment to meat rationing spawned literally thousands of recipes and pages of rhetoric in cookbooks. Into the fray stepped meatloaf, ideally suited to wartime duties. Cookbook authors and magazine writers had almost always praised the thriftiness of meatloaf. Now that the United States had entered the war, thriftiness meant more than good housekeeping. It meant helping the boys in uniform; it meant helping to defend the nation. To give up meat seemed practically unthinkable to Americans, but a meatloaf offered housewives a perfect way to "s-t-r-e-t-c-h" the meat ration. In the wartime recipe booklet *Your Share*, "Betty Crocker," the fictional spokeswoman for General Mills products, suggested meatloaf as one of the best ways to extend scarce meat. In a chart explaining how to get the most out of different types of meat, the editors of *Your Share* advised that any ground meat (beef, veal, pork, ham, or liver) could be made into a loaf and extended with bread crumbs, rice, oatmeal, cracker crumbs, ground peanuts or Wheaties cereal. Their "Pinwheel Meat Roll" recipe extended the loaf with a filling of either onion and celery cooked in butter or mashed potatoes.[16]

Other cookbooks also advocated for the now patriotic meatloaf dinner. In 1941, *A Cookbook of Leftovers* included a variety of meatloaf recipes, such as meatloaf stuffed with creamed vegetables and a "Mexican Meat Loaf" made with green peppers, chili powder, and condensed tomato paste.[17] But after December 7, 1941, using up leftovers became more than just an economy measure—it became essential to national defense. According to the authors and editors of cookbooks, no single female wartime task could so effect the outcome of the war as adherence to rationing regulations and producing good home cooking. Cookbooks in the 1920s and 1930s had encouraged women to think of home cooking as a creative and fulfilling task, but when the United States entered the war cookbooks began to reconstruct cookery as vital wartime defense work.

Wartime cookbooks underlined the two most essential aspects of the homemaker's cookery defense: one, maintaining the health of the family and two, keeping the family's spirits high with plentiful, well-cooked, and palate-pleasing meals. Women had to accomplish these tasks, moreover, with food supplies rationed to ensure enough food for all, including "our boys" in the service. Earlier cookbooks had also focused on the importance of balanced meals and good nutrition, but during the war, they upped the ante considerably, and consistently linked the health of the family with the defense of the United States against annihilation. Prudence Penny's meatloaf recipe, "Vitality Meatloaf," called for beef, pork, pork liver, wheat germ, oatmeal, onion, egg, evaporated milk, salt, parsley, pepper, sage, celery salt, and chili sauce. The author praised the meatloaf for its thrifty use of ground meat and for its vitamins and minerals.[18]

But the most economical meatloaf recipes published from 1942 through 1945 did not contain any meat at all. Meat-protein substitutes often appeared in loaf form during the war. Authors drew on the American familiarity with the shape and texture of meatloaf to introduce lima bean loaves and meat-loaves extended with soy flour. Ida Bailey Allen's lima bean loaf recipe called for mashed limas, crumbled bread, cooked carrots or peas, minced sweet green peppers, salt, pepper, thyme, and flour. The 1943 *Cooking on a Ration*, by Marjorie Hills, included recipes for asparagus, baked bean, peanut butter, nut, vegetable, and cottage cheese loaves. Mills asserted that her "V Loaf," made of rice, nuts, tomatoes, onion, green pepper and tomato sauce, "defies detection as a substitute meat loaf and is very good."[19] But some authors acknowledged that lima beans could never replace ground beef. Elizabeth Case and Martha Wyman admitted that their lima loaf recipe, in their 1943 *Cook's Away*, was "more nutritious and filling than epicurean."[20]

But although wartime cookery books admonished women to provide sound nutrition and economical dishes for the family, the housewife's wartime cooking duties did not end with providing essential nutrients. Many cookbooks argued that the attractive presentation of dishes and relaxing, satisfying repasts was as necessary to home front defense as vitamin-packed meals. In other words, Mom-cooked meals did more than safeguard the health of the family. They also kept spirits high, kept families strong, and helped to ensure cheerful war workers. When magazine articles and cookbooks discussed the emotional importance of the family dinner table, they did not often mention meatloaf specifically. Women wondering what to cook for their beloved departing servicemen were urged to fry chicken, broil steak, bake pies and cakes. But meatloaf stood ready to do duty as an everyday meal.

Numerous cookery books and articles lectured women on the use of beef heart, liver, and tongue during wartime, and meatloaf could easily incorporate these variety meats. When cookbook authors and magazine writers admonished women on the importance of making every ration point count, housewives could turn to friend meatloaf, and stretch every bit of ground meat with almost any other leftover: rice, mashed potatoes, cooked vegetables, cold oatmeal, or stale bread crumbs. And perhaps most importantly, this resilient main dish did its symbolic and emotional duty at the family dinner table. Hot, meaty (if not the best kind of meat), economical, irrevocably associated with family life and women's home cooking, meatloaf—the humble GI of the meat world—kept the flag flying on the kitchen front and kept the family supplied with comfort food. And after the war's end, when the United States had begun to enjoy an era of unprecedented prosperity and abundance, cookbooks and domestic magazines continued to emphasize women's cooking. And they continued to praise meatloaf as a quick and satisfying family meal—prepared, of course, by the woman of the house.

THE MEATLOAF MYSTIQUE, 1946–1960

The meatloaf recipes in the best-selling cookbook of the post–World War II era—*Betty Crocker's Picture Cook Book*, published in 1950 by General Mills—were not especially innovative. Crammed full of instructional photographs, cooking tips, and recipes using General Mills ingredients, the cookbook sold millions of copies. Though an overwhelming number of the recipes dealt with baking and desserts, "Betty Crocker" devoted an entire page to meat loaves. Most of the meatloaves called for standard ingredients—ground beef or veal, egg, milk, chopped onion, Wheaties (a General Mills product), salt and pepper. The "Peanut Ham Loaf" stood out: it called for the addition of peanut butter to a ham loaf. The editors also noted that a regular meatloaf could be transformed into a "Festive Meat Loaf" by baking the loaf in a ring mold.[21]

Meatloaf recipes in the 1950s continued to emphasize the same kinds of things that prewar recipes had: ease of preparation, thriftiness, and flexibility. But Betty Crocker's suggestion on how to make a meatloaf "festive" signaled a change. In the late 1940s and 1950, according to the cookery instruction of the time, it was no longer enough to simply pack some ground meat scraps mixed with bread and milk into a loaf pan. Every dinner, even meatloaf, had to reflect the care and love of the homemaker, and had to illustrate a woman's special touch; it had to be "festive." Meatloaf recipes in the 1950s reflected the "cooking mystique" created by recipe writers, food editors, and cookbook publishers: even as food preparation became easier and availability of processed food increased, women's cooking duties became invested with increased symbolic, gendered meaning. While cookery instruction for men—as evidenced in meatloaf recipes by and for men—continued to depict men as creative, fun-loving kitchen hobbyists, general cookbooks always depicted the act of cooking the family's daily meals as an essential expression of wifely and motherly caring. Men's meatloaf recipes continued to emphasize fine quality ingredients and exotic touches, and often a suitably masculine setting such as a campsite. But in cookery instruction for women, meatloaf remained firmly on the dinner table.

Historians of popular culture and of food have sometimes overstated the extent to which strange Jell-O salads and Velveeta cheese sauce marked food in the 1950s.[22] But without a doubt, some of the trends that shaped food fashions in the 1950s deserve their reputation. Tuna noodle casserole with crushed potato chip topping, flaming food, casseroles of every imaginable kind, and sandwich loaves all regularly appeared in 1950s cookbooks. Suburban cookery—backyard barbecues, cocktail parties, and Hawaiian influenced food—made a decided mark on recipes in the 1950s, as well. Though basic meatloaf recipes still showed up in postwar cookery instruction, many meatloaf recipes in the 1950s suffered from an overabundance of rich and sometimes bizarre ingredients. For example, a recipe for "Spiced Meat Loaf" in *Complete American Cookbook*, published in 1957, called for beef, beef suet, cream, basil, ginger, butter, cloves, cinnamon, sherry, and "homemade tomato catsup or chutney." A pork loaf in the same cookbook included turmeric, curry powder, Angostura bitters, meat extract, and two teaspoons "caramel or syrup." The author noted that this loaf had "rather an exotic flavor." Her recipe for a liver loaf required equally exotic ingredients: calf's liver, chicken livers, salt pork, allspice, nutmeg, pistachio nuts, cream, and anchovy paste. The editors of a 1955 Culinary Arts Institute recipe pamphlet suggested garnishing a ham and veal ring with pineapple slices, crab apples, parsley *and* a horseradish sour cream sauce.[23]

Like Betty Crocker, postwar cookbooks often advised serving meatloaf in a ring or in a mold. Meatloaf rings, surrounding a mound of vegetables or potatoes, offered one way to spice up a meatloaf recipe (figure 5.2). Food in ring molds and unusual jelled shapes epitomize, for many Americans, postwar cuisine. And baking meatloaf in a ring, or reshaping meatloaf into a pie and serv-

Meatloaf Ring (with corn in center), from "Dress Up a Meat Loaf—Five Good Ways," *Better Homes and Gardens* (April 1957), 190

Figure 5.2.   In the 1950s, meatloaf rings, like this one, offered housewives a way to give basic meatloaf a new look.

ing it in wedges did present a new way of cooking this familiar dish. Drawing on the well-known basic meatloaf recipe, authors and editors urged women to give the old standby a modern kick, a "festive" touch. As the editors of the 1959 *General Foods Kitchens Cookbook* counseled: "Hamburger doesn't always have to be a round patty-cake. It can come to the table as Swedish meat balls, or little meat loaves baked in muffin tins, or in a casserole snow-capped with mashed potatoes, or baked in a ring mold and filled with a creamed vegetable."[24] Individual-sized meatloaves, sometimes mentioned in 1920s and 1930s cookery books, enjoyed even more popularity in the 1950s, and authors and editors often suggested them as a way to create new interest among family members. One of the only main dish recipes in the 1955 *Better Homes and Gardens Junior Cook Book* was a simple recipe for "Little Meat Loaves" baked in muffin tins (figure 5.3).[25]

Figure 5.3.   The editors of the Better Homes and Gardens Junior Cook Book, published in 1955, recommended meatloaf baked in muffin tins as an easy main dish for the beginner. This photograph is copyrighted material of Meredith Corporation, used with their permission. All rights reserved.

Meatloaf recipes continued to use most meats in the 1950s, including canned pork products such as Spam. Though available for decades, wartime rationing had increased American familiarity with canned "luncheon meat," and like other convenience foods this product appeared more and more often in postwar meatloaf recipes. A meatloaf recipe in Dorothy Malone's 1947 *Cookbook for Brides* illustrated the minimum amount of cookery knowledge expected of new wives and America's increasing dependence on processed foods. The ingredients list for "Miniature Meat Loaves with Chili" read simply "1 can luncheon meat, 1/2 tbs. Shortening, 1 tbs. Chili Sauce." The directions read "Open the can of luncheon meat at both ends and gently push out the solid meat. Cut in half and coat first with the shortening, then with the chili sauce, just on top of each miniature loaf." Malone also gave variations on this recipe. A woman might substitute "a brown-sugar topping studded with a few cloves, basting the little loaves while they bake with pineapple juice or grape juice," instead of the shortening–chili sauce mixture. "Or you might coat the tops with orange marmalade, so that the meat loaves will bake with a most attractive glaze and have a most enchanting flavor," she advised.[26] This recipe required virtually no cookery knowledge and gave incredibly explicit directions—did she think brides would be unable to remove lunch meat from a can without instructions?

While Malone's "meatloaf" recipe did not tax the cookery knowledge of the kitchen novice, it did make it clear that the bride—the woman of the home—would be responsible for providing the household's meals. Even if she could not cook anything more complicated than a slab of Spam, she held responsibility for the daily meals. In the 1950s, cookbook publication shot up and food processing companies, grocery stores, and kitchen appliance manufacturers created thousands of recipes. Like cookbooks in the 1920s and 1930s, these recipes continued to offer simple dishes and explicit directions. But authors and editors also increasingly accentuated the importance of cooking as part of a woman's social role. Cookbooks stopped representing cookery as a creative, joyful task for women and started emphasizing women's duty in the kitchen; women's duty to make even a luncheon meat meatloaf reflect her devotion to the home and to her role as wife and mother. Serving your family luncheon meat straight from the can seemed to indicate an unwomanly interest in providing for your family. Hence, many recipes "doctored up" processed foods and required additional kitchen work in order to serve the very foods that supposedly made cooking more convenient.

Cultural historian Karal Marling argues that during the 1950s, "even convenience foods [had to] be slaved over to show love."[27] While cookbooks relied on canned and packaged foods, they also directed women toward elaborate ruses to cover up the fact that they were using those convenience foods.

The emphasis on glazing, decorating, and fussing with food indicated unease over the implications of processed foods. By "doctoring" food, women retained their position as the only real cook of the family. Any member of the family could slap together a meatloaf, but only Mom knew how to make a festive meatloaf ring. Even a luncheon meat meatloaf had to be basted with pineapple juice or coated with orange marmalade.

Every meatloaf had to reflect that little extra touch of Mother love. For example, the "De Luxe [*sic*] Meat Loaf" in *A Picture Treasury of Good Cooking*, published in 1953, called for a simple mixture of veal, pork, poultry seasoning, egg, milk, and bread crumbs. But the authors instructed the reader to remove the meatloaf from the loaf pan, decorate it with "crisp bacon" and "heated, canned broiled mushrooms," and return it to the oven for browning[28] The author of a 1958 article in *Better Homes and Gardens* on meatloaf began "Nothing everyday about this trio of meat loaves." About a recipe for a "Glazed Ham-Loaf Ring" with a sweet-sour glaze and mustard sauce, the author enthused, "No plain fare! The sauce and glaze add gourmet flair."[29] In the 1950s, according to the cookery instruction in domestic magazines and in commercially published cookbooks, family dinners called for more than "plain fare" or "everyday" recipes. And meatloaves required glazes, garnishes, or gravies—and dedicated home cooks to provide them.

Meatloaf recipes in the postwar period frequently appeared in cookery instruction for women. But authors and recipe writers rarely numbered meatloaf among the dishes suitable for the man in the kitchen. As in the 1920s and 1930s, a significant number of popular domestic magazines published articles about men's cooking, and several authors produced entire cookbooks devoted to the subject. But although meat met with universal approval in man's cookery instruction, and although meatloaf received constant praise in general cookbooks, few recipe collections for men included meatloaf in any guise. *Parents' Magazine* published one notable exception in 1946 in an article entitled "He Might Like Cooking." The author of the article described how her teenage son had taken up cooking as a hobby, then gave her son's meatloaf recipe (ground beef and sausage, flavored with sage, and held together with milk, egg, and crushed crackers).[30] Perhaps significantly, the male meatloaf maker in this article had not yet graduated from high school. In cookery books for *men* during the 1950s, men barbecued steaks over backyard grills or mixed potent drinks at the basement bar or tossed piquant green salads. They did not, for the most part, mess around with ground meat and loaf pans. As in the 1920s and 1930s, postwar cookbooks by and for men, and domestic magazine articles on the same topic, regularly depicted men as naturally talented and imaginative in the kitchens. Foreign foods, exotic ingredients, prime cut meats—these were the kinds of recipes suitable for men.

If a meatloaf recipe made a rare appearance in such instruction, the authors made it clear that man-made meatloaf differed significantly from the feminine variety. In the 1947 cookbook *A Man and His Meals*, Fletcher Pratt and Robeson Bailey introduced their meatloaf recipe by urging their male readers to use quality ingredients, not just leftovers:

> Meat loaf is a concoction beloved of females who run tearoom-like restaurants and who have no qualifications for the job but a taste for small tables, low lights, "atmosphere," and puttering, so they always buy wrong, and are faced with leftovers in massive quantities. Actually, a meat loaf can be quite a noble dish; it merely takes the care few cooks are willing to give it.

Their noble meatloaf called for high grade hamburger, perhaps stretched with ground leftover meat if necessary, cracker meal to hold the loaf together, and seasonings such as sage for beef, juniper berries for lamb, and marjoram for veal. They scorned cereal and oatmeal as fillers. The authors also recommended putting in strips of bacon or salt pork at the bottom of the pan and a lump of butter on the loaf, and basting the loaf with a mixture of butter or oil and wine. Their meatloaf, they instructed, should be studded with small stuffed olives, and the result could be served hot or cold, warmed up with bacon and gravy, or used as the foundation for a meat spaghetti sauce. "Nobody claims it is the equal of steak," they wrote, "but what the hell! One cannot afford steak or Christmas every day, and probably one would not like it if one could."[31]

Pratt and Bailey's attitude toward women's cooking, and women's meatloaf, reflected the scorn expressed in many such cookbooks for feminine cookery. Cookbooks had already designated meatloaf as a lowly leftover dish, a beginner's meal, and a family meal—not a manly recipe. Cookery instruction for men in the 1950s might mention cooking meatloaf over an open fire, as did Glenn Quilty in *Food for Men*, published in 1954. But a meatloaf cooked over a grill and turned "using two large pancake shovels" demanded masculine mastery of cooking over an open fire and wielding of large outdoor instruments.[32] Meatloaf "studded" with stuffed olives, basted in wine, or roasted over an open campfire, denoted men in the kitchen, men's recipes. Such recipes revealed how Americans often linked standard meatloaf recipes with humdrum daily cooking for the family—or with addled tearoom ladies. Still, men could safely eat meatloaf without imperiling their masculinity, at least according to the author of *1001 Ways to Please a Husband*, published in 1958, who included three meatloaf recipes in her cookbook. Or according to Dorothy Chaun Lee in her 1959 article for *McCall's*. In "It's a Date," Lee suggested that teenage women invite Dreamboat over for dinner: "A girl with an eye on a guy should show off her skill at the stove," she wrote. And on the menu? "Italian Meat Loaf" made with ground beef, Parmesan cheese, oregano, and rye bread.[33]

Of course, the authors intended these meatloaf recipes for beginners in the kitchen—teenagers and new brides. When *Good Housekeeping* ran a meatloaf recipe in their popular photo-instruction recipe series, they noted that "Susan" (the fictional woman behind the pair of hands demonstrating the steps of the recipe) was in this case "Teenage Susan."[34] Meatloaf, in the estimation of cookbook authors and magazine editors, did not demand too much cookery knowledge, but would produce a meal acceptable to male appetites. Not the equal of steak, perhaps, but still presentable. And in the post–World War II era, a woman-made meatloaf and meals meant more than simply filling stomachs. In the Cold War, as in World War II, they meant keeping families and the nation strong. As historian Elaine Tyler May has shown, fierce and widespread anticommunism sentiments, fears about social instability, and pervasive anxiety about nuclear war created intense domestic ideology during the Cold War. She asserts that the United States enacted a social policy of sexual and social "containment" of women during the late 1940s and 1950s.[35] In the 1950s, psychiatrists and cultural commentators spent considerable energy attempting to convince women that only by being a wife and mother—and nothing else—could a woman achieve true feminine completion. Marital sex manuals insisted that only by embracing the notion of motherhood could a woman enjoy real orgasmic fulfillment. Cookery books added to the chorus of popular literature that urged women to focus entirely on their family's welfare, for the good of their families and for the nation.

Cookbooks invested family dinners, where meatloaf seemed to truly belong, with particular importance. Everywhere in the 1950s Americans read and heard advice and discussions about the family. By the mid-1950s, the "baby boom" had reached its peak, and women married in increasing numbers but at younger ages than ever before. Everyone from politicians to women's magazine writers urged citizens to practice "family togetherness," and at the same time, Americans worried more than ever before about divorce and the newly termed "juvenile delinquency." Family dinners, lovingly prepared by Mother, not only kept the family healthy but also combated juvenile delinquency. Even with all the assistance of frozen dinners, canned vegetables, cake mixes, and ready-made rolls, cookbooks urged women to invest their daily meals with love and care. Cookery instruction urged women to be sure that their meals reflected the right attitude about cooking and the right demonstration of a wife and mother's love for her family and for her job as homemaker. In general cookbooks, women retained sole responsibility for the preparation of the daily meals—even as cooking itself became an easier undertaking. Meatloaf became even easier to cook in the late 1950s, when preground, prepackaged beef became more readily available. Many recipes demanded a minimal amount of cooking knowledge, but they also took on a symbolic burden which only a woman's cooking, and women's meatloaf, could fulfill.

MEATLOAF GOES GOURMET

In the 1960s and 1970s, recipe writers struggled to help meatloaf keep up with changing times. A recipe published in the January 1967 edition of *Better Homes and Gardens* epitomized the new look in meatloaves. Submitted by a reader from Atlanta, Georgia, "Hidden Treasure Meat Loaf" seemed like a basic meatloaf but it had a surprise center of processed Swiss cheese, ham, and parsley[36] (figure 5.4). To raise meatloaf to more gourmet levels seemed to be

Figure 5.4. Better Homes and Gardens *published a recipe for "Hidden Treasure Meat Loaf" in 1967. Baking meatloaf with a "hidden treasure" in the center was only one way recipe writers tried to spice up basic meatloaves in the 1960s and 1970s.*

the goal of many cookbook and magazine writers in the 1960s and 1970s. For instance, in a 1966 article, the editors of *Sunset* magazine claimed that their meatloaf recipes elevated the dish "above the usual classification of 'family fare only.'" A "mustard-sharpened sugary glaze" distinguished their "Grated Carrot Meat Loaf," while "a sour cream–cream caper sauce and crisp bacon topping" adorned the "Mushroom Veal Loaf."[37] Though nobody ever thought up a truly revolutionary meatloaf recipe, many tried to enliven the loaf and give it a less pedestrian image. But the fact that most meatloaf recipes began by acknowledging meatloaf's reputation as a dull "family fare" revealed the persistence of that image.

When popular domestic magazines offered meatloaf recipes to their readers in the 1970s, editors and writers took care to emphasize that *these* recipes would give new life to tired meatloaf. "Old-Time Meat Loaf Was Never Like This," exclaimed the title of a 1972 article by Frances M. Crawford in *American Home*. Crawford introduced the recipes for "Blue Cheese–Stuffed Meat Loaf" (rolled up like a jelly roll) "Olive-Mushroom Meat Loaf," "Dill Meat Loaf," and "Italian Meat Loaf" (made with frozen chopped spinach, tomato sauce, and bacon) by remarking on how modern these meatloaves were: "Most of us remember with fondness the old-fashioned meat loaf that Mother used to make. Though still a traditional dinnertime staple, it's taken on a new and thoroughly modern life—taste years away from the usual mixture of seasoned beef, bread crumbs and egg."[38] But despite the best efforts of these food editors and their test kitchens, meatloaf remained a fixture at the family dinner table. After all, meatloaf recipes appeared in magazines such as *American Home, Better Homes and Gardens*, and *Parents' Magazine*, not *Gourmet*. As Crawford had admitted, "most of us" still thought of meatloaf primarily as a humble mixture of ground beef and simple seasonings, made by Mother.

In 1987, *McCall's* magazine attempted to modernize meatloaf by pairing it with the latest in kitchen appliances: the microwave. All four recipes—"Mexican Turkey Ring," "Mini Lamb Loaves," "Glazed Ham Loaf," and "Beef Roulade Florentine" (made with chopped frozen spinach, Parmesan cheese, red and yellow peppers, and a jar of spaghetti sauce)—called for microwave cooking. Microwave meatloaves did not catch on in the 1980s, but in the 1980s and 1990s, meatloaf did enjoy a certain revival. Culinary historian Sylvia Lovegren explained, in 1995, that "comfort food" in general and meatloaf specifically became fashionable in the 1980s: "Despised as utterly pedestrian in the chic Seventies, meat loaf reappeared on the menus of down-home (and upscale) American restaurants in the late 1980s."[39] In the last two decades of the twentieth century, a time marked by corporate greed, increasing economic disparities, and bewildering technological changes, a filling meatloaf dinner seemed an island of peace in a world growing ever more chaotic and confusing. Moreover, in a world where fewer families—whatever configuration family might take—shared regular meals, let alone meals "from scratch," meatloaf seemed to hearken back to simpler, easier times. Simpler, easier times when women's home cooking kept the Cold War at bay.

In the 1920s and 1930s, cookbook authors, magazine editors, and recipe writers upheld meatloaf as a simple dish which would help show white, middle-class women the joy and creativity of cooking. During World War II, meatloaf did double-duty as a thrifty and healthful, thus patriotic, main dish and as an emblem of Mother's ability to keep the family's spirits high during wartime trouble. Meatloaf's symbolic importance only increased in the 1950s, when the "cooking mystique" gave meatloaf, and family dinners, a new significance. Blatant domestic and gender ideology loosened its grip on American cookbooks and recipes in the 1960s and 1970s. But Yuppie meatloaves of the 1980s revealed our continuing need to believe in Mom-cooked meals. We may be able to get gourmet meatloaves in homestyle restaurants today, we may make meatloaves with 93 percent lean ground beef and cook them in special double pans made to drain away excess fat, but these are only surface changes. We still expect meatloaf to stand for homely cooking, women's cooking. Meatloaf is our national "comfort food"—and what could be more comforting than a home-cooked meal, made with love by Mom?

NOTES

1. Mrs. D. A. Lincoln, *Boston Cooking School Cook Book: A Reprint of the 1884 Classic* (New York: Dover, 1996), 272–73. Mrs. Simon Kander and Mrs. Henry Schoenfeld, compilers, *The Way to a Man's Heart: The "Settlement" Cook Book: A Facsimile Edition* (Bedford, Mass.: Applewood, 1903), 59.

2. Ida Lee Carey, *Cook Book of Tested Recipes* (Poughkeepsie, N.Y.: A. V. Haight, 1920), 10.

3. Margaret Pratt Allen and Ida Orma Hutton, *Man-Sized Meals from the Kitchenette* (New York: Vanguard, 1928), 51; Helen Hilles, *To the Queen's Taste: A Cook Book for Moderns* (New York: Random House 1937), 124; Virginia Porter and Esther Latzke, *The Canned Foods Cook Book* (New York: Doubleday, 1939), 163.

4. *Good Housekeeping's Book of Menus, Recipes and Household Discoveries* (New York: Good Housekeeping, 1922), 148; Ida Miglario, Harriet W. Allard, Zorada Z. Titus, Irene Nunemaker, eds., *The Household Searchlight Recipe Book* (Topeka: Household Magazine, 1939), 193; *America's Cook Book* (New York: Scribner's, 1938), 226–304.

5. Nell B. Nichols, "Baked in a Loaf," *Woman's Home Companion*, September 1934, 35.

6. Roger Horowitz, e-mail to the Association for the Study of Food and Society discussion list in response to query from author, 8 December 1999.

7. Ida Bailey Allen, *Ida Bailey Allen's Money Saving Cookbook* (New York: Garden City, 1940), 82–83.

8. Hazel Young, *Better Meals for Less Money* (Boston: Little, Brown, 1940), 44.

9. Ruth Berolzheimer, *250 Ways to Prepare Meat* (Chicago: Consolidated, 1940), 16, 20–25.

10. Young, *Better Meals for Less Money*, 44.

11. George Rector, *Home on the Range with George Rector* (New York: Rogers-Kellogg-Stillson, 1939), 75; William Rhodes, *Of Cabbages and Kings* (New York: Stackpole, 1938), 131–32; Mac Sheridan, ed., *The Stag Cookbook: Written for Men by Men* (New York: George H. Dornan, 1922), 18.

12. John MacPherson, *The Mystery Chef's Own Cook Book* (New York: Longman, Green, 1934), 80.

13. Marjorie Mills and Bertina Foltz, *Corned Beef and Caviar* (Indianapolis: Bobbs-Merrill, 1937), 125; Ruth Taylor, *The Kitchenette Cook Book* (New York: Scribner's, 1936), 72; Louise Bennet Weaver and Helen Cowless LeCron, *When Sue Began to Cook* (New York: A. L. Burt, 1924), 78. A meatloaf recipe also appeared in Inez N. McFee, *The Young People's Cook Book* (New York: Thomas Y. Crowell, 1925). In *Jessie Marie DeBoth's Cook Book* (Racine, Wis.: Whitman, 1940), the author reminded readers that children might not care for highly spiced meatloaf and recommended making a seasoned loaf for adults and plain meatballs or miniloaves for the children (50).

14. "Yes sir, we men baked 38 cakes—and did the ladies' eyes pop!" *Ladies Home Journal*, April 1942, 41; Harry Botsford, "Just a Man with a Pan," *Woman's Home Companion*, November 1941, 82–83; Corey Ford, "You Say We Can't Cook?" *Better Homes and Gardens*, June 1941, 64, 94–95, 97; Carl Malmberg, "Dad and Daughter Cook," *Parents' Magazine*, February 1941, 44, 63–64.

15. See Amy Bentley, *Eating for Victory: Food Rationing and the Politics of Domesticity* (Urbana: University of Illinois Press, 1998).

16. *Your Share* (Minneapolis: General Mills, 1943), 3, 5–8.

17. Clare Newman and Bell Wiley, *A Cook Book of Leftovers* (Boston: Little, Brown, 1941), 54–55.

18. Florence Richardson (Prudence Penny), *Coupon Cookery: A Guide to Good Meals under Wartime Conditions of Rationing and Food Shortages* (Los Angeles: Hearst, 1943), 47.

19. Ida Bailey Allen, *Double-Quick Cooking for Part-Time Homemakers* (New York: M. Barrows, 1943), 56; Marjorie Mills, *Cooking on a Ration* (Boston: Houghton Mifflin, 1943), 64.

20. Elizabeth Case and Martha Wyman, *Cook's Away: A Collection of Simple Rules, Helpful Facts, and Choice Recipes Designed to Make Cooking Easy* (New York: Longmans, Gree, 1943), 55.

21. *Betty Crocker's Picture Cook* (New York: McGraw Hill and General Mills, 1950), 275.

22. See, for example, Joshua Gitelson, "Populox: The Suburban Cuisine of the 1950s," *Journal of American Culture* 15, no. 3 (fall 1992).

23. Stella Standard, *Complete American Cookbook* (Cleveland, Ohio: World Publishing, 1957), 87, 170, 101; *The Ground Meat Cookbook* (Chicago: Culinary Arts Institute, 1955, 1954), 32.

24. *General Foods Kitchens Cookbook* (New York: Random House, 1959), 3.

25. *Better Homes and Gardens Junior Cook Book* (Des Moines, Iowa: Meredith, 1955), 146.

26. Dorothy Malone, *Cookbook for Brides* (New York: A. A. Wyn, 1947), 68. In 1956, a meatloaf recipe submitted to *Sunset* magazine from a reader in Lakewood, California, included "pork luncheon meat," and called for a sauce made from cloves, cornstarch, red table wine, brown sugar, and canned cranberry sauce. See "Two Colorful Loaves, *Sunset*, March 1956, 162.

27. Karal Marling, *As Seen on TV: The Visual Culture of Everyday Life in the 1950s* (Cambridge, Mass.: Harvard University Press, 1994), 222.

28. Demetria M. Taylor and Lillian Zeigfeld, *A Picture Treasury of Good Cooking* (New York: Tested Recipe Institute, 1953), 16.

29. "Let's Have Meat Loaf," *Better Homes and Gardens*, October 1958, 74.

30. "He Might Like Cooking," *Parents' Magazine*, February 1946, 54.

31. Fletcher Pratt and Robeson Bailey, *A Man and His Meals* (New York: Henry Holt, 1947), 103–5.

32. Glenn Quilty, *Food for Men* (New York: Sheridan House, 1954), 18.

33. Dorothy Chaun Lee, "It's a Date," *McCall's*, May 1959, 100.

34. "Susan Makes Meat Loaf," *Good Housekeeping*, March 1948, 144.

35. See Elaine Tyler May, *Homeward Bound: American Families in the Cold War Era* (New York: Basic, 1988).

36. "Meat Loaves," *Better Homes and Gardens*, January 1967.

37. "Meat Loaves Using Vegetables," *Sunset*, October 1966, 243.

38. Frances M. Crawford, "Old-Time Meatloaf Was Never Like This," *American Home*, March 1972, 90–91. See also Rita Molter, "Meat Loaves: Old Standbys Can Be Standouts for Dinner," *Parents' Magazine*, June 1977, 44.

39. Sylvia Lovegren, *Fashionable Food: Seven Decades of Food Fads* (New York: Macmillan, 1995), 141.

· 6 ·

Bananas: Women's Food

Virginia S. Jenkins

$\mathscr{I}$n the late nineteenth and early twentieth century, bananas became known as women's food, a sweet substitute for meat and other more expensive fruits and vegetables. This chapter explores the introduction of bananas to the United States and their particular association with women.

Our consumption of food is continually shaped by a variety of external forces in an increasingly complex global economy. Multinational companies and imported foods are not new although their power and the concomitant homogenization of culture is a growing concern at the beginning of the twenty-first century. The introduction of new foods includes negotiation between the producer and consumer, governed by economics and culture.[1] Successful introductions occur when the food item fits into a recognizable niche, replaces a previously valued item, or serves a new purpose in a changing society.[2] Also, as Claude Levi-Strauss pointed out, a food has to think good before it can taste good. Imported bananas became the most popular fruit in the United States in the twentieth century because they were able to take the place of seasonal fruits replacing a previously valued item; were available year-round at an inexpensive price fitting into a recognizable niche; and met the new concerns raised by advances in sanitation, public health, and nutrition, serving a new purpose in a changing society. Publicists for the banana in the late nineteenth century described it in terms of other, known fruit and promoted its exotic, tropical origin, helping bananas to think good.

Bananas began to appear in cookbooks and on menus in the United States in the 1870s, but were not widely available until the 1890s, when the United Fruit Company and others put together a system of steamships, railroads, and refrigeration to make it possible to transport the perishable fruit to interior markets with decreased risk of the fruit rotting before it reached the consumer. In the 1870s and 1880s, bananas were an expensive luxury found on holiday and hotel menus and at other special occasions during the fall and winter months. In the 1890s, United Fruit made a decision to import bananas as cheaply as possible, relying on marketing and advertising to sell them in huge quantities.[3]

Bananas quickly made the transition from novelty to daily necessity in a number of ways. Americans ate a lot of fruit and were able to combine bananas with familiar fruit or substitute bananas for local, seasonal fruit in familiar dishes. United Fruit and others were able to bring a constant supply of inexpensive bananas to market year-round, supplementing the seasonal availability of most fruits known to the American public. In addition, United Fruit made good use of the new discoveries concerning germs and sanitation to market bananas as the fruit in the sterile wrapping or germproof container.

The major domestic reform movement that swept the United States in the late nineteenth century promoted the elevation of traditional household responsibilities to the status of a profession, in which all the new resources of science and technology were applied to the improvement and more efficient management of the home.[4] Housewives learned about the relationship of nutrition and diet to health through scores of articles in newspapers and magazines, and were exhorted to produce three "protective" meals a day for their families. United Fruit marketed bananas on the basis of the new discoveries of germs, vitamins, minerals, and calories, presenting the fruit in a modern, attractive way to appeal to women newly educated to be responsible for the health and nutrition of their families.

Most residents of the United States had never seen or eaten a banana before 1880, although bananas were sporadically available in East Coast ports when fair winds favored sailing ships that brought in small quantities of the fruit on speculation. A Boston publication of 1872 described bananas to readers who had never eaten one as having "a taste somelike [*sic*] muskmelons. They are not improved by cooking."[5] The author continued with instructions for preserving this rare fruit by placing it raw in a bottle and then filling it with boiling water and sealing. A teaspoon of sugar to each banana could be added. In 1877, *A Domestic Cyclopaedia of Practical Information* described bananas as

> the fruit of the palm-tree [*sic*], found in the West Indies and South America.
> ... It is eaten raw, either alone or cut in slices with sugar and cream, or wine
> and orange juice. It is also roasted, fried or boiled, and is made into fritters,
> preserves, and marmalades. It is dried in the sun and preserved as figs; meal is
> extracted from it by pounding and made into something resembling bread;
> and the fermented juice affords an excellent wine. With us it is brought to the
> table as dessert, and proves universally acceptable.[6]

Before 1880, few cookbooks included recipes that called for bananas and it appears that most were eaten as is. Marion Harland, domestic expert and well-known cookbook author, published *The Dinner Year-Book* in 1878, in which she included bananas in January, May, and July dinner menus. Her recipe for Tropical Snow called for oranges, grated coconut, sherry, powdered sugar, and bananas. Mrs. Harland suggested supplementing "this pretty, but not substantial dessert by a salver of lady's-fingers and macaroons, and a good cup of coffee."[7] In the May menu, the housekeeper was instructed to serve oranges and bananas "whole upon china plates with a knife for each." In July, the fruit was to be placed in a dish with oranges and served with iced coffee and fancy biscuits. This book was clearly not intended for the vast majority of working-class Americans.

Whole bananas were listed on 1880 dinner menus from the Windsor Hotel, Jacksonville, Florida, and Glen House in the White Mountains of New Hampshire, and etiquette books instructed diners faced with a whole banana on their plates to use a silver fruit knife and fork to open the peel and slice and eat the fruit.[8] A menu of October, 1885, from Willard's Hotel in Washington, D.C., cautioned that "all fruit or lunch taken from the table or sent to the rooms, will be charged extra."[9] The menu listed bananas, apples, Delaware grapes, Concord grapes, Malaga grapes, pears, raisins, and a selection of nuts and cheeses, in addition to Cafe Ice Cream.

As bananas began to be more plentiful in the 1880s, cooks became more inventive and bananas were included in dessert recipes as filling for cakes or mixed with custard, whipped cream, or gelatin. Expensive bananas could be "stretched" further by using one or two in a dessert rather than providing one for each diner. *The Cook: A Weekly Handbook of Domestic Culinary Art for All Housekeepers* began publication in New York in the spring of 1885, and included a weekly retail market report for New York, Philadelphia, and Boston that listed the availability and prices of fruits and vegetables. Yellow bananas cost between twenty-five and forty cents a dozen, depending on the city. Recipes for bananas included "Cuban" baked bananas and banana fritters.[10] Weekly menus were provided that occasionally included bananas for dinner (frozen bananas [banana ice cream] and banana Charlotte), or whole and raw for breakfast. In 1886, the hotel Genesee in Buffalo, New York, included a Charlotte of Bananas as an accompaniment to Filet of Beef a la Naverin, Turkey Wings a la Chevalier, Lobster a la Bordelaise, and Sweetbreads with Asparagus tips.[11] *Good Housekeeping* published a recipe for "'Heavenly Hash,' the newest fashionable dish: oranges, bananas, lemons, apples, raisins and pineapples are cut up into little bits, and then served with a little grated nutmeg." This was to be served in a hollowed out orange shell on "a pretty little glass fruit dish, with lemon or orange leaves."[12] Heavenly Hash was not an everyday dish, nor within reach of most Americans.

Americans were known as a nation of fruit lovers despite concerns about the connection between intestinal disorders and fruit consumption. In 1885, an editorial in *The Cook*, claimed:

> One of the best evidences that the American people of this generation live better than their fathers did is found in the steady and rapid growth of the trade in tropical fruits. It is not many years since the great majority of people scarcely knew what a banana was, and considered oranges and lemons as luxuries to be afforded only in sickness or on great occasions. Now, not only these, but other tropical fruits, are bought and eaten almost as generally and freely as apples, and the consumption of melons, peaches, pears, plums and berries is on the same universal and extensive scale. This is a change which tends to gratify the taste, and to promote health, which is the foundation of human happiness, and is of advantage to everybody.[13]

The notion that fruit promoted health was uncommon in the nineteenth century. Most advice manuals recommended that children not be given any fruit until they were at least two years old, sometimes as old as five.[14] An "Inexperienced Mother" writing to *The Ladies' Home Journal* in 1902, asked: "Some of my friends tell me that I ought not to allow my little girl, five years old, to eat bananas. Why are they more indigestible than other fruit?" She was advised to cook bananas for her daughter because under-ripe bananas were too starchy. Alternatively, "a single banana eaten slowly would do no harm if taken raw and thoroughly masticated so that the starch may be well moistened by the saliva."[15] It wasn't until 1917 that the American Medical Association endorsed bananas as food for infants and young children. An article on bananas in *Parents' Magazine* in 1929, recalled that the mother of twenty-five years ago often believed bananas to be indigestible, but "the up-to-the-minute mother of today probably says, "Yes, certainly, [you may have a banana] but pick one with brown spots on the skin, and eat it slowly and chew it well."[16] The article included a recipe for baked bananas with the instruction that they "may be served as main dish of [a] meal for children supplemented with green vegetable and simple dessert, or as a dessert for the whole family after a light meal."

Maria Parloa, who began teaching cookery in New England in the 1870s, became a famous lecturer, teacher, and author. In a cookbook published in 1887, Miss Parloa provided recipes for banana fritters, banana cream pudding, bananas and whipped cream, baked bananas, frozen oranges and bananas, and sliced oranges and bananas sprinkled with sugar.[17] These recipes either substituted the new bananas for the more mundane apple (banana fritters, baked bananas) or combined them with the more familiar but still exotic orange.

By 1889, the price of bananas had fallen. They were no longer an exotic luxury, but had begun to come within reach of the poor. The 1890s was a period of transition as bananas continued to appear as special occasion food despite their growing association with women and children and inclusion in the diet of the working classes. *The Ladies' World* in 1896 suggested that "a dish of apples, oranges, bananas and white grapes, placed at one end of the table, and another dish filled with cracked hickory nuts, walnuts and butternuts, make a pleasant finale to the Christmas dinner."[18] Marion Harland also included fruit for Christmas dinner: "bananas, white grapes, oranges, and late pears, will probably be partaken of sparingly, but must not be omitted."[19]

In 1892, *Housekeeper's Weekly* published a description of an elaborate Spring-Time Breakfast that could only have been a fantasy for most Americans. It included an appetizer of thin slices of banana, sprinkled with pepper and salt, followed by oatmeal with whipped cream and buttered toast; steak with lettuce sauce; cheese toast; potato chips; hot chocolate; breaded, fried sardines; omelets; and breakfast rolls. "Afterward came oranges, bananas and pineapples, chopped very fine and served with a rich lemonade. This delicious mixture was served to each guest in an orange rind, from which the fruit had been carefully removed with a spoon through a circular opening at the top, the lid was put on again after the chopped fruits had been packed in, so the orange seemed to be a whole one."[20]

Bananas came to be associated with dainty, delicate, sweet, women's food despite repeated injunctions to put them in the laborer's dinner pail. The anthropologist Sidney Mintz, in his seminal book, *Sweetness and Power: The Place of Sugar in Modern History*, suggests that the introduction of sugar in Europe followed a similar pattern as that of bananas in the United States. Sugar was at first very expensive and conspicuously consumed by the wealthy on formal occasions. In England, as the supply of sugar increased and the price decreased, sugar was included in the diet of the middle class in the eighteenth century, and finally embraced as a daily necessity by the working class in the nineteenth century as a quick source of energy in place of more expensive protein. Nineteenth-century working-class men were served meat "because of a culturally conventionalized stress upon adequate food for the 'breadwinner'" while their wives and children ate bread and jam and heavily sweetened tea.[21] Women and children became associated with sugar, criticized for having more of a sweet tooth than men and for preferring sweets to more nutritious meat, when in fact, there was not enough meat for all.

Delicate Dishes, complied by the Ladies of St. Paul's Church, Chicago, 1896, included five banana recipes. The forerunner of the ubiquitous Jell-O salad was the fruit jelly of the nineteenth century. A recipe for Fancy Pudding called for "2 oranges sliced, 1 banana sliced, a few figs cut, 1/4 pound candied cherries, and if liked 1/4 pound chocolate creams" to be folded into sherry gelatine and served with whipped cream sweetened and flavored with wine.[22] Chocolate creams were the ultimate women's food, associated with leisure and luxury and marketed exclusively to women.[23] A recipe for Banana Whip, printed in 1907, called for three bananas, the juice of one lemon, one-half package of Larkin Gelatine, one pint of freshly boiled water, one-half cup of cold water, one cup of sugar, and one-half package of pink coloring-powder. The mashed bananas were beaten into the gelatine and sugar mixture, poured into a mold, and when firm, served with cream.[24]

Mrs. S. T. Rorer suggested in 1898 that fruit salads, including bananas, "are largely used at ladies' luncheons."[25] A "delicate and rich" recipe for Banana Layer Cake appeared in Maud C. Cooke's cookbook published in the 1890s, along with a banana Blanc Mange covered with a meringue of pink sugar, banana salads (including one flavored with "genuine eau de cologne"), a "dainty dessert" of banana fritters, and "frozen bananas . . . very nice, served as a sweet course at a luncheon in the place of ice or ice cream."[26]

As Laura Shapiro points out in *Perfection Salad: Women and Cooking at the Turn of the Century*, this was the era that placed Jell-O fruit salad with marshmallows at the heart of our national cuisine. Sugary food was considered light, dainty, and appropriate for women who avoided eating large quantities of meat, either through necessity or for appearance's sake. The fiction that women had no appetite made it almost possible to believe that women had no right to substantial food. "In 1903, Marion Harland observed that lunch was of no interest to a normal woman, and that since men were tending not to come home in the middle of the day any longer, the middle meal might have disappeared entirely if it were not for hungry children."[27] *A Bill of Fare for Everyday in the Year*, considered that "two or three bananas, sliced in a bowl of bread and milk, make a delicious and sufficient lunch" for women or children at home alone.[28] An article about young women living on their own described a luncheon for two women of "an attractive array" of rolls, butter, bouillon, tongue, oranges, grapes, bananas, fruit cake, and macaroons for a total cost of 32 cents, heavy on sweets and carbohydrates, with tongue considered daintier and consumed in smaller quantities than beef, mutton, or pork.[29] This was quite extravagant considering that it was considered possible to feed a family of six on thirteen cents per person per day.[30] Sweet, inexpensive bananas, usually in combination with sugar, added some nutritional substance to these feminine meals and were filling.

The Chicago Record Cook Book: Seasonable, Inexpensive Bills of Fare for Every Day in the Year included a number of light luncheons for ladies.[31] One listed Scotch eggs, bread and butter, radishes, favorite cookies, banana cream and cocoa. Another suggested cheese sandwiches, Saratoga [potato] chips, wafers, banana float, and tea. Still another suggested egg vermicelli, brown bread and butter, baked bananas, and cocoa. Women might also enjoy a luncheon of cereal with fruit, thinly sliced bread and butter, frozen bananas, and Angel Food [cake]. Banana Sandwiches (bananas and mayonnaise) were said to be "new and very nice" and were included in a menu with bouillon, wafers, marshmallow cakes, and tea. Menus for breakfast and dinner, when the man of the house was at home, were more substantial, and all included meat, fish, or eggs. In 1894, *Harper's Weekly* published an article about banana freighters and quoted a New York importer as saying, "If it wasn't for the women and children in this country the banana trade wouldn't be worth a rap."[32] Bananas were closely associated with women and children, homey food that was cheap and easy to prepare.

After 1900, bananas appeared in salads almost as frequently as in desserts. *Good Housekeeping* published a set of menus for August 1904, with a suggested luncheon of vegetable salad, nut sandwiches, olives and bananas with cream.[33] *Practical and Dainty Recipes: Luncheons and Dinner Giving in Woodward, Oklahoma* provided a recipe for bananna [sic] pudding and included banana salad in a sample luncheon menu.[34] *Salads, Sandwiches and Chafing-Dish Dainties*, published the same year, provided women with information on "When to Serve a Fruit Salad: A fruit salad, with sweet dressing, is served with cake at a luncheon, or supper, or in the evening; that is, it may take the place of fruit in the dessert course. A fruit salad with French or mayonnaise dressing, may be served as a first course at luncheon, or with the game or roast, though in the latter case the French dressing is preferable."[35] The book included recipes for Orange and Banana Salad, Fruit Salad (June), Fruit and Nut Salad, Fruit Salad (winter), Fruit Salad (sweet, to serve with cake), and Tapioca and Banana Sponge, all containing bananas. In 1910, Fannie Merrit Farmer of the Boston Cooking School noted that "Fruit-cocktails are served as a first course at many fashionable luncheons today, and indeed, they crowd their way into a dinner of ceremony. They are very refreshing, particularly when thoroughly chilled."[36] She suggested "Sato Salad" made of cubed bananas, canned peas and French dressing served in banana-skins placed star-shape on a lettuce leaf. *Dainty Dishes For All The Year-Round*, published in 1915, included recipes for banana ice cream, banana sherbet, frozen bananas, and iced fruit salad under the category of "Some New Recipes."[37] A booklet of eighty-three banana recipes with sample menus, published in 1926, suggested cream of tomato soup, banana and date salad, crisp crackers, cream cheese, and tea as a light lunch for a business woman or a student.[38]

The idea of bananas as dainty, feminine food persisted. In 1939, the Home Economics Department of the United Fruit Company provided teachers with a series of lessons for the "Study of the Banana: Its Every-day Use and Food

Value." In the accompanying teachers' manual were instructions on "How To Flute Bananas: Run the prongs of a fork lengthwise down a peeled ripe banana, then slice crosswise. You'll have dainty, 'crinkly edged rounds' to decorate desserts and salads."[39] As late as 1952, *The Perfect Hostess* suggested "When You Entertain At Luncheon," that guests be served a large fresh fruit salad of cantaloupe ring, peach half, apricot halves, pineapple ring, banana and bing cherries with orange sherbet topping, along with hot tiny butterscotch pecan rolls, mints, nuts, and coffee.[40] Ladies' luncheons continued to feature sweet, "dainty" food for women continually on a diet.

Mintz postulates that sugar and sweetened processed food such as jam and baked goods, were adopted by the working poor in England at the end of the nineteenth century because they provided quick energy, were inexpensive, and allowed women to work outside the home. Traditional food such as porridge, which required long slow cooking, was replaced by heavily sweetened tea and bread and jam, or commercially baked goods, which were quick and easy to prepare, even by children. In the United States, the new home economics experts pressed the working poor to substitute bananas for meat and even for the traditional pie in the workman's lunch pail. United Fruit promoted bananas as a substitute for meat, claiming that a banana and a glass of milk made a complete meal, and advertised a banana in every lunch pail.

Shapiro explains that at the turn of the century an expanding middle class used food as a way to define itself, not only imitating the dainty preferences of the rich, but by carefully avoiding the hallmarks of the poor. Pork, brown bread, thick soups, heavy pies—all these were seen as lower-class or old-fashioned.[41] Marion Harland included a chapter on The Dinner Pail in her 1889 cookbook and housewife's guide in which she recommended: "Instead of the blunt triangle of leathery pie which will emerge from nineteen out of twenty dinner pails opened by his comrades, provide John with fresh fruit in its season. Oranges, bananas, and grapes cost no more than pie; apples, berries, and, in summer, peaches, less, when the original price is counted. If we estimate the ruin wrought upon digestion by pastry and doughnuts, we are ready to affirm that he could better afford hot-house fruits at their dearest, than to satisfy the cravings of nature with these home-made 'delicacies.'"[42] In "Cheap Living In Cities," the author pointed out that during the winter months, fruit cost as much as meat. She asked,

> hygienic writers urge with great truth, that fruit should be made a part of every meal, but how is this to be done when four oranges cost from ten to twenty cents? They must take the place of a pound of meat. Will they do so to the average American? . . . If a woman has but twenty-five cents for her dinner expenses, meat, vegetables, etc., she would find it difficult to squeeze more than a quarter of an orange, half a dozen grapes, or part of a banana for each per-

son, unless meat be left out. Will an orange and a plate of mush and milk take the place of a meat stew and vegetables, with the milk made into a pudding? Bananas are sometimes very cheap, and they take the place of meat better than any other fruit, being it is said, very nutritious.[43]

Bananas, a foreign fruit available year-round, symbolized technological progress and the United States' growing overseas power. In addition, bananas were filling, cheap, safe to eat, and needed no preparation. Little wonder that they were embraced by the modern housewife for her husband's and children's lunches as well as her own.

Before the late nineteenth century, fruit was considered pleasant to eat, but was not believed to have any nutritive value. With advances in nutrition research, and increasing knowledge of calories and vitamins, fruit acquired a stronger claim for inclusion in the daily diet. A pamphlet, compliments of the United Fruit Company c. 1917, claimed that bananas were "wholesome, cheap, nutritious, delicious, easily digested, always in season, available everywhere, no waste, convenient for the dinner pail, good food when cooked, good food when not cooked, the poor man's food, the children's delight, endorsed by physicians, put up and sealed by nature in a germ-proof package, and produced without drawing on the Nation's resources."[44] Directed at working women or working-class women, it appealed on the basis of price, convenience, and concerns about health for themselves and their husbands and children. Bananas could be eaten anywhere, anytime, without any mess or fuss, the original fast food.

With many more people working in offices than on the farm after the turn of the century, there was growing concern about the connection between weight and health. An article on "The Versatile Banana" published in *The Ladies' World* in 1910, assured readers that

> Bananas are a food as well as a fruit. While the apple or the orange aid digestion by means of their splendid acids and salts, rather than by actual food value in themselves, the banana can nourish. For this reason it can be used rather as a portion of the meal than as an adjunct, after the fashion of fruits. Bananas and brown bread will furnish a meal alone without other aid. The banana can show a fifth of its full weight in pure nourishing sugar that is in a form readily absorbable, requiring no digestive change at all.[45]

In 1907 the *Ladies' Home Journal* published an article "How to Live Without A Fire," for the new breed of young working women living in city rooming houses.[46] Breakfast might consist of sliced bananas in cereal with cream and coffee, and dinner would be tomatoes stuffed with sardines, mayonnaise dressing, brown bread, banana fluff (use white of egg), and cream. A 1917 menu for an office worker's lunch included hot consommé in a thermos bottle, celery and boned turkey salad (in a cup), thin bread-and-butter sandwiches, olives, a cup of baked custard, two cookies, and a banana.[47] In 1922, the author of "The Green Gold of the Tropics," asked: "Are you concerned with calories, vitamins, and such-like scientific novelties? Then behold in the banana a food brimful of nourishment. It contains three times the protein of the apple, nearly twice as much carbohydrate and three times as much fat as the orange, and exceeds the potato by about twenty percent in fuel or food value."[48]

Food advertising, specifically written for women shoppers and cooks, reflected women's concerns about their own health and diets. A magazine ad campaign for United Fruit in 1930 targeting the "better-class" market, depicted two women having lunch in a department store restaurant (eating fruit salad?), and a woman being served breakfast in bed by a uniformed maid.[49] Bananas were promoted as a dieting aid to women, even during the Depression when many were concerned about getting enough to eat. "Milk has long been used in reducing diets and within the past few years medical authorities have demonstrated the importance of bananas in conjunction with milk for this purpose. Bananas quickly satisfy the appetite, their satiety value, or filling effect, is comparable to that of fatty foods of much higher caloric content. This fact gives bananas unique importance as a means of satisfying the hunger craving of a normal person while reducing."[50]

Bananas were difficult to obtain during World War II due to naval blockades in the Caribbean and a shortage of commercial freighters. Following the war, bananas once again became available in quantity in U.S. grocery stores. With an expanding middle class, and more purchasing power for blue-collar workers, postwar advertisements dropped the class consciousness of the early part of the century and concentrated on appealing to consumers on the basis of health, nutrition, and name branding rather than convincing people to try bananas. Miss Chiquita had her first starring role in Chiquita Banana's Beauty Treatment, a 1945 technicolor movie advertisement in which the Latin lovely burst into song to revive an exhausted housewife. "You'll find by eating fruit you'll have a more beautiful appearance and complexion," she counseled. A daily dose of banana "will help you look perfection."[51]

In the 1960s Chiquita urged consumers to eat bananas "for goodness sake." High vitamin content made them ideal baby food. Banana advertising also appealed to young women who were watching their weight, promising fewer calories than cottage cheese and "not a trace of cholesterol." Chiquita said "wear it in good health."[52]

A Dole Banana advertisement in a 1977 issue of *House Beautiful* showed three women wearing leotards at a gymnasium weight clinic. Two women are quite heavy, the third standing on a scale in the middle and holding a banana is thin. The caption: "Waist Not, Want Not."

Some things are not as they appear. Take a Dole banana. Sweet and plump and creamy enough to satisfy the hungries. Maybe you think it's loaded with calories. Uh-uh. A medium-size Dole banana contains only about 101 calories, no cholesterol and about as much fat as you'll find in lettuce. So when that 10 A.M. craving comes and you want to keep the scale tipped in your favor, grab a Dole banana. It's one snack that won't go to your waist.[53]

Sweet, plump, and creamy, words that describe women's food with the assumption that women crave sweets.

Despite the successful introduction and enthusiastic reception of bananas into the diet of the people of the United States, there remain some lingering questions about the propriety of women eating bananas, particularly in public. Associations with monkeys and "shiftless" natives in tropical settings, as well as the phallic shape of the fruit can be embarrassing. (As late as 1937, a cookbook author wrote: "In hot climates the natives live mostly on bananas, and a nation is said to be cursed where they grow, because the ease with which they get their living makes them lazy."[54])

There are several extant photographs taken about 1900 of young college women eating bananas that flaunt the convention that a lady should not eat a banana like a monkey.[55] The phallic symbolism of these photographs is overwhelming, with the young women holding half-peeled bananas and in some cases offering each other a bite. Advice books counseled that except at very informal occasions such as picnics, bananas should be peeled, then broken up "as needed into small pieces" and "conveyed to the mouth with the fingers."[56] An article in *The Ladies' World* recommended that "fruit should be eaten in as dainty a way as possible. Peaches and pears are peeled with a silver knife, cut in quarters and the pieces taken up with the fingers. If the fruit is very juicy a fork may be used. Oranges are cut crosswise and the sections are eaten with an orange spoon or teaspoon. After eating fruit the tips of the fingers are dipped in a fingerbowl and dried on the napkin."[57] Bananas are not included in these instructions, the inference being that ladies did not eat whole bananas, or that bananas would not be served at a formal dinner having lost their early luxury status. The recipes for bananas called for them sliced with lemon juice and sugar, sliced with breakfast cereal, or cooked in pudding.[58]

Vaudevillian Annette Kellermann (who officially retired in the 1930s), once set a record swimming the English Channel, and performed on stage in a glass tank. Her act included eating a banana underwater to the titillation of the audience.[59] In the 1950s Florida's Weeki Wachee, Spring of the Mermaids, featured an underwater show with "lovely talented Mermaids" who enjoyed a picnic lunch that included bananas.[60] Aside from being relatively easy to eat underwater, bananas were extremely suggestive and fascinated audiences on a number of levels.

United Fruit incorporated some of the exotic and sexual connotations of the banana in the advertising character Chiquita Banana, modeled after the singer and actress Carmen Miranda. Miranda was known for her exotic dancing, her costumes that bared her midriff, and her elaborate hats. The saucy cartoon character Chiquita sang and danced with a Latin beat with the suggestion of a bare midriff. The Chiquita banana advertising jingle became so popular that it was sung by a number of groups during the 1940s and 1950s and went to the top of the hit parade charts. GIs voted Chiquita the girl they would most like to share a fox hole with.[61]

Figure 6.1.   Chiquita Banana Sheet Music.

In 1952, Butterick and McCall's sold patterns for Chiquita Banana costumes for children and women. These costumes had wide flounced skirts, blouses with scooped necks and puffy short sleeves, and fruit-bowl hats. These feminine costumes made with lots of fabric may have been appealing to women after the drabness of the Depression and War years when women's clothing was more severe, used less fabric, and resembled military uniforms. Women were encouraged to be more feminine in the 1950s, spending less time in the kitchen and more time as "courtesan types" with their husbands.[62] *Better Homes and Gardens* Magazine offered "half a dozen sure ways to add glamour to your springtime meals. . . . Bananas are the star ingredients in each."[63] There were Chiquita Banana contests and the

Figure 6.2. Child's Costume Pattern, United Fruit Company, McCall's Pattern no. 101, no date, Lovell Banana Museum.

United Fruit Company hired young women to tour as Chiquita Banana to promote their product, playing on romantic, sexual associations with tropical Latin America.

Bananas have never lost these associations. They are used in high school sex education classes to demonstrate condom use. In July 1995, Jay Leno, host of the *Tonight Show*, had fun insisting that a woman guest eat a banana while he interviewed Ken Bannister, owner/curator of the International Banana Museum in Altadena, California. She was clearly reluctant, and the two men enjoyed her discomfort while she ate the fruit "like a monkey."

Since the introduction of bananas to the United States market in the 1880s, banana advertisers have consistently addressed the female audience as the purchasers, preparers, and consumers of their product. Concurrent with the widespread availability of cheap bananas, new concerns about nutrition, health, sanitation, and weight loss or gain for the whole family became the women's responsibility in the late nineteenth century, and the new field of home economics and domestic science taught women to count calories and balance meals. Bananas were promoted as a substitute for meat, as a fruit in a germ-proof wrapper, and as a dainty aid in dieting. Despite their risqué size and shape, imported bananas became the women and children's food and remain the most popular fruit consumed in the United States.

Figure 6.3.   Unidentified photograph of women eating bananas, Lovell Banana Museum.

Figure 6.4.   100 Ways to Enjoy Bananas, Bauerlein, Inc., New Orleans, 1925, Lovell Banana Museum.

NOTES

1. Comment by Arwen Mohun, University of Delaware, at Food and Drink in Consumer Societies, a conference sponsored by the Center for the History of Business, Technology, and Society, Hagley Museum and Library, Wilmington, Delaware, 12 November 1999.

2. Alonzo E. Taylor, "Consumption, Merchandising, and Advertising of Foods," *Harvard Business Review*, April 1924, 33.

3. "Fruit Dispatch Company 1898–1923," *Fruit Dispatch* (December 1923), 365; Grace Agnes Thompson, "The Story of a Great New England Enterprise," *New England Magazine*, May 1915, 19.

4. Mary Corbin Sies, "The Domestic Mission of the Privileged American Suburban Homemaker, 1877–1917: A Reassessment," *Making the American Home: Middle-Class Women & Domestic Material Culture 1840–1940*, ed. Marilyn Ferris Motz and Pat Browne (Bowling Green, Ohio: Bowling Green State University Popular Press, 1988), 196.

5. S. D. Farrar, *The Homekeeper* (Boston: Published for the Author, 1872), 125.

6. Todd S. Goodhome, ed., *A Domestic Cyclopaedia of Practical Information* (New York: Henry Holt, 1877), 14.

7. Marion Harland, *The Dinner Year-Book* (New York: Scribner's, 1878), 39.

8. Menus from the Winterthur Library Manuscript Collection; Walter R. Houghton et al., *American Etiquette and Rules of Politeness* (Indianapolis: A. E. Davis, 1882), 171; Mrs. Florence Marion Hall, *The Correct Thing in Good Society* (Boston: Estes and Lauriat, 1888), 100; Maud C. Cooke, *Our Social Manual for All Occasions or Approved Etiquette of To-Day* (Chicago: Monarch, 1896), 226.

9. Winterthur Library, Manuscript Collection.

10. *The Cook: A Weekly Handbook of Domestic Culinary Art for All Housekeepers* 1, no. 17, 20 July 1885, 9; *The Cook* 1, no. 16, 13 July 1886, 6.

11. Winterthur Library Manuscript Collection.

12. *Good Housekeeping*, 23 July 1887, ii.

13. *The Cook* 1, no. 12, 15 June 1885, 8.

14. "Our Baby in June," *Housekeeper's Weekly*, 4 June 1892, 8.

15. "Bananas for Children," *The Ladies' Home Journal*, April 1902, 37.

16. Ruth Washburn Jordan, "Bananas Up to Date," *Parents' Magazine*, February 1929, 40.

17. Maria Parloa, *Miss Parloa's Kitchen Companion* (Boston: Estes and Lauriat, 1887).

18. *The Ladies' World*, December 1896, 8.

19. Marion Harland, *House and Home: A Complete Cook-Book and Housewife's Guide* (Philadelphia: P. W. Ziegler, 1889), 505.

20. "A Spring-Time Breakfast," *Housekeeper's Weekly*, 7 May 1892, 14.

21. Sidney W. Mintz, *Sweetness and Power* (New York: Viking, 1985), 130.

22. *Delicate Dishes: A Cook Book / Compiled by Ladies of St. Paul's Church* (Chicago: E. B. Smith, 1896), 82.

23. David H. Shayt, "Of Dragons and Bluebirds: Deconstructing Whitman's Samplers," paper given at "Chocolate: Its Mystery and History," the Smithsonian Forum on Material Culture and The Smithsonian History Roundtable, 16 October 1999.

24. *Good Things to Eat and How to Prepare Them* (Buffalo, N.Y.: Larkin, 1908), 48.

25. Mrs. S. T. Rorer, *Good Cooking* (Philadelphia: Curtis, 1898), 140.

26. Maude C. Cooke, *Twentieth Century Cook Book*, n.p., c. 1890.

27. Laura Shapiro, *Perfection Salad* (New York: Farrar, Straus and Giroux, 1986), 233.

28. B. W. Bryant, *A Bill of Fare for Everyday in the Year*, n.p., October 1892, 1–14.

29. Mary Cruger, "Mid Busy Streets and Crowded Marts," *The Home-Maker*, September 1889, 485.

30. Mary Hinman Abel, *Practical Sanitary and Economic Cooking Adapted to Persons of Moderate and Small Means* (Rochester, N.Y.: E. R. Andrews for the American Public Health Association, 1890), 144.

31. *The Chicago Record Cook Book: Seasonable, Inexpensive Bills of Fare for Every Day in the Year* (Chicago: Chicago Record, 1896).

32. "Unloading a Banana Steamer," *Harper's Weekly*, 21 April 1894, 366.

33. "Menus for August," *Good Housekeeping*, August 1904, 233.

34. Mrs. Edgar N. Blake, ed., *Practical and Dainty Recipes: Luncheons and Dinner Giving in Woodward, Oklahoma* (Woodward, Okla.: Wm. A. Pyne, 1907).

35. Janet McKenzie Hill, *Salads, Sandwiches and Chafing-Dish Dainties* (Boston: Little, Brown, 1907), 10.

36. Fannie Merritt Farmer, "The Banana in Cookery," *Woman's Home Companion*, March 1910, 60.

37. Mrs. S. T. Rorer, *Dainty Dishes for All the Year-Round* (Philadelphia: North Brothers, 1915), 57.

38. Fruit Dispatch Company, *From the Tropics to Your Table* (New York: W. F. Powers, 1926), 30.

39. *A Study of the Banana: Its Every-day Use and Food Value* (Teacher's Manual) (New York: United Fruit Company, Home Economics Department, 1939), 15.

40. Nancy Prentiss, *The Perfect Hostess* (New Kensington, Pa.: Westmorland Stirling, 1952), 32.

41. Laura Shapiro, *Perfection Salad* (New York: Farrar, Straus and Giroux, 1986), 231.

42. Marion Harland, *House and Home: A Complete Cook-Book and Housewife's Guide* (Philadelphia: P. W. Ziegler, 1889), 387.

43. Catherine Owen, "Cheap Living in Cities," *The Home-Maker*, May 1889, 126.

44. "Bananas—Wholesome, Nutritious, Cheap: A Few Appetizing and Inexpensive Recipes," compliments of United Fruit Company, 131 State Street, Boston, c. 1917, 4.

45. Marion Harris Neil, "The Versatile Banana," *The Ladies' World*, August 1910, 17.

46. "How to Live without a Fire," *The Ladies Home Journal*, August 1907, 28.

47. *The Business of Being a Housewife: A Manual to Promote Household Efficiency and Economy* (Chicago: Armour and Company, 1917), 16.

48. Newton Fuessel, "The Green Gold of the Tropics," *Outlook*, 4 October 1922, 188.

49. Scientific Market Research Brief for Fruit Dispatch Company, typescript, December 1929, no page numbers.

50. "The Story of the Banana" (Boston: United Fruit Company, Education Department, 1936), 52.

51. Laura Bird, "Chiquita's Ad Archive: The Picture of Health," *Adweek's Marketing Week*, 7 January 1991, 32.

52. Bird, "Chiquita's Ad Archive," 33.

53. *House Beautiful*, October 1977, 120.

54. Mary Ronold, *The Century Cook Book* (New York: D. Appleton-Century, 1937), 531.

55. "Yes, We Do Have Bananas," *Strange Stories, Amazing Facts of America's Past*, Reader's Digest, 1989, 237; unidentified photograph in The Banana Museum, Auburn, Washington.

56. Raymond Sokolov, "Bananamania," *Natural History*, May 1977, 81; *Manners and Rules of Good Society* (New York: New York Book Company, 1913), 72.

57. *The Ladies' World*, September 1912, 28.

58. *The Ladies' World*, May 1912, 21.

59. Anthony Slide, *The Vaudevillians: A Dictionary of Vaudeville Performers* (Westport, Conn.: Arlington House, 1981), 83.

60. Florida's Weeki Wachee, Spring of the Mermaids, brochure, c. 1950.

61. David Widner, "America's Going Bananas," *Readers Digest*, July 1986, 118.

62. Laura Shapiro, *Perfection Salad* (New York: Farrar, Straus and Giroux), 226.

63. Frances O'Connor, "Bananas Add Glamour to Your Springtime Meals," *Better Homes & Gardens*, April 1950, 71.

7

There's Always Room for Resistance: Jell-O, Gender, and Social Class

Kathleen LeBesco

$\mathcal{J}$ust about every American I have ever met has some kind of Jell-O "story" to tell, but two anecdotes in particular start me thinking about Jell-O and resistance: one that is personal and one from the news. Let me start with a bit of family history. In my maternal grandparents' house, the serious art of cooking was the delight of my grandfather, Brooks. A butcher by day, he spent evenings and weekends perfecting the balance of spices in his chicken noodle soup recipe, showing me how to clove a ham with an artist's eye, and lovingly glazing his sweet potatoes. Food seemed to envelop his life, to be his livelihood both at work and at home, and he cared about it deeply.

In contrast, my grandmother Kathleen made Jell-O. While her culinary creations also encompassed boiled hot dogs and butter sandwiches, as a young child I recall being struck with the realization that my grandmother was notably different from the sweet old grannies of my friends who slaved over hot, crusty apple pies and Thanksgiving dinners. A pianist by design but a full-time secretary by economic necessity, Grandma seems now to me to have been resisting something, with Jell-O as her accomplice.

I ate a lot of Jell-O at my grandmother's table in my first ten years of life, during the 1970s: red, yellow, green, you name it. In an act most likely committed out of sheer exhaustion from Jell-O monotony, at age ten I decided to mix Grandpa's juicy prime rib and golden corn niblets into my yellow Jell-O in an attempt to create some space mission-like complete meal in a bowl. Grandma yelled at me, unhappy that I had "ruined the Jell-O" and forced me to eat the troubled concoction, effectively terminating my experience as a Jell-O consumer.

As if that were not enough to turn me from Jell-O forever, I recently read that in New Bedford, Massachusetts, a middle-aged woman pleaded guilty to killing her boyfriend, at whose hands she said that she had suffered years of sexual abuse.[1] The weapon of choice was neither a gun nor a knife—nothing so gruesome and invasive. Instead, the woman served her boyfriend a heaping bowl of Jell-O laced with a little something extra: LSD. What better context for a deadly dose than this deceptively cheery dessert? The deed of this New Bedford woman highlights one of the ways in which Jell-O can be used as a tool of resistance. Though this is an extreme example of how women use Jell-O to resist oppressive gender and social-class paradigms, it is nonetheless instructive about the seriousness with which we should examine Jell-O.

Now, twenty years after my troubled tangle with Jell-O and beef, and just a year after learning of its deadly possibilities, I maintain a strange (some might say "morbid") fascination with Jell-O. My interest in Jell-O now centers on its historical function as a gendered, classed, cultural product, rather than merely the colorful, sugary, translucent dessert item most know it to be. In this chapter, I consider Jell-O from two perspectives: on one hand, Jell-O seems to solidify some very traditional notions about gender and social class, and so I intend to highlight how women have resisted these delimitations. On the other hand, Jell-O itself has been and continues to be used as a tool for resisting expectations about gender and social class. Much stands to be learned from thinking about the ways in which Jell-O both congeals and shakes loose gendered and classed social behaviors and attitudes. Such a task would allow us to understand not only the role of Jell-O as the perfect (female, middle-class) homemaker's helper, but also its functions as simplifier of the homemaker's cooking duties and medium for expressing oneself in opposition to the homemaker role.

JELL-O AND THE STATUS QUO: SOMETHING WORTH RESISTING

Advertisements

The connotations of Jell-O—domestication, orientation toward family, lack of sophistication, earnestness—may send women who consider themselves "modern" scurrying away from identification with the old-fashioned lives they think are signified by its use and enjoyment. Historically, has the woman who makes Jell-O been empowered to alter the conditions of her own existence? Has she been able to break free from the status quo of high expectations of the housewife but low expectations of the woman?

Anthropologist Carole Counihan suggests that the capitalist conception of food as commodity means that food is a vehicle of power, as control over access to food varies from person to person.[2] She further argues that an individual's capacity to set the conditions of her/his own food consumption and that of others helps to position that person within the prevailing social hierarchy as relatively autonomous. I choose not to examine the differences between those who have access to Jell-O and those who are denied access, as its relatively low cost and widespread availability mean that even working-class people in the United States can consume Jell-O if they choose to. Indeed, Kraft Foods statistics indicate that more than a million packages of Jell-O are purchased or eaten every day, that the brand is recognized by 99 percent of Americans and is used regularly in 72 percent of American homes.[3] Instead, my focus is on what it means to select a particular commodity/food item in working- and middle-class America today, specifically, what it means to consume (or disavow consumption of) Jell-O in terms of power.

In exploring Jell-O's advertising, we can gain some clues to the intended meanings for its consumption, which will later prove useful in gauging why women would want to resist these meanings. Jell-O has long, and intentionally, been associated with childhood and femininity in its advertising.[4] The product named by a woman was a poor seller in the late 1890s until advertising campaigns featuring fabulously coifed ladies in women's magazines helped Jell-O to catch on. The relieved expressions on the models' faces seem to result directly from the caption "No Recipe Book Required." The next ad campaign featured the darling Jell-O Girl, delighted to play with Jell-O boxes instead of toys, insisting that "you can't be a kid without it." A few years later, artist Rose O'Neill, creator of the impishly cheerful Kewpie Dolls, began to illustrate Jell-O ads and booklets. By 1912, ads and booklets featured the recipes of the country's most famous female cooks and home economists, and even those of actresses and opera divas.

Overall, the copy of the ads from 1904 through the 1920s suggested ease of preparation above all else, "so easy to prepare that even the children can make it."[5] The idea that even the least experienced housewife can handle Jell-O preparation abounds in Jell-O advertising, as in this 1904 *Ladies Home Journal* ad: "How often some ingredient is forgotten or not rightly proportioned and the dessert spoiled. That will never occur if you use Jell-O."[6] But female ineptitude was not limited to preparation ability, according to the Genesee Pure Food Company folks; it also encompassed women's decision-making abilities as far as food was concerned. A 1908 Genesee booklet argues that "all women will agree that one of their most perplexing duties is the selection, day after day, of a suitable dessert."[7] Of course, Jell-O saves the day for these poor, perplexed women.

Advertising in the more lighthearted 1950s sold women Jell-O as a "busy day dessert," promoted National Trim-Your-Torso-with-Jell-O Week, and encouraged a waste-not-want-not attitude during National Use-Up-Your-Leftovers-in-a-Jell-O-Salad Week. Interestingly, 1960s ads deviated from the norm of solely addressing women and children. A popular print ad of the era depicts a clean-cut but befuddled-looking man in a dress shirt and tie mulling over a thick, tattered cookbook, surrounded by presumably foreign implements including a measuring cup, mixing bowl, and mixer. The caption reads "Now's the time for Jell-O." The absence of women in this advertisement reflects larger societal changes, with women moving into the paid workforce in record numbers. By the 1960s, the "nutritious" properties of Jell-O were de-emphasized in advertising, making room for a focus instead on its "lightness."[8] This laid the groundwork for the introduction in the 1980s of sugar-free Jell-O, which was marketed to higher income, calorie conscious consumers.

By the late 1970s, ads targeted women's need for efficiency in the kitchen. One print ad of this newly microwave-savvy era features a sweetly (or sheepishly) smiling grandmother-type holding a tray of enticing Jell-O pudding parfait glasses, with the caption "I zapped it." Ten years later, Jell-O pudding pitchman Bill Cosby had so appealed to young mothers and children that he became the Jell-O gelatin spokesperson, as well. Jell-O ads in the 1980s bore the directive "Make someone happy"; the "someone", though, was presumably not the female reader herself. Print and television ads of the late 1980s and '90s both featured and targeted kids, based notably on the introduction of Jell-O Jigglers gelatin snacks, part of a larger field of "Snacktivities" recipes and games designed to bring parents (read: mothers) and children together.

Consumer Connotations

If the makers of Jell-O enforced connotations of childhood, traditional femininity, ease of preparation, and dieting with their product during the 1900s, did women consumers simply internalize these as desirable meanings? Or did they resist these means by which contemporary women were infantilized, de-skilled, made passive, and distracted by concerns over weight?

I interviewed a number of women about the meanings they have for Jell-O, and found that the latter instance of resistance is indeed more prevalent. The actual tastes for Jell-O of women to whom I spoke are quite varied, with responses ranging from "revolting" to "nondescript and bland" to "delicious." However, more interesting than the attributes assigned to the food product are the connotations these women assigned to those who prepare and consume Jell-O. Scholars of the post-capitalist U.S. economy have suggested that Americans now tend to forge their identity around consumption of commodities, rather than production of goods. Strikingly, the trend among those to whom I spoke was for women to contrast their own modern identities to those old-fashioned identities they imagined were possessed by others who did enjoy making and eating Jell-O. This, however, does not mean that the women I talked with disavowed any enjoyment of Jell-O themselves; but many categorized their own relationship with Jell-O as ironic rather than earnest.

A large number of the women who enjoyed Jell-O discussed the product as something which, despite its ease of preparation, is usually prepared by women (sometimes with children), but rarely by men. "When men cook, they go gourmet—no messing around with Jell-O for them," said one woman, herself a former caterer. Another spoke of her beliefs about gender and Jell-O.

> When I was single, I think I made Jell-O about four times in my entire life. (Well, no, I did have to make it for my job in a cafeteria at college, but that was professional, not personal.) At home, I never made it (but when I think about it, my mother made it all the time). When I got married, it was kind of weird, but I started making it, even though my husband never really asked for it; it was almost like I thought that's what a married woman was supposed to do. I would get recipes from the boxes or from magazines, and try out some new stuff from time to time. It was like I was reliving my mother's life: being the perfect woman, Jell-O molds and all. Then I got divorced, and even though it was much saner for me to be single again, I didn't feel so perfect anymore (I'm Catholic), and I stopped the Jell-O.

This quotation illustrates the link one woman forged between ideal femininity and Jell-O production. What I find most interesting is that she discounts the Jell-O making experiences for which she was paid, at the college cafeteria, as irrelevant to her feminine identity; instead, what matters in defining her gender identity is her unpaid domestic dessert production. This woman's comments indicate some degree of critical distance on her part from the "perfect woman" Jell-O was supposed to have helped her to be.

Other women, many notably from the working class, connected their experiences as Jell-O makers to their savvy ability to get along on a tight budget. One informant noted that "When you have four kids and only one income, you have to feel like you're taking care of things. I feel like a good mom when I can put a decent meal on the table, and even give them some snacks, too. That's when Jell-O is good." This woman is not alone in relating Jell-O production to social class, as in this instance when an interviewee tells of an incident in which she realized how Jell-O marked her status:

> When my daughter was little, her club at school was having a bake sale, and I was supposed to send in something for her to sell. I figured everyone would

send cookies and brownies, and I wanted to do something different. I had a lot
of Jell-O packets on hand, so I did up a bunch of Styrofoam bowls of rainbow
colored Jell-O and sent them in with her. She came home from school all up-
set, crying that some other kids had teased her and called her 'trailer park girl'
for bringing in the Jell-O. I was furious. It wasn't like we couldn't afford to do
cookies. I just wanted to be original.

This anecdote supports Sarah Newton's contention that "the image of the
food product [Jell-O] has changed from being the ultimate in the American
housewife's repertoire of tasty and elegant salads and desserts to an embar-
rassment, a symbol of gauche unsophistication often tied, not to the trendy
coasts, but to the rural—the hick—Midwest."[9] In different ways, contemporary American women resist the implications of low socioeconomic status and
bumpkin locale conferred by Jell-O: some by elevating the 1950s ideal of domestic elegance to new heights, others by avoiding Jell-O altogether.

Beyond its implied connotation with traditional femininity and its inferred
connection with low socioeconomic status and lack of sophistication, women
may also resist some of the less-than-savory aspects of Jell-O as a gritty
chemical concoction. Orator Woodward, the man who owned the patent for
Jell-O at the turn of the century, is also responsible for a composition nest egg
with "miraculous power to kill lice on hens when hatching."[10] Even more
striking than this heretofore-unknown relationship between Jell-O and de-
lousing agents is the fact that the LeRoy Historical Society, based in the
home of Genesee Pure Food Company, would claim bragging rights about
this odd connection on their Jell-O Centennial Celebration website. Aes-
thetically speaking, there is something to resist in *any* food that touts its connection to lice-killer. The same can be said for the attempt of the Jell-O bu-
reaucracy to appeal to children with "Dirt Cups," made with crushed
chocolate sandwich cookies, milk, Jell-O chocolate pudding and gummy
worms, to create the effect of worms wiggling out of surprisingly sweet soil.[11]
Though the latter dish is arguably quite tasty, I suspect that adult women
might resist its pull because of the association of dirt and worms with food
products. These aesthetic reasons to resist Jell-O are perhaps less serious than
the gender- and class-based ones discussed earlier, but taken together, they
point to a range of interruptions of food rules surrounding Jell-O. Counihan
believes that "food rules are part of a usually unscrutinized cultural ideology
that continuously leads to the reinforcement of life as it is."[12] In resisting the
rules for making sense of Jell-O, women also resist the cultural ideology that
prescribes their continued domesticity and passivity.

We have examined some of the emotional connotations of Jell-O, but not
how rules and meanings attach to Jell-O in ways that maintain the status quo
of American gender and class relations. Beyond the meanings intended by

Jell-O advertisements, when I asked women in interviews to think about this issue, they presented interesting responses. Many interviewees understood Jell-O as a "maintenance food," something to eat in order to preserve the status quo. While Jell-O was seen by most as having relatively low nutritional value, it was represented as useful for not gaining weight, for not interfering with the ability of the body to recover after illness, for not breaking a budget, and for not requiring a lot of time to prepare.

The most frequently repeated statement in all of my interviews was that Jell-O was a good snack food for dieters. The majority of women cited it as low-calorie and claimed that it would not make a woman gain weight. "When I found out I was pregnant, I still had cravings for sweets but since I was already heavy the doctor said I should be careful about putting on any more weight—so I ate a lot of Jell-O" said one woman. Others pointed to the notion that Jell-O is light and does not present the possibility for an uncomfortable sense of fullness after eating it. One claimed that "even if I'm not hungry I can eat it, because it's like candy, but it doesn't get me fat like candy," suggesting that Jell-O does not interfere with her body's usual signals of satiety. Another woman recounted her belief that Jell-O is good for people prior to certain medical procedures or after surgery for fast healing; while perhaps Jell-O does not have miraculous curative powers, this woman understands that it is also something to eat that will not interfere with recovery from illness. Another woman summed it up by doubting the nutritional value of Jell-O, but simultaneously suggesting that it has no outright negative health effects. Others compared Jell-O to more detrimental snack foods: "Okay, so it's not exactly celery, but it won't clog up your arteries like potato chips or fatten you up like cookies."[13]

There seems to me to be something worth resisting in a product marketed to help already diet-obsessed women further discipline their personal eating behavior. American women have historically been distracted from more pressing battles for political empowerment by the lure of beauty, and throughout most of the twentieth century, mainstream American beauty has been conflated with slenderness. In many cases, saying "no" to Jell-O would be symbolically akin to saying "no" to diets, thus affirming women's right to take up space and to concentrate on more potent forms of social change.

Several women applauded Jell-O's affordability, describing it as "cost-effective," "inexpensive," and "very cheap." One claimed "when I had my third child, I couldn't spend as much money on junk food, and I found that Jell-O was pretty easy to stretch for dessert." A detached, privileged critique might call into question why women should skimp on food, sustenance of energy and life. A critical perspective more attuned to the exigencies of a tight budget might ask women to examine their spending habits and to eschew Jell-O in favor of more wholesome, nutritious foods made newly affordable by decreased spending, say, on diet products. In addition to affordability, numerous interviewees used the phrase "easy to prepare" when discussing Jell-O, praising the short time it took to mix the dessert before refrigerating it. The decadent response to this view might be to suggest resisting the rush in favor of communing with the sensual pleasures of culinary creativity. A more acceptable proposition might be to involve other family members in food preparation, so the brunt of responsibility no longer falls on a wife or mother so exhausted that "easy to make" is the quintessential recipe criterion.

Not only have American women long been expected to prepare family food, they have been expected to serve it, as well, regardless of the amount of time they spend working outside of the home. William McIntosh and Mary Zey contend that middle-class women experienced a change in domestic roles as a result of the Industrial Revolution and capitalist marketing. Before, their status had been determined through their proficiency in acquiring, storing, preserving, and preparing food to be eaten by the family, but afterwards their roles in production shifted to responsibility for the emotional well-being of family members.[14] Media from the mid-1800s to the mid-1900s elevated domesticity "to the level of a religious calling," according to McIntosh and Zey, with special focus on a wife's ability to keep her family happy and together with food. "Women were told that the 'health of the nation' depended on the quality of meals they prepared," but were warned away from attempting the scientific endeavor of cooking without the proper training.

According to Alan Warde, the decline of the full-time housewife in the last century has actually led to an increased load in paid and unpaid labor for women who now juggle responsibility for work outside the home and in the domestic sphere. The consequence, he believes, "in the absence of concessions and compromises by men, has been the need for women to seek their own personal solutions to the intensified time pressure to which they have been subject."[15] Jell-O fits as a less labor-intensive way for women to "care" for their families, taking the place of time-consuming cake, pie, and cookie preparation. Scholars contend that Jell-O functions "as a way for women to show creativity in the kitchen, nurturance of the family, and a clever if innocent sophistication."[16] One woman I interviewed described Jell-O's simultaneous usefulness as both food and an activity for entertaining her children: "It can be a fun snack, especially because children like to help make it. Except for the boiling water, they can really do the rest." Another reflected back on her own mother making Jell-O for the family, and said that she carried on the "family tradition" by making Jigglers with her son when he was a child.

However, Warde speculates that women are frequently reluctant to rely on available food commodities as a solution to their problems for a variety of reasons, including moral and practical suspicion about convenience food and distrust of its tendency to de-skill cooks. One woman I interviewed agrees with Warde's speculation, representing Jell-O consumption as a signifier of ignobility: "I wouldn't be caught dead eating that crap; trash eats trash." Another reminisced about her rise from inauspicious beginnings:

> As a kid, my family didn't have a lot of money, and my parents weren't too strict about us eating right, so we ate a lot of chips, candies, Jell-O, donuts, and pizza. When I came into my own, got a job, started earning more money than my dad ever made, I started eating right. You know, the cheapest stuff in the market is loaded with the most stuff that's bad for you. You have to pay more to get good, fresh things like nice vegetables and good cuts of meat.

Even lumped in among a list of other "junk" foods, Jell-O stands out for this woman as a signifier not only of childhood but also of low income. A different woman's complaint with the foodstuff centered more around her concern about losing her cooking skills: "If you get into the habit of making food that way, you won't feel like cooking a nice meal when it counts; it promotes laziness."

One interviewee claimed "I am not interested in eating nonfood; I'll leave that to the women who are so concerned with being thin that they can't enjoy eating real food." Another informant sounded a similar note: "Jell-O has no nutrients. How am I supposed to function and do all the things I do if that's what I'm eating for fuel? If I were sitting at home all day watching soap operas, then maybe." Her comments suggest a belief in the appropriateness of Jell-O for a certain type of woman—a less active woman, and arguably a more traditionally feminine woman—a stereotype she clearly resists with gusto.

Cookbooks

Not only do Jell-O advertising and consumer-constructed connotations provide reasons to resist Jell-O; one can also see the recipes of more traditional cookbooks as emphasizing the feminine flair of the cooks and the reputed but dubious great taste of the final results, as well. In the descriptions of recipes that follow, consider whether the culinary efforts of the presumably female cookbook reader are ultimately noble. *Yankee Magazine's Good Neighbors USA Cookbook* bills itself as "a stimulating collection that reflects the taste and tables of America";[17] its Dried Beef and Celery Mold contains lemon Jell-O, dried beef, and Miracle Whip, labeled an "attractive, novel invention to grace your dinner table." Beef? Jell-O? Miracle Whip? Should we honor the possibility that women so strongly desire a novel invention to grace their dinner tables that they would confidently combine these ingredients? Eleven years later, the 1996 *Yankee Magazine's Church Suppers and Potluck Dinners Cookbook* presents a variety of Jell-O recipes intended to please the eye, the palate, and the children, too. Take, for instance, the Cranberry Gelatin Salad, which "simply sparkles on a buffet table"; the Layered Strawberry Dessert, which "kids adore"; or the Sunshine Salad, of which we are told that "The ladies of Gilsum, New Hampshire tell us this salad is a great complement to the ham and beans they serve at the town's annual rock swap supper."[18] Though I admit ignorance about what exactly a "rock swap supper" is, I can nonetheless see that the descriptions accompanying these Jell-O-centric recipes emphasize very traditional and restrictive roles for women. In what universe might a woman's most pressing concern be the extent to which her dessert outsparkles others at the buffet? What are the gentlemen of Gilsum doing while the ladies industriously spread their Sunshine Salad?

The 1950 *Perfect Hostess Cookbook* contains numerous Jell-O recipes, all interestingly in the form of rings: Beet Ring, Borsch Ring, Cucumber Ring, Lime Ring, Pineapple Ring, Relish Ring, and Tomato-Apricot Ring. Is there some kind of subliminal message here? Must the perfect hostess have not only a Jell-O ring, but a wedding ring? Apparently so. With cloying tone and condescending timbre, its author assuages inexperienced cooks, assumed to be young, newly married women, in the introduction. "It isn't difficult—please remember that—because the recipes that follow are set forth in such a way that you have only to follow one direction at a time—just one at a time, and try not to look ahead."[19] Here, the young woman reader is trained to realize that, even without the brains of a rocket scientist, she is capable of fulfilling her station in life: routine food preparation for the family. The author's assurances go even further in her admission that "few foreign words are used; at least four young friends have begged me not to use directive foreign words such as 'sauté.'"[20] The tone and content of this Jell-O-oriented cookbook leave a bad taste in the mouth of anyone who believes that women are not inept. While one might argue that it is the overall cookbook that deserves critique more so than the ingredients, in noticing that difficult concoctions such as soufflés are studiously avoided, one realizes that Jell-O is concomitant with a derisibly doltish definition of womanhood.

Further cookbook evidence that Jell-O goes hand in hand with traditionally feminine roles comes in the 1995 *Miss America Cookbook*. A compendium of "fascinating" tidbits about Miss Americas through the ages, the book intersperses conservative observations about women's changing roles in society with good-ole heartland recipes from contestants in the annual pageant. That the book champions Miss Americas for "sid[ing] with conservative values and patriotism"[21] during second wave feminist attacks on the degradation of women in beauty pageants, amidst all the Jell-O recipes, is quite telling about the reasons many women have to resist Jell-O's connotations today. Miss Iowa 1955 contributes her Blueberry Lemon Mold; Miss Kentucky 1974 shares her Cinnamon Applesauce Salad; Miss Nebraska 1969 presents her Original Pineapple Dessert. Even the pageant winners get in on the act, with the Festive Cranberry Relish of Miss America 1964 and the Blueberry Dessert Salad of Miss America 1979. The enterprise of compiling a Miss America cookbook is premised upon old-fashioned notions of femininity—a link between conventional feminine beauty, ideal wife material, and the duties that accompany womanhood as defined by attachment to men. Few other food products stand in so perfectly for this connection, and thus few raise as many feminist eyebrows as does Jell-O.

Sugar and Social Class

In addition to gender-related reasons for resistance, there also exist some concerns about social class status. Carole Counihan writes of a positive correlation between thinness and class status for both women and men. She suggests that the thin body is associated in White middle-class American culture with control and moral authority, ultimately prompting expressions of self-righteousness and moral rectitude among its bearers.[22] The poor, who are presumed to have shoddy diets, and members of non-White ethnic and racial groups, who have higher obesity rates than Whites, are thus slotted in to lower positions in the social hierarchy. These hierarchical assumptions become clear when women themselves discuss their experiences, or lack of, making and eating Jell-O. Interestingly, though, the role of Jell-O is complex: many women consider Jell-O to be part of a shoddy, low-class diet, but at the same time, the product is not, especially in its sugar-free varieties, considered to be fattening. Eating Jell-O does not mark one's body indelibly as fat (and thus poor, following Counihan's logic).

Counihan suggests that the case of sugar deftly illustrates how food reproduces and sustains hierarchies.[23] When little sugar could be produced, it was a food of the rich, who squandered it in sculptures as a means of signifying their wealth. Then, when increased colonization and enslavement made possible more sugar production, the poor were able to consume it as well, and did so "to emulate the rich." However, the poor sacrificed other vital foods in order to eat more sugar, and their diets suffered. The rich were able to eat sugar as well as the more vital foods, and turned to less commonplace foods as new signifiers of class difference. This anecdote demonstrates the connection between food preferences and social class affiliation, and has resonance with Jell-O, which is approximately 90 percent sugar.[24] As I discussed earlier, many women were pleased with the affordability of Jell-O;

however, in choosing it over more vital foods, their diets suffer and they mark themselves as having a low position in the social hierarchy.

Ben Fine, Michael Heasman, and Judith Wright note a marked difference in sugar consumption between the 1930s and the 1980s: in the 30s, considerably more sugar was consumed in processed foods by richer people, while in the 80s, the targeting of high-income consumers for new, "healthy" sugar-removed products meant that more processed sugar was consumed by the poor.[25] They go on to state that "sugar is also considered a lower-class food, with . . . the fastest decline in retail sugar purchases in higher-income groups."[26] The authors point out the ironic preference among higher-class consumers for artificial, inorganic chemical additives rather than natural, organic sugar.

Fine, Heasman, and Wright locate a capitalist underpinning for the popularity of sugary foods like Jell-O, writing that "many of today's modern, taken-for-granted foods and drinks have been 'invented' around sugar as a major ingredient. Sugar has successfully functioned and performed within the underlying tendencies toward mass-produced, mass-consumed industrial products and not least in producing 'durable' and 'hardy' products."[27] It seems that amenability to mass production, distribution, and consumption is the basis upon which class distinction is to be found;[28] thus, Jell-O, easily adaptable in the aforementioned functions, articulates lower social class. Pâté and caviar, for instance, would articulate higher social status, as they are more difficult to produce, scarce to find, and expensive to consume. Consumers, women in particular, would do well to contest their own further economic disenfranchisement on the grounds of the foods they eat.

A 1923 Genesee Pure Food Company publicity piece invites consideration in this light. The text tempts consumers to gaze deeply into their Jell-O: "If you will look intently, you may discover crowds of brown-skinned tropical natives cultivating and cutting sugar cane under the blazing torrid sun, and a great white fleet of ships coming up through the Caribbean and through the Pacific Ocean bearing the tons of sugar that go into Jell-O."[29] The parent company cultivated attitudes whereby comfortable, White, middle-class American consumers felt economic and racial superiority over the "brown-skinned natives" laboring in difficult conditions.

Contrast this with the 1923 publicity assurance that "The Jell-O employees are all Americans. Strikes or labor troubles do not occur. Their work reminds one of a big sociable sort of jelling-bee."[30] Compare it with the recollection that Jell-O was a symbol of national unity in the early part of the twentieth century. Allegedly, Ellis Island immigrants were typically served bowls of Jell-O under signs that read "Welcome to America."[31] It was important for Genesee Pure Foods Co. to emphasize happy, middle-class American-ness among its producers as a selling point, but bewildering in regards to the dark-skinned natives working under the torrid sun. If the *white* ships were indeed sailing up through the Caribbean, then these weren't American folks, they were economically exploited residents of some island country. The class implications are strikingly deserving of opposition. More recent Jell-O advertising highlights the same issues of class in new ways. Pierre Bordieu proposes that professionals, with their taste for the light, the refined and the delicate, define the popular taste by negation as in favor of the heavy, the fat, and the coarse.[32] It is interesting, then, that Jell-O is marketed by executives as light and nonfattening, as in "good taste," when the product itself is clearly understood by the public to indicate lower social class.

Jell-O, in its "regular" incarnation, has been described as incredibly troubling: "It is the demise of the food supply, the distancing of ourselves from the natural world, the demeaning and de-skilling of women, the suffering of animals, and the desecration of the environment. All in one box."[33] This section has also argued for an outlook on Jell-O as troubling; from the angle of continued gender and social class hierarchies, there are many valid reasons to resist Jell-O. Nonetheless, I believe that in order to grasp fully the cultural significance of Jell-O, one needs to take into consideration the ways in which people use Jell-O itself as a tool for resistance.

JELL-O AS ACCOMPLICE: SOMETHING TO RESIST WITH

Hold the skepticism and pass the Jell-O. Think again about my grandmother. How might Jell-O have helped her to register her displeasure at her economically mandated job path? Did it filter off some of her rancor toward the traditionally feminine roles expected of her? And what about that New Bedford woman who served Jell-O with LSD to her sweetie? Though undoubtedly a criminal act, wasn't it the cover provided by happy, reliable Jell-O that empowered her to end years of abuse at his hands? These are extreme examples, but they are suggestive of how women use Jell-O as a tool for resisting social subjugation.

While Jell-O has clearly been marketed as a food item designed to please the family, there exists a darker side of Jell-O in the minds of many people. Recipes designed to disgust, including one for Toilet Bowl Jell-O (involving a plastic toy potty, yellow Jell-O, and submerged miniature Tootsie Rolls—you get the picture), circulate in the far corners of the Internet. *The Detroit News* features dissent from residents of the working- and middle-class neighborhood bordering the Woburn, Massachusetts Atlantic Gelatin (Jell-O) factory, who complain about the pervasive stench of rotting animal flesh.[34] In less wholesome incarnations, Jell-O has been part of fads from Jell-O shots (hard liquor mixed into the sweet treat to the delight of college students nationwide) to Jell-O wrestling (which Ann Landers declared an abominable "waste of food") in the latter part of the twentieth century. Given this variety of uses and reactions, the possibilities of using Jell-O to resist particular ideas about gender and social class are worthy of investigation.

Resisting Drudgery

The women I interviewed shared some interesting ideas about Jell-O. Many associated Jell-O with fun, drawing connections between humorous ad campaigns and other media representations, the qualities of the foodstuff itself, and their own experiences eating and preparing it. Several respondents mentioned the affable personalities of Jell-O pitchmen Jack Benny and Bill Cosby when discussing the fun to be had with the product. One older woman said "I got a kick out of the Jack Benny radio spots—it was a funny guy selling a funny food" while a younger woman referred to Cosby's commercials as cute, recalling instances in which smiley kids ate the Jell-O before he got the chance. Others recalled humorous Jell-O moments in film, like the scene in *National Lampoon's Christmas Vacation* when Jell-O with cat food is served for Christmas dinner. One woman described her perception of Jell-O: "Jell-O has personality. It is not really a food; it's entertaining. You eat it as fun. It's silly and slimy. Those are not qualities of food. If they were, you would probably be eating worms." The same woman later doubted the nutritional value of eating ground up horse hooves and chicken feet, but stated that spiritually Jell-O is good for the soul because it's playful. A different interviewee nostalgically recalled an experience from when she was very young: "my grandmother made Jell-O and it would be shaped in a design, or made into a star and other shapes. It was always neat to watch it jiggle." Another recalled an enjoyable adult experience, a wild ski trip during which she imbibed Jell-O shots all night long. It is possible that this mental association with fun allows women to resist the serious, labor-intensive responsibility for food preparation typically expected of them.

A handful of the women I interviewed mentioned the significance of Jell-O as an artistic medium, referring to its bright colors, molds, and versatility. "I went through a phase where I was trying out new Jell-O recipes every time we had company over. The most creative I got was a beach scene where I used light brown sugar as sand and did a molded tidal wave with blue Jell-O," claimed one woman. Another confessed to having a fascination with the way Jell-O colors could be played against one another in a dessert dish, admitting that she had tried out a few Amish quilt-like designs despite the lack of black Jell-O.

For not only these women but for women and starving artists nationwide, Jell-O is emerging as a medium for self-expression. Postmodern food product extraordinaire, Jell-O isn't just for breakfast anymore. (Or was that dessert?) Eschewing stone and clay, artists around the country have turned to Jell-O as an expressive artistic medium, and have displayed their works in shows from Oregon to New York.[35] Some artists prefer to work with Jell-O in its dried form, creating sand art and even Zen gardens, though most are lured by the jiggly jelled form. Jell-O art takes a surreal turn at the Maude Kerns Art Gallery in Eugene, Oregon, every April Fools Day. Notable entries in the Jell-O-Rama contest include: "It Came From the Fountain Pool," where Ken's Jell-O guts spurt as he is mauled by an evil creature while he and Barbie relax next to a Jell-O filled pool. Also worthy of attention are a wearable shirt made out of thin congealed Jell-O layers, a "Mad Cow" panel in which Jell-O resembles stained glass, and a display in which a Jell-O figure resembling the Pope rides along in his Popemobile.

On the face of it, little connects the displays of the women I interviewed with the offbeat creations of these West Coast artists. However, both are playfully exploring the trash/art contradictions of Jell-O, an act with larger implications for dismantling the connected cultural ideologies that keep gender and class hierarchies in place. Despite the aforementioned assumptions that making Jell-O characterizes a woman as traditionally wifely or merely trashy, those women who create Jell-O art embrace the contradictions of the food product and wink slyly at the idea that their involvement with it could categorize them as in any way traditional. They resist expectations that they should cook wisely to fuel the family, instead using Jell-O in an arguably frivolous manner to toy with aesthetic predilections. Likewise, artists have thumbed their noses at the class-linked concept of "high" art, preferring to work in a medium whose supplies are cheap and whose look is tacky but indelibly of-the-people.

Resisting the Middle-American Housewife Role

Women dramatize their resistance to the traditional, nurturing, and housewifely symbolic meanings of Jell-O in a variety of ways. In admittedly different terms, the women I interviewed recognized that Jell-O is considered to be a mass cultural product,[36] an agent in the erosion of good taste. However, I argue here that many of them do not accept Jell-O and its accompanying personifications passively. Instead, in the excerpts that follow, consider how their uses and meanings for Jell-O resist traditional expectations and exercise power in a novel manner.

The women to whom I spoke resisted the notion that Jell-O makes a woman a better wife/mother/domestic goddess in a variety of ways. One declared that she enjoyed making Jell-O because the four hours that it takes to congeal "are my time, and my time alone. When I bake, I am constantly attending to what's in the oven. With Jell-O, I can read or watch TV while [the fridge] does the work." This response is notable in that the woman claims no compulsion to use her newfound time to do the endless work of the ideal woman; instead, she kicks back and relaxes. Another woman admits a small degree of guilt when she indicates her decision to buy Jell-O because she can get her kids to make it, instead of solely playing the cook herself. Nonetheless, the ease of preparing the product allows her to escape (at least for the time being) the traditional role of domestic chef.

A related rationale for resistance stems from Marcia Millman's contention that women who feel embarrassed about eating in front of men often prefer to prepare and serve food instead of eating it, thus denying themselves the pleasure that they offer to men.[37] Women and men are judged by how much they eat, rather than what they eat,[38] with women expected to eat lightly and men expected to "chow down." Perhaps Jell-O, with its physical properties of lightness and its reputation as a low-calorie dessert, is a way for women to subvert the gendered demand that they not eat too much (which would often mean a restriction on dessert), while simultaneously functioning to keep firmly in place the idea that a real woman doesn't eat "too much." This said, the popularity of Jell-O with women who cook can be read as an act of resistance, in that they decide not to expend much energy preparing food that they might then feel ashamed of eating.

Laura Shapiro writes that "women's cooking remains an anonymous service to their families, while men's cooking tends to become a highly personal gift to a grateful audience."[39] This statement rings true in many American households, where Mom's fare gets the family through the week without applause, but where Dad's Saturday night grilling foray is met with great appreciation. In order to resist this highly inequitable valuation of cooking, women now have at their fingertips a variety of bizarre, creative recipes intended to produce a result that bespeaks anything but run-of-the-mill service. For instance, a classic Jell-O recipe called "Ring-Around-the-Tuna"[40] involves a "spicy" ring of lime Jell-O speckled with onion, cucumber, celery, pimiento, olives, and tuna. Chef Andy, on-line archivist of Jell-O recipes, nominates this for worst recipe of all time, asking "What were they thinking? If you showed up to a potluck dinner with this in hand, why on earth didn't they shove you back out the door and fling it after you in disgust?"[41] Also notable for their questionable edibility are Cherry Cola Salad (incorporating canned cherries and pineapple, black cherry Jell-O, cream cheese, mayonnaise, and either Coca-Cola *or* port wine!) and Cherry Rice Fluff (utilizing rice, milk, cherry Jell-O, almond extract, and heavy cream). For festive occasions, Chef Andy advocates the creation of a Meathead Centerpiece; this involves a plastic skull layered with strips of cranberry Jell-O and ham, for the "severe burn victim" effect, topped off with boiled egg yolk & olive eyeballs. (Tapioca pudding brain is optional.)[42] Though originated by a man, this recipe provides Chef Andy's legions of female followers with a way to resist the normative expectations of attractive, cheery, wholesome, and nutritious provisions for friends and family.[43] Such recipes, along with helpful tidbits like "Jell-O prepared with tonic water glows under black light, but tastes really awful"[44] encourage whimsicality, not the boring, functional food service typically expected of women.

Chef Andy is not alone in his realization of the self-aware kitsch quotient of Jell-O, though. Jane Stern and Michael Stern, in their 1984 *Square Meals: A Cookbook*, argue that "Jell-O and the suburban chef were made for each other. Jell-O is fast and convenient, pretty, and it mixes so well with other media."[45] They feature campy recipes for Sour Cream Jell-O D'Akron, Sandusky Strawberry Daiquiri Bavarian, Barbecue Cubes, Red Hot Salad, Poke Cake with Jell-O, Cut Glass Dessert. My favorite, though, is Undescended Twinkies, in which the authors ask "why bury the Twinkies? Why not partially chill the Jell-O and lay them across the top, exploding the planar arrangement into three dimensions? Thus Art is made, and a new Jell-O dessert is born."[46] This type of recipe encourages the "chef" to have some fun with her creation, eschewing rote food preparation.

Where Jell-O used to be symbolically aligned with the concerned, caring homemaker, comedic subcultural texts now mock that reading of the product. The mysterious "Mrs. Megabyte" hosts a parodic website featuring Martha Stewart's Alcoholic Green Jell-O Recipes, replete with collage graphic of do-it-yourself doyenne Stewart wearing a Carmen Miranda-esque molded Jell-O platter hat, advising readers that "each person can use a knife, or their tongue, to loosen edges of the Jell-O to suck [the Green Jell-O shots] down."[47] Other texts make sport of traditional associations between Jell-O and nature. In "How Jell-O Killed the Dinosaurs," Frank Wu and Ben Lethbridge jokingly determine a causal relationship between the impact of prehistoric Jell-O comets ("Jell-O-roids") and the extinction of dinosaurs due to sugar-induced stupor.[48] These texts need be neither exclusively created nor enjoyed by women in order for women to use them as resources for counteracting conventional wisdom about women's relationship to cooking, and to Jell-O more specifically.

While these acts of subversion described by women I have spoken to range from those made earnestly or without much consideration to the highly kitschy, another interviewee suggests a more ironic design for her involvement with Jell-O:

> I'm single, but part of why I like to make Jell-O is to make fun of that outdated 1950s 'little lady' of the house that, thank God, I know I'll never be. My friends and I get together and put on our aprons that we only wear for Jell-O making, and get our Tupperware containers all lined up for storage, and go crazy with the Jell-O. We've even dyed our hair using Jell-O—hey, it's cheaper than hair dye and it comes in colors that Clairol ladies never dreamed of.

This statement indicates that while Jell-O may be marketed with slimming body modifications in mind, it can be mirthfully used with quite different intentions. It also suggests that one's attitude, more so than obvious behavior, is a better indicator of how one uses seemingly overdetermined cultural products like Jell-O.

In many conversations, I also found women resisting the social class significations of Jell-O in engaging ways. An interviewee shared the following ideas that suggest the association of Jell-O with a "higher" artistic aesthetic:

> I love Jell-O for its over-the-top quality, its pure kitsch level. When I think of Jell-O I think of trailer parks and pink flamingos on the lawn, though I'm sure it's the solid middle class that's eating it. It has this connotation of being cheesy, but look at other cheesy things. They're coming back. It's hip to go buy a pink flamingo and put it on your lawn. My plaid lunchbox from third grade was cheesy at the time, but now it would sell for like $50. I think it's the same with Jell-O: it's cool because mainstream people think it's not.

This woman frames the meaning of Jell-O as having shifted from a low-rent dessert to a "hip," "cool," and valuable commodity. Here, one might apply Warde's recognition that "mass-production commodities can be customized, that is appropriated for personal and private purposes"[49] to the artful work done with Jell-O. By adding labor to the mass commercial product, one creates social and symbolic value. These instances of women resisting the gendered and social class significations of Jell-O are admittedly local and partial. It would be difficult to argue that these few examples successfully undermine all traditional ideas about Jell-O as a cultural product and a corollary of identity, but there would be little reason to anticipate such a large-scale change. In their small ways, many of these women do succeed in challenging the oppressive system of underlying meanings.

Back to Grandma's house, Jell-O congealing in the refrigerator while she sits in the breakfast room, intently spying on her shell-shocked neighbor as he paces back and forth in the driveway. Like some of the women whose stories I solicited for this chapter, she may have been doing with Jell-O exactly what advertisements, tradition, and "common sense" told her to do. It is possible that she prepared it lovingly for her husband and family (but rarely ate it herself, unless it was the sugar-free variety), relishing its ease of preparation, thrilled that she had extra time to sweep the kitchen or wash an extra load of laundry. She very well may have felt like a better woman, a better mother, and a better American when she made Jell-O. But then again, she may have been throwing a monkey wrench in the works of tradition, silently scoffing at the expectation that it was *her* job to provide healthy food for her family to maintain our emotional well being. Maybe she chowed down on the sweet stuff in direct violation of restrictions on how much women of her era were supposed to eat. Perhaps it was her way of saying "You want dessert when I've been typing all day to earn a living, even though I have the talent to be a pianist? You'll take what you get!"

More than likely, it was a little bit of both. The strange relationship with Jell-O cultivated in me by my grandmother many years ago encouraged me to consider the ways in which contemporary American women make sense of this unusual food product, and the results are complex, reflective of neither pole exclusively. I hope to have presented a picture of Jell-O as a cultural product whose involvement in the resistance of gender and social class paradigms is equally complex.

NOTES

1. Anonymous, "Woman pleads guilty to killing man with LSD-laced Jell-O," *Court TV Online* (available at http://208.229.230.57/people/1999/0219/jello_ap.html, February 19, 1999).

2. Carole M. Counihan, "Food Rules in the United States: Individualism, Control and Hierarchy," *The Anthropology of Food and Body* (New York: Routledge, 1999), 113.

3. Anonymous, "The Cool History of Jell-O," *Jell-O Introduction* (available at www.kraftfoods.com/jell-o/history/intro.html, July 1, 1999).

4. Anonymous, "The Cool History of Jell-O."

5. *Ladies Home Journal* ad from 1926, cited in Rosemarie D. Bria, *How Jell-O Molds Society and How Society Molds Jell-O: A Case Study of an American Food Industry Creation,* unpublished doctoral dissertation, Teachers College, Columbia University, 1991, 81.

6. Bria, *How Jell-O Molds Society*, 102.

7. Bria, *How Jell-O Molds Society*, 107.

8. Bria, *How Jell-O Molds Society*, 145.

9. Bria, *How Jell-O Molds Society*, 255.

10. LeRoy Historical Society, "History of Jell-O," *Jell-O Centennial Celebration Web Site* (available at www.iinc.com/jello/index.html, 1997).

11. Anonymous, "Dirt Cups," *Kraft: Recipe Card* (available at www.kraftfoods.com/cgi-bin/recipe-card.cgi?id=25500W, March 14, 2000).

12. Counihan, "Food Rules," 114.

13. While most women emphasized Jell-O's nutritional impact ambivalently, there were a few respondents who lauded its health-promoting powers. One mysteriously claimed, "I think there is a special ingredient that is actually good for the body," while others discussed the usefulness of gelatin for growing strong fingernails.

14. William A. McIntosh and Mary Zey, "Women as Gatekeepers of Food Consumption: A Sociological Critique," in *Food and Gender: Identity and Power*, ed. C. Counihan and S. Kaplan (Amsterdam, Netherlands: Harwood, 1998), 127.

15. Alan Warde, *Consumption, Food and Taste: Culinary Antinomies and Commodity Culture* (Thousand Oaks, Calif.: Sage, 1997), 151.

16. Sarah E. Newton, "'The Jell-O Syndrome': Investigating Popular Culture/Foodways," *Western Folklore* 51 (July 1992): 252.

17. Clarissa Silitch, ed., *Yankee Magazine's Good Neighbors USA Cookbook* (Dublin, N.H.: Yankee, 1985).

18. Andrea Chesman, ed., *Yankee Magazine's Church Suppers and Potluck Dinners Cookbook* (New York: Villard, 1996).

19. Mildred Knopf, *The Perfect Hostess Cookbook* (New York: Knopf, 1950), xiv.

20. Knopf, *The Perfect Hostess*, xiv.

21. Ann Marie Bivans, *The Miss America™ Cookbook* (Nashville, Tenn.: Rutledge Hall, 1995), 185.

22. Counihan, "Food Rules," 113.

23. Carole M. Counihan, "Food, Culture and Gender," *The Anthropology of Food and Body* (New York: Routledge, 1999), 8.

24. Bria, *How Jell-O Molds Society*, 46.

25. Ben Fine, Michael Heasman, and Judith Wright, *Consumption in the Age of Affluence: The World of Food* (London: Routledge, 1996), 80.

26. Fine et al., *Consumption in the Age of Influence*, 119.

27. Fine et al., *Consumption in the Age of Influence*, 85.

28. Fine et al., *Consumption in the Age of Influence*, 227.

29. Genesee Pure Food Company, quoted in Bria, *How Jell-O Molds Society*, 47.

30. Bria, *How Jell-O Molds Society*, 30.

31. Anonymous, "On the Jell-O Trail," *Roadside America: Your Online Guide to Offbeat Attractions* (available at www.roadsideamerica.com/rant/jello.html, July 1, 1999); Anonymous, "Famous Cooks Favor Jell-O," *Jell-O 1910–1920* (available at www.kraft foods.com/jell-o/history/1910.html, July 1, 1999).

32. Pierre Bordieu, *Distinction: A Social Critique of the Judgment of Taste* (London: Routledge and Keegan Paul, 1984), 185.

33. Bria, *How Jell-O Molds Society*, 197.

34. R. Estrin, "Jell-O's Top-Secret Plant, Work Methods Make Some of Its Neighbors Suspicious," *The Detroit News Online* (available at detnews.com/menu/stories/33131.htm, January 24, 1996).

35. Shannon Sneed, "Jell-O Masterpieces," *Oregon Daily Emerald* (available at www.dailyemerald.com/archive/v99/3/980403/jello.html, April 3, 1998); Barbara R. Ackroyd, "Jell-O Fest Fosters Gelatin Creativity," *Brigham Young University Newsline* (available at http://newsline.byu.edu/newsline/Archives/news/9704/970402JIGGLERS.HTM,

March 14, 2000); Anonymous, "Jell-O-Rama," *Mad Martian: Fun with Jell-O!* (available at www.madmartian.com/jello.htm, March 14, 2000).

36. Here, *mass* implies that the cultural product has been deemed by the taste elite to be debased; the term *popular* would indicate a more sympathetic position toward Jell-O.

37. Marcia Millman, *Such a Pretty Face: Being Fat in America* (New York: Norton, 1980).

38. Counihan, "Food Rules," 124.

39. Laura Shapiro, *Perfection Salad: Women and Cooking at the Turn of the Century* (New York: Farrar, Straus and Giroux, 1986), 235.

40. *Joys of Jell-O Gelatin Dessert, Second Edition* (General Foods Corporation, 1962).

41. Chef Andy, "Tricks and Tips: Fun Things You Can Do with Jell-O Gelatin Dessert," *Jell-O Pages* (available at http://cascade.mit.edu/cookbook/jello/tips.html, February 29, 2000).

42. Andy Oakland, "Meathead! Yum Yum Yum!" *Meathead! Yummy Halloween Fun* (available at http://cascade.mit.edu/halloween/meathead.html, March 14, 2000).

43. Over a dozen women on a Usenet recipe group attested to their use of Chef Andy's recipes as a way to buck food norms.

44. Chef Andy, "Tricks and Tips: Fun Things You Can Do with Jell-O Gelatin Dessert," *Jell-O Pages* (available at http://cascade.mit.edu/cookbook/jello/tips.html, February 29, 2000).

45. Jane Stern and Michael Stern, *Square Meals: A Cookbook* (New York: Knopf, 1984), 313.

46. Stern and Stern, *Square Meals*, 318–19.

47. Anonymous, "Martha Stewart's Alcoholic Green Jell-O Recipes," *Martha Stewart's Favorite Party Recipes* (available at http://mrsmegabyte.tripod.com/gjello.html, March 14, 2000).

48. Frank Wu and Ben Lethbridge, "How Jell-O® Killed the Dinosaurs," *How Jell-O Killed the Dinosaurs* (available at www.frankwu.com/Jell-O.html, March 14, 2000).

49. Warde, *Consumption, Food and Taste*, 152.

8

Beating the Biscuits in Appalachia: Race, Class, and Gender Politics of Women Baking Bread

Elizabeth S. D. Engelhardt

To celebrate Christmas, my extended family gathers at my grandmother's house for breakfast. This year, with my scrambled eggs and grits, I ate my grandmother's biscuits with apple jelly canned by my aunt and uncle. When I was twelve, my grandmother taught me to make biscuits. Sifted flour, milk, baking powder, soda, some salt, and lard (vegetable shortening, these days) in mathematical proportion—measured carefully by me, eyeballed from years of practice by my grandmother—all are baked in a hot oven until fluffy and flaky. Biscuits are a deceptive recipe; they may be short on ingredients, but they are long on touch. I may know her recipe, but I am still working on the touch; every time I move, I have to learn a new oven, and keep practicing my skills. To celebrate the New Year, I fixed for myself a dinner of collard greens, hoppin' john (a black-eyed pea dish), and a skillet of corn bread. My mother made cornbread for dinner regularly; in fact, I cannot remember when I first ate it. I have been working on my cast iron skillet to perfect its seasoning; my mother seems to be able to make good corn bread in any pan that comes to hand, but this is a trick I have not learned. That New Year's menu should bring me luck throughout the year, so perhaps good biscuits and corn bread will follow.

Talking about the food we prepare and eat to celebrate our chosen holidays can help women understand the differences and similarities between us. Having told you about corn bread, collards, apples, black-eyed peas, and biscuits, you might place me—correctly—as being from the southern United States. Depending on what you know about local crops, the combination of apples and corn bread might even help you deduce that I am specifically from the southern Appalachian mountains. Two of these foods, however—the biscuit and the corn bread—have shifted in meaning over the course of the twentieth century. Today they are, at least for Americans of European and African descent, both primarily southern foods, hallmarks of down-home or country cooking, and sources of nostalgia for "simpler" times. But when the nineteenth century turned into the twentieth, they had very different and distinct meanings. To some observers, one was a mark of high culture, modern hygiene, and progressive womanhood. Biscuit baking demonstrated class consciousness, leisure time for women, consumer marketed equipment, and nationally standardized consumption. Corn bread, on the other hand, symbolized ignorance, disease, and poverty. It could be made with locally produced ingredients, equipment made at home, and brief moments of time seized between other work; even at the turn of the century, it was regionally identified and nationally disparaged. A social history of class, race, and gender hides in the different recipes and uses of corn bread and biscuits. Using diaries, fiction, memoirs, and recipe books, this chapter seeks to tease out that social history by examining women, beaten biscuits, and corn bread.

The 1890s until the 1920s were the heyday of the Progressive Era—a time of settlement houses, New Women, public libraries, antituberculosis campaigns, "Lifting As We Climb," temperance, and, of course, suffrage. Regionalist women's writing enjoyed great success; many local color authors chose Appalachia as a setting for their fiction. Although university education for select women emerged out of the 1860s and 1870s, a national consensus about what women would do with their educated lives remained elusive. Women like Amelie Troubetzkoy, Miss Matt Crim, Emma Bell Miles, Grace MacGowan Cooke, and Maria Louise Pool chose careers in writing. Margaret Morley combined writing with the scientific practice of being a naturalist.

Other women became teachers and activists; one of those was May Stone. In 1884, Kentucky native Stone entered Wellesley College, scarcely nine years after it opened. Despite leaving college a year before she was to graduate, Stone gained entrance into the group of socially conscious, educated women looking for careers.[1] She found it in her participation first in women's clubs and then in the "mountain work" they sponsored in eastern Kentucky. Historian Anne Firor Scott has documented the projects taken on by southern women's clubs by 1900: "they organized libraries; expanded schools; tackled adult illiteracy; organized settlement houses; fought child labor; supported sanitary laws, juvenile courts, pure water, modern sewage systems; planted trees; and helped girls to go to college."[2] As if modeling the combination of turn-of-the-century projects mapped by Scott, Katherine Pettit worked with May Stone to lead Appalachia's settlement house movement, establish libraries, teach elementary school, facilitate girls' applications to college, and plant trees. When the opportunity arose, both left for a lifetime of work in Kentucky's Appalachia. Pettit and Stone were middle-class, white, educated women who came to Appalachia with the idea of helping the less fortunate Appalachians; each stayed there for the rest of her life. They were not alone in their efforts; as Nancy Forderhase has researched, dozens of similar women came to Appalachia. Some, such as Lucy Furman, combined their activism with writing. All were ready to help the Appalachians.[3] That "help" often took the form of cooking lessons.

One of the most well-known experiments run by Progressive women in Appalachia was Pettit and Stone's Hindman Settlement School. The journals Pettit and Stone kept were used for fund-raising; today, they give us a picture of the school's early years.[4] At the school, Appalachians were introduced to "domestic science." By the turn of the century, early advocates of domestic science, such as Harriet Beecher Stowe and Catharine Beecher, who emphasized women's work inside homes, had given way to new reformers, who shaped a model of women's domestic work beyond the home. One of these new reformers was Jane Addams; her successful use of the settlement house model for educating women particularly influenced Appalachian activism. By Pettit and Stone's own account, they were summoned in 1899 by a letter sent from the Reverend J. T. Mitchell to the State Federation of Women's Clubs in Kentucky. Although Stone and Pettit educated both men and women, cooking lessons for women were a core element of their mission from the beginning. Rev. Mitchell requested they "conduct . . . meetings of wives, mothers, housekeepers, young ladies, and little girls. Lectures and lessons in cooking and homemaking should be made particularly enthusiastic and then the intellectual and moral features can be made interesting" (*QWJ*, 59). Not only are women defined by Mitchell, Pettit, and Stone in the restrictive categories of wife, mother, and housekeeper before all others, but also cooking and homemaking are presented as the path for Appalachian women to follow to reach the intellectual and moral positions occupied by Pettit, Stone, and their teachers.

Evidence from their letters, diaries, and fiction suggest that the teachers began the enthusiastic lessons by targeting the staple food of mountain residents, corn bread. They sought to replace it with what they considered a more healthful, appropriate, and civilized alternative, the wheat-based biscuit and light bread. Early in their journals Pettit and Stone reported as a success that "Mrs. Green and two girls came and wanted to learn to make light bread, but it was so late that we taught them how to make good soda biscuit instead" (*QWJ*, 177). The Hindman women considered soda biscuit, using wheat flour and baking soda, and light bread, using white wheat flour and yeast, worthy of being taught. My grandmother's biscuits resemble the soda biscuits they describe; their light breads preceded store-bought bread loaves. But more appropriate for the mountain women, judging by its appearance in Pettit and

Stone's journals, was the beaten biscuit. This was the recipe they crowned as the height of domestic achievement. For a special occasion, Katherine Pettit noted she was "up earlier than usual this morning to make beaten biscuit for Miss McCartney's luncheon" (*QWJ*, 213). She and Stone were pleased when native mountain woman, "Ida Francis . . . walked down with a pint of flour to learn to make beaten biscuit for her sick brothers" (*QWJ*, 232). For other families, they "promised to send them some beaten biscuit and go Wednesday to show the mother how to make them" (*QWJ*, 230). So important was the beaten biscuit to their efforts that contemporaries looking to criticize the Hindman women focused on the biscuits to do so: they derided the entire project as the "beaten biscuit crusade."[5]

Only when we examine the recipe for beaten biscuits do we begin to understand why Katherine Pettit had to get up early to prepare them. Bill Neal, in his *Southern Cooking*, writes that the beaten biscuit involves flour, salt, sugar, lard, and cold water. He lists the necessary equipment as a "mixing bowl; blending fork; wooden spoon; mallet, cleaver, or rolling pin, biscuit cutter, and baking sheet." It is also apparent that anyone cooking this recipe needs a way to regulate the temperature for baking (such as an oven), and a board or flat table that is sturdy enough for the beating process. In 1913, Martha McCulloch-Williams claimed that, for the perfect beaten biscuit, "householders, and especially suburban ones, should indulge in the luxury of a block or stone or marble slab—and live happy ever after." These perfect blocks, stones, or slabs are crucial because what distinguishes the beaten biscuit is that not only is it mixed in a bowl and kneaded on a board (Neal suggests twenty-five strokes), but it is also beaten with the mallet on a hard surface. Neal calls for at least three hundred strokes for one's family and five hundred for company.[6] As my godmother suggested when I told her I was writing this chapter, the beaten biscuit is nothing like a good cat-head biscuit that we might long for today (in other words, each one as big as and as fluffy as a cat's head). The Hindman women's beaten biscuit had no leavening and thus was much more like today's crackers or an unsweetened English biscuit.

Reading Katherine Pettit and May Stone's journals today, one might think that the mountain women cooked no bread at all until Progressive activists came along to teach them. In fact, as most of the local color fiction about Appalachia (written both by women from the region and elsewhere) makes clear, Appalachian women baked plenty of bread. The action in Maria Louise Pool's novel, *In Buncombe County*, centered on the visit of two white, upper-class women tourists to the mountains outside of Asheville, North Carolina. One of these women observed upon watching two mountain girls fix dinner, "They mixed a pone and set it down in its kettle by the fire; they called it 'making bread.'"[7] This was not wheat bread. Instead, these characters, and Appalachian women in general, cooked corn bread. And corn pone, and hoe cake, and dog bread, and hushpuppies, and corn fritters, and spoon bread. The basic ingredients of all of these recipes—corn meal, buttermilk, lard, and salt, occasionally embellished with an egg or two and additional (although not strictly necessary) leavening—need only a bowl and spoon and a source of heat. Unlike biscuits, corn bread can be cooked in a variety of conditions— over an open fire or in an oven; and in a variety of containers—a skillet, Dutch oven, or the proverbial hoe.

Although these are just a few variations of the basic recipe, almost all of the corn breads can be mixed in the time it takes to heat a skillet. Unlike in other parts of the South, most Appalachian corn breads, as my mother puts it, have hardly any flour or sugar added. Tommie Bass, from northeast Alabama's mountains, recalled for his memoirs his mother's basic recipe: "When mother made cornbread, she added baking soda, not always. It was about a teaspoon-ful to a cupful of meal. And she added a little salt and sugar and buttermilk, to make a thick batter. Then she melted a little grease (lard) in the hot skil-let, and drained that into the batter. And she put a little dry cornmeal in the hot skillet, and put it back on the stove." He continued, "When the dry corn-meal was brown, she knew the skillet was hot enough to pour in the batter. She put the skillet of batter in the stove and cornbread would just swell up, you know, and become just as light as it could be."[8] It is an adaptable and for-giving recipe.

Other writing of the era gives us a sense of the ubiquity and flexibility of corn bread baking in Appalachia. Tennessee author Grace MacGowan Cooke's short story entitled "The Capture of Andy Proudfoot" told the story of a northern, Irish bounty hunter searching for and then helping a mountain man. Cooke mentioned meals of corn pone and fish that Andy and his po-tential captor ate in a mountain hideaway. At most, Andy and his captor had camp equipment; their corn bread had to be cooked over an open fire. If they had milk or eggs, they stole them. Theirs was probably a very simple combi-nation of meal, water, and lard. Margaret Morley described such a recipe in her 1913 naturalist text about the areas around Asheville, North Carolina, *The Carolina Mountains*. A mountain man in her book told her, "'Stoves? . . . I ain't never owned a stove and I don't never aim to. I don't see no use in stoves noway. I wouldn't have one in the house. You can't bake bread in a stove. I don't want nar' thing but meal and water mixed together and baked in the fire. I don't want salt in the bread. I was raised on that bread and it is the best in the world.'" From her position of outsider, Morley commented archly, "Imag-ine a condition where one's physical wants are reduced to cornmeal and wa-ter."[9]

On a different end of the spectrum, Miss Matt Crim, in "The Strike at Mr. Mobley's" (an antifeminist story about a mountain community) opened with Mrs. Mobley cooking her family vegetables and corn bread in her well-appointed kitchen. Similarly, Amelie Rives Troubetzkoy's novel, *Tanis, the Sang-Digger*, told the melodramatic story of a mountain woman who made a living digging ginseng root in Virginia until she met a northern, middle-class family. In it, mountain resident Sam chose to eat corn pone and honey while waiting for his girlfriend to finish her domestic duties serving the wife of a railroad engineer.[10] Even in Pettit and Stone's journals, we glimpse how pervasive corn bread was; they mentioned a "Mrs. Godsey, over seventy, [who] brought her turn of corn to the mill and then came here to learn to make bread" (*QWJ*, 190). If we could ask her, Mrs. Godsey might have said that she was not ignorant of bread making, but that she first took care of her family's staple and then learned a new luxury—wheat bread.

For turn-of-the-century mountain women, choosing whether to cook corn bread or biscuits was not simply a question of what a woman or her family preferred on any given day. Instead, as close reading of these texts and memoirs of the time reveal, the decision made a statement about class in the Appalachians. The biscuit, in other words, marked middle- and upper-class status in 1900. Pettit and Stone judged the households into which they were invited by the breads they were served for dinner. For instance, they report that "The Cornets are all clean and thrifty"; the evidence of cleanliness and thriftiness that they give readers is: "They had a good dinner, beautiful honey and whole wheat biscuit from the wheat they had raised themselves" (*QWJ*, 202). According to the Hindman teachers, the Cornets were in contrast to most of the mountain residents, who "live on fat bacon, corn bread and a few vegetables, all cooked in the most unwholesome way. Everything is fried in as much grease as they can get." Prioritizing their cooking plan, the Hindman teachers noted, "Our efforts in the line of cooking were to teach them to make good bread, to cook the vegetables in as many ways as possible, and the meat without so much grease" (*QWJ*, 63). For Pettit and Stone, these domestic practices marked the achievements of superior social classes. Moral and intellectual lessons could follow once bread making was standardized.

John and Olive Campbell, acquaintances of the Hindman women and author and editor, respectively, of the widely influential *The Southern Highlander and His Homeland*, proposed that class and bread can be charted on a continuum: "It is probably safe to say that the main sustenance of many a rural household a good share of the winter is fat pork, beans, potatoes, and corn-bread, with the addition of sorghum or honey and strong cheap coffee. Soda biscuit of wheat flour, and 'grits' are also used extensively among families in better circumstances. 'Light bread' or raised white bread, is very unusual."[11] In

other words, corn bread was available to almost everyone; middle-class mountain residents added in wheat-based soda biscuits; but only the most finan-
cially and socially upper-class mountain people could choose to eat the yeast
breads. In fiction, it is often passed as unremarkable that people of higher
classes will avoid corn bread. While Sam in Troubetzkoy's *Tanis, the Sang-
Digger* eats corn pone in the servant's area, Alice Gilman, the middle-class
railroad engineer's wife who is new to the mountains, offers her guests biscuits and milk.[12] Although both corn pone and biscuits emerge from the same
kitchen, the mediating figure of Tanis, an Appalachian woman hired to serve
biscuits but eat corn bread, further codifies this class-bread continuum.

While Pool, Troubetzkoy, and even Pettit and Stone imply that all
mountaineers were poor—eating corn bread, unaware of the modern
world—memoirs of the time give support to the Campbells' implication
that there was a range of class positions in the mountains. Breads can be
traced through these varied positions. Joe Gray Taylor in his *Eating,
Drinking, and Visiting in the South: An Informal History* says, "the amount
of wheaten bread consumed rose with wealth and social position." Anec-
dotally, he also remembers that "everyone of substance that I knew ate
them [biscuits] for breakfast." Herbalist Tommie Bass reminisced, "Back in
my days, biscuits made from wheat flour was special for the poor people."
Alabama resident William Bradford Huie grew up in the southern tip of
the Appalachians. In his semiautobiographical novel, *Mud on the Stars*, he
wrote, "Biscuit for breakfast is a social and economic self-measurement
among croppers and hands. Those who always have biscuit for breakfast regard themselves as successful persons of dignity. They pity and look down
on the unfortunate who have to go back to corn pone during hard times."[13]
A friend of mine, who is a medical doctor, recalls her grandfather-in-law
asking her upon her marriage whether she could make biscuits; when she
said no, he said, "Well, can you at least make corn bread?"

Thus, we find a dividing line primarily between corn and wheat, with gra-
dations on each side. Yeast bread and beaten biscuits occupy one end of this
food-and-class continuum; the many varieties of corn bread occupy the other.
Soda biscuits and quick breads occupy the middle ground. The logic of these
divisions reveals much about gender and race in Appalachian culture around
1900. This logic can be seen when we examine the ingredients, equipment,
leisure time, and national standards encoded in the recipes themselves.

The most obvious difference between biscuits and corn bread is their ingredients. Biscuits usually require wheat flour, but it was difficult for mountain residents to grow wheat. Significant annual rainfall and frequent shade
around Appalachian fields meant that wheat was particularly susceptible to
the growth of fungi. Joe Taylor documents the effect of rust fungus on wheat

and suggests that, compared to corn, wheat with rust yielded much less usable food.[14] A mountain family needed large, cleared, unshaded fields and the economic security to afford less efficient planting if they were to grow wheat— or they needed the financial security to purchase imported food instead of food grown in their own gardens or farms. Although research is thin for early in the century, it suggests that African American Appalachian families in both rural and urban Appalachia tended to be in worse economic shape than their white counterparts[15]—and thus even less likely to afford growing or using wheat regularly in their baking. For all Appalachian families, Taylor points out, "Corn demanded little skill in cultivation, and it was certainly easier to gather a given amount of corn than to harvest half as much wheat. Perhaps most important of all, corn was much easier to process with the crude machinery available." Wheat, then, required a greater investment of labor at all stages of its production. Tommie Bass reveals another reason that mountain farmers favored corn when he remarked, "Corn is a wonderful plant, we didn't waste any of it"; he then describes the medicinal value of cornsilk tea, recipes with hominy, corn as feed for both people and stock, and even corncob toilet paper.[16] All of these factors are behind Pettit and Stone admitting that "very little wheat is raised in the mountains" (*QWJ*, 86).

For women, the differences between wheat and corn were particularly significant. Unlike wheat, corn is a garden plant; even a woman living in a rigid patriarchal system—which some parts of Appalachia surely were—could "handle" growing corn. Frances Goodrich, in her memoir of founding a woman-based handicraft industry in the mountains at the turn of the century, *Mountain Homespun,* portrayed Aunt Liza, who shows off her garden with pride. Liza says, "Ever since my old man died I've made enough corn to do me, and sweetening too. The boys they come and plough for me in the spring of the year; they'd be willing to do more than that, but I believe in working, then a body has something."[17] Women in mill towns, women with children or other domestic responsibilities, black Appalachian women working in white women's homes (a common occupation throughout this time period), and women on their own could grow a patch of corn without too much physical or social difficulty. For mountain families without many resources, the return on the investment made planting corn by far the better decision.

Once grown, both corn and wheat were ground into flour. Yet, race, class, and gender differences in the choice between corn and wheat were not left behind at the mill. Visitors to and writers from Appalachia at the turn of the century often commented on the mountain residents' lack of proper cooking utensils. The Campbells noticed that, in one mountain family they visited, they "found the mother baking pies. She was rolling out the crust, not on a molding board but on a piece of cloth spread on the table, her rolling pin being a round bottle." Tennessee native Emma Bell Miles, writing in her semi-autobiographical, theoretical *The Spirit of the Mountains*, concurred with the Campbells, since, "I have seen a woman carry water, dress a fowl, mix bread, feed her cow and pick up chips all in the same big tin pan, simply because it was the only vessel she had; I have seen pies rolled out and potatoes mashed with a beer bottle found in the road." But these were not isolated instances; Olive and John Campbell suggested that even in the country stores in Appalachia, "Cooking utensils are exceedingly scarce."[18] Equipment for cooking targeted women's daily lives particularly; both Miles and the Campbells imply that even if mountain women wanted to move up the class scale from corn bread to biscuits, they might have had difficulty acquiring the additional equipment that biscuit-making entailed.

Pettit and Stone, reflecting the philosophies of like-minded Progressive women, linked moral and mental strength to domestic science's emphasis on cleanliness, purity, and standardized cooking. Even if these women were baking wheat-based pie crusts or bread, beer bottles would not have been acceptable equipment to do so. Thus, the class-bread continuum was not simply a matter of the end-product placed on one's family's table. The *equipment* employed to cook was as important an element in the class-bread continuum as that which was being cooked. Recalling her experiences as a teacher during the early Hindman years, Lucy Furman described the proper equipment and method of cooking in her novel *The Quare Women:* "[a] very pretty young woman, in a crisp gingham dress and large white apron, was kneading a batch of light-bread dough, and explaining the process of bread-making as she worked." Furman emphasized the clothes one needed to cook properly, the tables, ingredients, and recipes that would help in the kitchen. But the process, for Furman, did not stop when the kneading was over. She continued, "After the dough was moulded into loaves and placed in the oven of a shining new cook-stove," the crowd moved on to another tent to learn the proper way to set tables to receive the bread.[19] This emphasis on process reminds us that the ultimate goal of these lessons extends beyond the recipe in question.

The Hindman teachers worried about their students, saying, "Add to bad air, dirt and bad cooking, the use of tobacco by men, women, and even children as soon as they can walk and talk, and how can we expect good health? And without any regard to the laws of health, how can the people be strong, mentally or morally?" (*QWJ*, 63). As their Rev. Mitchell suggested, moral and educational gains were supposed to follow from women teaching other women how to cook. But how were the activist teachers supposed to measure their moral successes? The visible signs of new cooking equipment became not only a way to judge material success—they also stood in for the mountain residents' spiritual accomplishments. Thus, rather than quizzing the Cornet family on their morals and beliefs, Pettit and Stone treated them as a successful mountain family on the evidence of the table their women present.

Yet, few of these writers suggested how to make the biscuit's additional equipment available to all of the mountain women. Few interrogated how the very class system into which they were placing biscuits contributed to some women having to use beer bottles and others getting to judge the moral character of women without rolling pins. The difference between equipment for biscuits and corn bread was essentially, with the exception of the pan, a matter of local versus imported goods—and that was a question of barter and handicraft versus cash money. Biscuits work better with marble rolling boards, rolling pins, biscuit cutters, mallets or cleavers, and ovens with consistent and steady temperatures. Corn bread needs only a bowl, a spoon (although fingers will do), a skillet of some kind, and a heat source. Unlike many of the biscuit items, corn bread's bowls, spoons, and fires could be created out of resources readily available in the mountains. Wooden bowls, wooden spoons, and open fires or fires in hand-built hearths and chimneys work fine for corn bread; all can be made or traded for by the women themselves. National currency need not be involved. Even the poorest mountain woman could fashion the container, spoon, and heat source to produce corn bread for her family.

Another significant difference between the two recipes concerns the time necessary to produce each. In her journal, May Stone related an incident in which "Miss Pettit went to make beaten biscuit for the sick boys while they all looked on." She noted that the boys then "asked if it was worthwhile to go to so much trouble" (*QWJ*, 233). And in fact, while writing this chapter, I tried out Bill Neal's recipe for beaten biscuits; while I am sure that Katherine Pettit was more practiced than I, she could not have significantly shortened the time and direct attention it took me to make them (and I just barely made it to the three hundred strokes for family; much less the exemplary five hundred strokes that were recommended).

Household economies encompass more than the labor of an individual. I had no help in beaten biscuit making, but some turn-of-the-century women did. The leisure time to put beaten biscuits on the table often suggested hired women's time and labor; in the South, that often implied black women's time and labor. Although many of Appalachia's corps of activist teachers were from the Northeast, Katherine Pettit and May Stone came from downstate Kentucky. While it is difficult to trace the origin of the first beaten biscuit recipe, some suggest that it began in the low country South. As Joseph Dabney writes in his reflection on southern Appalachian

cooking, *Smokehouse Ham, Spoon Bread, and Scuppernong Wine*, "My first inclination . . . was to omit any mention of 'beaten biscuits,' since they appeared to be more of an upper-class tidewater status symbol dish that depended on a lot of labor." He lists recipes for them from Philadelphia,
Virginia, and Kentucky. In other words, the recipe that was so championed
by activists in Appalachia seems to have developed in the race politics of
the nineteenth-century South. Writing in the 1930s about south Georgia
and Florida in *Their Eyes Were Watching God*, Zora Neale Hurston said her
character Janie "went to see [her grandmother] Nanny in Mrs. Washburn's
kitchen on the day for beaten biscuits"; this functions to remind readers of
the time-consuming tasks the Mrs. Washburn's of the world could ask of
their black Nannies.[20]

Teaching Appalachian women that they should find time—their own or
someone else's—to make beaten biscuits subtly supported the racial politics
associated with other parts of the South (and existing throughout the United
States). In fact, in cooking and elsewhere, Pettit, Stone, and other white activists replicated these politics. Although Appalachia did not have so firmly
entrenched a tradition of slavery and class division based on domestic workers, Pettit and Stone found African American Appalachian women servants
to hire. These women, who are rarely named in Pettit and Stone's journals,
primarily washed clothes; nevertheless, one of their teachers "made bread this
morning and showed the wash woman how to make it" (*QWJ*, 180). Corn
bread, on the other hand, was something that could be easily prepared by anyone after other paid or unpaid work was completed.

This issue of available leisure time to prepare breads other than corn
bread belies one of the tensions across women's activism throughout the
nineteenth century: where and how should a woman spend that leisure
time. Upper- or middle-class white women activists worked *outside* their
homes—to improve society for other women and to spread the values of
feminine virtue—but the ideal they presented to working women defined
success as having the leisure to spend more time *inside* the home. Activists
came to Appalachia to escape domestic life; they enjoyed the outdoors, they
hiked, sketched, and rode horses unaccompanied by fathers, husbands, or
brothers. But they taught Appalachian women how to bake biscuits—and
in so doing pushed the local women to stay inside domestic spheres. Had
everyone the ability to bake biscuits, their own presence in the mountains
would become unnecessary—so rarely do we find these activists question-
ing the economic and social reasons behind Appalachians' seeming preference for corn breads. Staying in Appalachia meant prolonging their own
freedom and mobility; staying was an escape from domestic duties awaiting
them at home. Ironically, this took away from some Appalachian women

freedoms they had previously enjoyed. Emma Bell Miles suggested of mountain women that "at an age when the mothers of any but a wolf race become lace-capped and felt-shod pets of the household, relegated to the safety of cushioned nooks in favorite rooms, she is yet able to toil almost as severely as ever." Miles found in this a "strength and endurance . . . beyond imagination to women of the sheltered life," and was generally critical of making women stay indoors.[21] Although not everyone would have agreed with Miles, many Appalachian women might well have wondered at this double standard proposed by activist women.

Finally, biscuits and corn breads differed in their participation in national, as opposed to regional or local, standards; definitions of race, class, and gender in Appalachia were nationalized as a result. Stone and Pettit returned after their first summer to find one mountain woman who "told us that she had tried to cook everything like we had taught her and that she had learned from the cookbook we sent her. She had a rice pudding with blackberries around it, just as we had served it the day she was with us. She said she had taught her friends our way of cooking and that she had made beaten biscuit for many weddings" (*QWJ*, 84). Not only did this woman follow the educational lessons of the Hindman women, but she also followed a cookbook that was standard for all of the United States. This practice implied standard ingredients, equipment, and expectations, as well as definitions of proper white womanhood that could be generalized across the United States.

Imported wheat, marble slabs and rolling pins, technologically advanced and consistent cook stoves, and cookbooks were all parts of a national distribution system fueled by the buying decisions of women. Grace MacGowan Cooke said explicitly in her novel about mills in Appalachian Tennessee, *The Power and the Glory*, "Illustrated magazines go everywhere these days"; the era's women's magazines especially portrayed "the 'homemaker,' a newly coined term" and her responsibilities for material consumption. In this rhetoric about women's important role in consuming wisely for one's family, female homemakers with more money (often a combination of class and race privilege during this era) were more valued. As Martha McCulloch-Williams suggested, "happy ever after" could come from the proper kitchen equipment in a turn-of-the-century home. In the burgeoning consumer culture in 1900, things moved in to supply satisfaction to women across the United States and "value [was] inexorably linked to both elaborate embellishment and to sheer quantity."[22] More tools, more equipment, and mass market sources for both meant that Appalachians were participating in the nation's consumerist culture and that the Progressive activists who were helping them to do so could claim success in their goals of "civilizing" the Appalachians. This new homemaker and her buying power had to decide between biscuits and corn bread in many mountain families.

Fiction of the period reflected the nationalization of taste and class. For instance, in Louise Baker's *Cis Martin*, a novel about a sophisticated northeastern family having to live in Appalachian Tennessee until their finances recovered, a mountain woman offered to serve "fried chicken and soda biscuits for breakfast," presenting them as something special, if only the newly arrived Cis will stay and help her play a prank. The action in Grace MacGowan Cooke's novel centered around the class tensions inspired by national and regional values in an Appalachian mill town as northern mill owners clashed with local workers. Her heroine, who eats corn pone at the beginning, is recognized as a member of "what we are learning to call the 'leisure class'" by the end of the novel—but refused to renounce her local tastes and values.[23]

Despite the general adoption of biscuits as a marker of higher class by mountain residents and newcomers, there was resistance to this hierarchy. Based on the erosion of women's precious free time, controversies over health effects, and, in at least one case, an overarching social critique regarding local values, corn bread did have its defenders.

Olive Campbell recorded in her travel journal from her research trip around Appalachia with her husband John, which resulted in *The Southern Highlander*, that she found "quite a prejudice against domestic science"—which would have included biscuits and cooking lessons—"as being merely 'dish washing' of which [the mountain women] say they have plenty at home."[24] Such a sentiment was also expressed by the boys watching Pettit make biscuits; whether a food is worth the trouble to make is in fact a trenchant question. Studies such as Arlie Hochschild's *The Second Shift* or Alan Durning's *How Much Is Enough?* have shown that timesaving devices for women, especially ones that target housework and food preparation, have, in fact, rarely decreased the amount of time that diverse women across the United States spend on these tasks.[25] Resisting a new recipe such as the beaten biscuit that has the effect of eroding one's quality of life seems a reasonable tactic. Or, as an anonymous mountain woman told Pettit and Stone after watching their extensive preparations for bed, "Ye all must be a lot of trouble to yerselves" (*QWJ*, 139).

The varied resistance to the soda biscuit in the mountains reached opposite conclusions, but was united in the belief that soda biscuits were not a healthy food for long-term consumption. Independently, Maria Louise Pool and Margaret Morley used the assumed unhealthiness of soda biscuits to justify the superiority of yeast breads on the continuum of class and bread. Emma Bell Miles used the same assumed unhealthiness to argue for a return to corn-based breads, therein inverting the hierarchy.

Pool's narrator noted, "I had apple butter and saleratus biscuit for my repast. I know they were saleratus biscuit because frequent yellow lumps appealed both to the eye and the palate. But I am not complaining. I knew that the apple butter would not hurt me, and I was just as sure that, at one meal, I could not eat enough sal-soda to destroy the coats of my stomach." Morley made a similar comment when she reported, "The most frequent disorder among them is dyspepsia, for which the pale green, or saffron yellow, brown-spotted, ring-streaked and speckled luxury known as 'soda biscuits' undoubtedly bears a heavy burden of blame. These wonders of the culinary art are freely eaten by all who can afford to buy white flour, and their odorous presence is often discernible from afar as you approach a house at mealtime." Pool, Morley, and others like them (in other words, upper-class, white women travelers) felt that the leavening used in biscuits—in particular in the newer commercial baking powders—was quite dangerous to the digestive system. Beaten biscuits, made with little or no leavening, would have an advantage over the risen biscuits Pool's character encounters near Asheville, North Carolina, but are not offered. Behind this brief comment in Pool's novel lay national concerns about cuisine, health food, and nutrition; this ongoing conversation stretched back through the nineteenth century. Harriet Beecher Stowe and her sister Catharine Beecher were concerned about breads at mid-century; they worried about the damaging effects of eating bread hot (as corn bread and soda biscuits certainly were in Appalachia), as they claim is especially the practice in the "South and West." Their solution was to advocate for cold, sliced yeast bread, suggesting that "lightness is the distinctive line between savage and civilized bread."[26]

Emma Bell Miles, who grew up in and lived most of her life in Appalachia, agreed with Pool and Morley about the dangers of risen soda biscuits, even as she reached a different conclusion about what to do with this knowledge. Miles worried that "Civilization is not likely soon to remedy this evil" of unhealthy food in Appalachia. But she blamed industrialization outside of Appalachia for "introduc[ing] cheap baking powders and the salicylic acid which is so dangerously convenient in canning fruit."[27] She wanted mountain residents to avoid all of the store-bought food (including flour) and thus supported the continued use of corn-based bread. Later in the twentieth century, this conversation about various breads in Appalachia moved into controversies over pellagra and the relative healthiness of any store-bought and commercially ground flours and meals. Today health food experts advocate for locally produced, organic food, arguing it provides protection against allergies, as well as more vitamins and minerals. Miles would have agreed.

Emma Bell Miles did not stop at insisting imported ingredients could be dangerous to individual women and families. She extended her argument to make a social critique that overarches the individual women involved. She suggested that, while "it is easier, far, to buy city tools with city money," they come with a high long-term cost. She argued, "the old-time mountaineer never knew the taste of ice cream in summer, he was, on the other hand, never without corn pones and side-meat in cold weather." She mourned to "see them buy meal by the half-peck to eat with the invariable white gravy" and concluded that the newcomers who have initiated this market economy in her community "would not think the pay so well proportioned to the sacrifice, after all" if they stayed to see the effects of their changes. She found local ingredients, indigenous traditions, and a barter economy to be more ecologically, socially, and individually sustainable. Corn bread, grown at home, using handmade equipment, as a part of a self-sufficient community, is a centerpiece of her argument. And while Miles used the third-person pronoun to write, we know from her biography that she was speaking out of the individual experience of running a household of six in extreme poverty. In a diary entry from May 8, 1915, Miles noted, "I had only corn bread and wild greens, with a very little potted ham; but we used big green leaves for plates, leaving them in the hollow of our left hands, and the children enjoyed it."[28] Cooking nonlocal, more expensive, and time consuming food was hardly an option for this social critic.

In fact, Joe Taylor suggests that, like the corn breads before it, the various forms of the biscuit, too, were eventually discredited and displaced. He argues that creating standardized housewives across the country helped fuel the market for and influence of media targeted to those women, all of which resulted in the promotion of mass-produced, commercial, sliced bread. He concludes, "In the 1920s small-town and country stores began to carry commercial bread, brought out from the nearest city in trucks, and soon it was presliced . . . as more housewives were influenced by women's magazines and home economics courses, toast rather than biscuits became breakfast fare."[29] It may be that this ascension of toast into Appalachian and American kitchens facilitated the movement of both biscuits and corn bread into their present day categorization as southern, home food, into both being sources of nostalgia. Both foods continue to be gendered— women are responsible for preparing them and are identified closely with them in our nostalgia about their symbolic meanings. It is a rare man (with the exception of professional male chefs and cookbook authors) who is nostalgic for the *process* of making the biscuits or corn bread for a family's table. Many of us, male and female, have strong memories and emotions associated with *eating* these foods.

In Atlanta, where I have been living, two restaurants tease me with the possibilities of biscuits and corn bread. One has people lined up for a three-hour wait each weekend to receive their order of huge, fluffy, but disappointingly (to my mind) sweet, risen biscuits. The other serves corn bread with its three-vegetable plate during lunchtime only; that corn bread, although still a bit sweet to my taste, is much closer to my childhood memories. Although the evidence is only anecdotal, I have begun to wonder why the first restaurant attracts so many of Atlanta's white yuppies, transplants, and recently arrived residents. And why does the other draw working-class folk of diverse races, local and long-time Atlantans? Gender, race, class, and biscuits may still be entangled if only we look for the web. For myself, I have decided that I can enjoy the first restaurant's pastries as long as I do not call them "biscuits," and I will continue to eat my lunchtime plate with corn bread—while enjoying the rich social history behind both choices. My grandmother, I suspect, approves.

NOTES

I wish to thank my godmother, Imogene Eaker, my friend Bonnie Hayes, my mother, Betty W. Delwiche, and my grandmother Iva S. Whitmire for their gracious storytelling and research help.

1. David Whisnant, *All That Is Native and Fine: The Politics of Culture in an American Region* (Chapel Hill: University of North Carolina Press, 1983), 34.

2. Anne Firor Scott, *Making the Invisible Woman Visible* (Urbana: University of Illinois Press, 1984), 217.

3. For information on the lives of Pettit and Stone, see Whisnant, *Native and Fine,* and Elizabeth S. Peck, "Katherine Pettit," in *Notable American Women, 1607–1950: A Biographical Dictionary*, vol. 3, ed. Edward T. James (Cambridge: Belknap, 1971), 56–58. For general information on women activists in Appalachia, see Nancy K. Forderhase, "Eve Returns to the Garden: Women Reformers in Appalachian Kentucky in the Early Twentieth Century," *Register of the Kentucky Historical Society* 85, no. 3 (1987): 237–61.

4. Quotations from Katherine Pettit and May Stone's journals are cited in the text with the following abbreviation: QWJ. *The Quare Women's Journals: May Stone and Katherine Pettit's Summers in the Kentucky Mountains and the Founding of the Hindman Settlement School,* ed. Jess Stoddart (Ashland, Ky.: Jesse Stuart Foundation, 1997).

5. Whisnant, *Native and Fine,* 25.

6. Bill Neal, *Bill Neal's Southern Cooking,* rev. ed. (Chapel Hill: University of North Carolina Press, 1989), 34–35; Martha McCulloch-Williams, *Dishes and Beverages of the Old South* (1913; reprint, Knoxville: University of Tennessee Press, 1988), 30.

7. Maria Louise Pool, *In Buncombe County* (Chicago: Herbert S. Stone, 1896), 95.

8. A. L. Tommie Bass, *Plain Southern Cooking: From the Reminiscences of A. L. Tommie Bass, Herbalist,* comp. and ed. John K. Crellin (Durham: Duke University Press, 1988), 37–38.

9. Grace MacGowan Cooke, "The Capture of Andy Proudfoot," in *Southern Lights and Shadows*, ed. William Dean Howells and Henry Mills Alden (New York: Harper and Brothers, 1907), 6; Margaret Morley, *The Carolina Mountains* (Boston: Houghton Mifflin, 1913), 161.

10. [Miss] Matt Crim, "The Strike at Mr. Mobley's," *Century* 50 (July 1895): 378; Amelie Rives [Chanler Troubetzkoy], *Tanis, the Sang-Digger* (New York: Town Topics, 1893), 92.

11. John C. Campbell, *The Southern Highlander and His Homeland*, comp. and ed. Olive Campbell (New York: Russell Sage Foundation, 1921), 201.

12. Troubetzkoy, *Tanis*, 40.

13. Joe Gray Taylor, *Eating, Drinking, and Visiting in the South: An Informal History* (Baton Rouge: Louisiana State University Press, 1982), 21, 110; Bass, *Plain Cooking*, 40; William Bradford Huie, *Mud on the Stars* (1942; reprint, Tuscaloosa: University of Alabama Press, 1996), 42–43.

14. Taylor, *Eating*, 21.

15. William H. Turner, "The Demography of Black Appalachia: Past and Present," in *Blacks in Appalachia*, ed. William H. Turner and Edward J. Cabbell (Lexington: University Press of Kentucky, 1985), 237–61.

16. Taylor, *Eating*, 21; Bass, *Plain Cooking*, 34.

17. Frances Louisa Goodrich, *Mountain Homespun* (New Haven, Conn.: Yale University Press, 1931), 40.

18. Campbell, *Highlander*, 201–3; Emma Bell Miles, *The Spirit of the Mountains* (1905; reprint, Knoxville: University of Tennessee Press, 1975), 22.

19. Lucy Furman, *The Quare Women: A Story of the Kentucky Mountains* (Boston: Atlantic Monthly Press, 1923), 8.

20. Joseph E. Dabney, *Smokehouse Ham, Spoon Bread, and Scuppernong Wine: The Folklore and Art of Southern Appalachian Cooking* (Nashville: Cumberland House, 1998), 118; Zora Neale Hurston, *Their Eyes Were Watching God* (1937; reprint, New York: Perennial Classics, 1998), 22.

21. Miles, *Spirit*, 54.

22. Grace MacGowan Cooke, *The Power and the Glory* (New York: Doubleday, Page, 1910), 27; Jean Gordon and Jan McArthur, "American Women and Domestic Consumption, 1800–1920: Four Interpretive Themes," in *Making the American Home: Middle-Class Women and Domestic Material Culture, 1840–1940*, ed. Marilyn Ferris Motz and Pat Browne (Bowling Green, Ohio: Bowling Green State University Popular Press, 1988), 38, 35.

23. Louise R. Baker, *Cis Martin, Or, The Furriners in the Tennessee Mountains* (New York: Eaton and Mains, 1898), 89; Cooke, *Power*, 13, 368.

24. Olive Dame Campbell, Diary, ms, 1 February 1909, John Charles and Olive Dame Campbell Papers #3800, Southern Historical Collection, Wilson Library, The University of North Carolina at Chapel Hill.

25. Arlie Hochschild, *The Second Shift: Working Parents and the Revolution at Home* (New York: Viking, 1989); Alan Thein Durning, *How Much Is Enough? The Consumer Society and the Future of the Earth*, Worldwatch Environmental Alert Series (New York: W. W. Norton, 1992).

26. Pool, *Buncombe*, 12; Morley, *Carolina*, 163; Catharine E. Beecher and Harriet Beecher Stowe, *The American Woman's Home: Or, Principles of Domestic Science; Being a*

Guide to the Formation and Maintenance of Economical, Healthful, Beautiful, and Christian Homes (1869; reprint, New York: Arno, 1971), 176, 170.

27. Miles, *Spirit*, 24.

28. Miles, *Spirit*, 191, 196; on Miles' biography, see David E. Whisnant, introduction to *The Spirit of the Mountains*, by Emma Bell Miles (1905; reprint, Knoxville: University of Tennessee Press, 1975), xix; Emma Bell Miles, Diary, 8 May 1915, Miles (Emma Bell) Papers, Hist. C. acc. 43, Chattanooga-Hamilton County Bicentennial Library, Chattanooga, Tennessee.

29. Taylor, *Eating*, 111.

• 9 •

"Suckin' the Chicken Bone Dry": African American Women, Fried Chicken, and the Power of a National Narrative

Psyche A. Williams-Forson

Chicken has always been an integral part of my life. Like that of other African Americans,[1] Sunday dinner at my house often included fried chicken, macaroni and cheese with plenty of paprika, collard greens with pork neckbones (until diabetes hit my home, then it was smoked turkey or some other seasoning), potato salad, corn pudding, rolls, or corn bread. And, if it wasn't this meal, it was some variation of this theme. I remember those days very well with the familiar sounds of bones crackling under my mother's teeth as she sucked out the marrow. The bones were eaten clean, chewed, and marrow juices savored until nothing was left or what remained was completely bone dry. My mother always said, "Sunday isn't the same without some chicken. You need something you can go back to later on." Usually, long after the dishes had been washed, someone would be in the kitchen wrapping a piece of bread around a chicken leg or wing, dousing it with hot sauce, and washing it down with iced tea or Coca-Cola. In the confines of the safe space of home all stereotypes about Black folks and chicken were forgotten.

Recalling these personal experiences has led me to think more carefully about how stereotypes are underpinned by variables such as gender, power, and history. These same dynamics are often at work in food interactions. So, I began more seriously considering "what food means"; how do the foods we procure, prepare, present, and consume have an impact on our cultural identity? What are the symbolic messages encoded in the foods we consume? Moreover, given their socially sanctioned status as nurturers, caretakers, and preparers of food what is the role of women in interpreting how and what these foods mean? To begin, I explored African American/Black/Negro foodways in an effort to unearth something about our foods and their meanings to our communities. I was shocked to learn that little existed to explain *and* interpret this history.[2] This lack of scholarly interpretation prompted me to seriously research foods consumed by Black people in the United States. I began by considering the gendered element of foodways. Taking as true Pamela Quaggiotto's notion that, "the mother determines when, what, and how much family members will eat. . . . She controls the symbolic language of food, determining what her dishes and meals will say about herself, her family, and world," made clear that women must be placed at the center of this analysis.[3] Armed with this notion in hand, I first set out to examine the food dynamics in my own home.

INVESTIGATING CONNECTIONS

My research into the realm of African American foods was about more than merely locating and identifying them. It was about understanding the connections between the foods and the people who consume them. This went beyond the theory of "you are what you eat" to "how does what we eat reflect our cultural identity?" How does our historical, socioeconomic, and political space influence the foods that we consume? Black people are engaged in an ideological warfare between race, identity, and food. For example, stereotypes concerning Black peoples' consumption of fried chicken—stereotypes that have been around for centuries—still pervade the American psyche today. Consider, for instance, the ease with which pro golfer Fuzzy Zoeller could make the comment to the media about the assumed food practices of pro golfer Tiger Woods. It was shortly after Tiger Woods (assumed to be fully African American because of his skin color) won the Master's Golf Tournament in 1997 that Zoeller commented to the media: "That little boy is driving well and he's putting well. He's doing everything it takes to win. So, you know what you guys do when he gets in here? You pat him on the back and say congratulations and enjoy it and tell him not to serve fried chicken at next year's dinner. Got it? . . . or collard greens or whatever the hell those people eat."[4] Comments such as this one made by Zoeller are unfortunately commonplace, functioning continuously to thwart and deflate African American economic, political, and cultural success. As Doris Witt successfully argues,

> Woods had the temerity to reign supreme at a sport thought to be innately "white." . . . The situation demanded some form of redress, which Zoeller took it upon himself to provide. Smart enough not to acknowledge directly his apprehension that Woods' victory marked a significant incursion against the faltering forces of white racial supremacy, Zoeller had recourse to chicken and greens.[5]

The media's—particularly those commentators with Southern roots—attempt to dilute this recourse by suggesting, "they themselves certainly liked fried chicken and collard greens" did little to appease Zoeller's racist intentions or Woods' compliance with such behavior, his declaration of "Cablinasion" heritage, notwithstanding.[6] Yet, the introduction of his Asian heritage brings his mother into the fore as a mediator introducing the intersection of gender, race, and food. Bringing her Thai heritage and thus Woods' multiethnic roots serves, on some level to reduce the severity of the comments to little more than "Black people's overreacting." In reality, however, it seems that Zoeller's comments, Woods' reaction, and his mother's entree, serve to heighten the relationship between food, race, nationality, and gender in today's society. My conjecture is that bringing Woods' mother into the debacle inadvertently illustrated the power of women at the center of mediating food interactions.

Black feminist scholar Patricia Hill Collins suggests the critical need for Black women to be aware of the importance of self-definition and self-valuation in historical and contemporary statements of Black feminist thought.[7] This assertion has utility for this discussion in that Black people also need to be aware of this importance in the statements used by White popular culture to describe and characterize Black cultural life. As Collins suggests, we need to be attuned to the way in which processes of power underlie our social interactions and more importantly, are involved in the process of external definition. These external definitions can, however, be challenged through a process known as "self-definition." These acts of "challenging the political knowledge-validation process that result[s] in externally defined stereotypical images"can be unconscious or conscious acts of resistance.[8] By utilizing and identifying symbols commonly affiliated with our cultural heritage, we engage in the process of self-definition or refusing to allow the wider American culture to dictate what represents our expressive culture and thereby represents us as Black people. But, this process of defining one's self is fraught with complications and complexities particularly if the group fails to understand or acknowledge that there is a power structure at work behind the creation of the stereotype.

Collins explains these complications further in her delineation of self-valuation or the replacement of negative images with positive ones. This process of replacement can be equally as problematic as external definition if we fail to understand and to recognize the stereotype as a controlling image. This was illustrated at a recent conference where I pointed out the hip-hop voiceover that can be heard in some of KFC's (formerly Kentucky Fried Chicken) commercials. I suggested that this depiction had stereotypical undertones. I also suggested that the visual image of the Colonel doing the "hip hop dance" was as bedeviling an image as that of the Black-faced man with big, shiny, red lips used to symbolize the restaurants of the Coon Chicken Inn. While many in the audience agreed with my assessment, some of the elder Black attendees championed the cause of "moving on" and "not letting the past control us." Perhaps in their minds, the hip-hop Colonel was a much-improved image over those with which they had coming of age viewing. Yet, in my mind, Collins' caution is registered here. This exchange of one set of controlling images for another does little to eradicate the defining image itself. We as Black people need to attend to the ways in which historical, social, political, and economical contexts have established these images (or narratives as I have termed them) and how they are embedded in our process of food selection, preparation, and consumption.

Black independence from negative controlling images is further challenged by Collins' suggestion to "push the envelope" by examining the content or basis for these external definitions. She suggests that usually stereotypes are "actually distorted renderings of those aspects of Black female behavior seen as most threatening to White patriarchy."[9] This assertion has model utility for this discussion in that the same holds true of the stereotypes that assassinate the character of Black people.

Figure 9.1.   *"I'se Boun' to Hab a Christmas Dinna!" ca. 1905, author's collection.*

EVOLUTION OF A STEREOTYPE

Initially, it seems these stereotypes involving Black people's affinity for chicken began as ideologies shaped from laws and ordinances passed during the seventeenth and eighteenth centuries as a way to control the economic gains of enslaved and free men and women who bartered and traded in the marketplace. Market trading in some of the heaviest areas like Charleston, South Carolina; Wilmington, North Carolina; New Orleans, Louisiana; and, varying parts of Virginia, Maryland, and Georgia provided one of the greatest and most essential forms of social interaction between Whites and Blacks. Meat and poultry procurement required a number of social interactions both on and off the plantation. Many of these market activities involved enslaved and free women of African descent. Enslaved women were frequently allowed to trade and engage in business using the possessions given them by their masters or those foods cultivated in their own gardens. In his study of eighteenth-century Black culture in Chesapeake Virginia and the Lowcountry of the Carolinas, Phillip Morgan points to the records of market activity that suggest that in the latter part of the century slaves controlled the poultry trade.[10] Accordingly, travelers' accounts indicate that "flocks of poultry [are] numerous" and "there are very few [slaves] indeed who are denied the privilege of keeping dunghill fowls, ducks, geese, and turkeys."[11] Moreover, some Black people would often sit by the wharf for days on end waiting to buy foods like chicken and then sell them for exorbitant prices.[12] Morgan notes a similar practice whereby some travelers would instruct their stewards to hold in reserve various foods like bacon so they would have bartering power with "the Negroes who are the general Chicken Merchants [*sic*]."[13]

As a result of this monopoly over the sale of poultry as well as the continuous increase in the Black population in many of these towns, regulations appeared which sought to limit the hawking of items being sold door-to-door. Anne E. Yentsch says that in 1717, Annapolis town fathers moved to restrict the market activities of its "Negroes" by limiting door-to-door sales by "confining purchases of flesh or fish, living or dead, eggs, butter, or cheese (oysters excepted) to the market."[14] She suggests the reason for these activities being stalled was the ambiguous ownership of goods prior to sale. Food items were not supposed to be sold prior to passing through the town gates, and in particular customers were not supposed to purchase goods whose ownership might be difficult to trace. This included items such as chickens, which were often sold outside the market. Yentsch maintains that goods such as oysters, salted fish in large barrels or casks, cattle, sheep, and hogs that were alive could easily be traced because they were by-and-large produced by small farmers. However, given that numerous Blacks had chicken coops as did many of their masters, the suggestion was that in buying dead chickens no one knew for sure whose chickens they were buying.[15]

Yet, despite these laws and ordinances, Black monopoly over the sale and trade of poultry increased and continued to cause numerous problems for customer and planter alike. Since the legal tactic failed, the town fathers began to accuse Blacks of theft. This accusation was fueled by Black people's use of trading practices like forestalling and extraplantation trading. Forestalling was the practice of anticipat[ing] the market by buying outside the city gates, which allowed sellers to place early bid on the goods which they in turn sold for higher prices within the market area.[16] The problem with this practice was that when Blacks were selling chickens, as many of them were, the goods were untraceable having been purchased (and possibly sold) well before the legal market trading activity began. Another practice described by Morgan, which had similar dire consequences for White planters, was extraplantation or off-site trading. According to Morgan, enslaved people took it upon themselves to branch out well beyond the neighboring plantation areas in search of more lucrative trading venues. Because it was hard to determine where the chickens and hens came from—the coffers of the enslaved or planters—these practices also proved to be an economic anathema.[17]

Legal ordinances did little to reduce the trading practices of Blacks. Many, both enslaved and free, continued to receive various gains from their trading acumen, furthering the ire of slaveowners. Thus, town managers instituted even newer laws as late as the mid-nineteenth century forbidding huckstering or the selling of day-old food at reduced prices in the market places, door-to-door or curbside.[18] Lastly, in part from truth as much as fiction, slaveowners—who considered any and all commodities, including the slave, to belong to them—began to associate Black trading practices with theft. Admittedly, some slaves did engage in pilfering and stealing of wares. Some scholars, however, have referred to these acts of pilfering as acts of skill and cunning. Eugene Genovese's study of African American life and culture, suggests this when he writes, "for many slaves, stealing from their own or other masters became a science and an art, employed as much for the satisfaction of outwitting Ole' Massa as anything else."[19] In *Weevils in the Wheat*, one slave affords us a glimpse at the "anything else." According to ex-slave Charles Grandy hunger was one motivating factor for the enslaved to use skill and cunning to steal food. He says, "I got so hungry I stealed chickens off de roos'. . . . We would cook de chicken at night, eat him an' bu'n de feathers. . . . We always had a trap in de floor fo' de do' to hide dese chickens in."[20]

It is this notion of the "chicken thieving darky" that provides a valuable segue into helping us historicize our present day stereotypes of the "chicken loving darky." This ideology began to crystallize during the Reconstruction era as the need to reclaim the "Old South" and "The Lost Cause of Southern White heritage" plagued the minds of many White Americans. With the mass exodus North and West of many newly freed Blacks, the South suffered a devastating loss of free labor. Jobs in the South were few. Many Black men had joined the "Yankees" or fled to the North in search of employment often as cooks on railroads or ships, in hotels and restaurants. Most Black women entered domestic service, many marshaling their culinary experiences of cooking either in the Big House or in the slave quarters. What was once championed by many as talented cooking of the South quickly turned to an object of ridicule and defacement.

According to historian Kenneth Goings, the loss of control over Black people due to the ending of slavery, the emergence of political and Black political participation, and outward migration by Blacks registered a blow among White Southerners. Threatened by Black newfound freedom, Southern Whites used advancing communications to forge a means of reasserting control and reclaiming power.[21] In an attempt to subjugate Blacks and conjure memories of the Ole' South, White Americans vented their anger using artifacts of visual media like brochures, pamphlets, trading cards, greeting cards, and food products. Emerging from this "new White backlash" was an ideology of Black inferiority, which prompted the formulation of racist stereotypes. These stereotypes were perpetuated by advertisements, trading cards, and sheet music like that of Fred Fischer which pictures an old Black man with his hands in a hen house, caption reading: "If the Man in the Moon Were a Coon."

Goings, whose study *Mammy and Uncle Mose* historicizes the cultural and political economy of Black collectibles, maintains that the coon image was one of the most offensive stereotypes. Most prevalent from 1880 to 1930, Goings considers "Zip Coon" "the alter ego to Jim Crow." He elaborates,

> Zip Coon was a "citified," "dandified" slave, who wore a fashionable (but worn) morning coat and top hat.... The word "coon" comes from the South, a shortening of "raccoon." This scavenger steals food at night, has enormous whites of the eye that contrast with its dark face, and is best when chased up a tree by dogs." ... The "coon" like the "sambo" was an attempt to reduce African-American men to ridiculous, stupid, and even beastlike comic figures.[22]

M. L. Graham used this coon motif as the mascot for his little-known "Coon Chicken Inn" restaurants. The emblem, a Black-faced man with large, extended red lips, was typically symbolic of how Whites would stereotype Black people with food to endorse various products like fried chicken. Considered a most affective advertising technique, images like this one reinforced the "stereotypical Old South/New South myth of the loyal, happy servant just

Figure 9.2.   Coon Chicken Inn Restaurant, 1925–1949, Portland, Oregon, Lake County (IL) Museum, Curt Teich Postcard Archives.

waiting to be used by the master—and now the consumer. The restaurant with all of its accoutrements becomes a metaphor for Whites using and discarding Black service. When the meal was complete, the napkins, plates, and utensils bearing the Black-faced logo were discarded, White patrons were symbolically discarding Blacks (who had fulfilled their duty of seeing that their "White masters" were well fed). This act of physical disposal provided Whites with what Goings describes in a similar discussion as a sense of "racial superiority" and a "therapeutic sense of comfort." This motif served to be even more effective because it seared in the minds of many White Americans the notion that "under the cover of night, the darky would supposedly steal a chicken from the master's coop for a purloined Sunday dinner"; and thus, the stereotypical belief that Black people are "chicken loving" and "chicken thieving darkies."[23] Manipulating these objects of material culture enabled White Americans to not only forge an alliance between White people that surpassed class lines, but also enabled them to more collectively subjugate and vilify the lives and cultures of Blacks. This notion of Black inferiority provided a safeguard for White America during a time when their racial, economic, and political balance was perceived as threatened. From this, it seems that a distinct historical narrative developed and continues to evolve around Black folks' consumption of fried chicken.

However, this narrative and its accompanying stereotypes have produced a paradoxical response from many White people. On the one hand, they want to attribute Black consumption of fried chicken as normative; on the other hand, they want to equate this consumption with something negative. However, the issue becomes more complex when fried chicken—as one of the most heralded foods of the South—is listed among the many contributions of Black folks. At issue here is how to malign Black people and their consumption of fried chicken without crediting them with contributing the method of deep-frying to New World Cuisine. Well into the nineteenth century as Blacks in general continued to monopolize and control the distribution of poultry, Black women dominated the cooking of chicken, being widely credited with lining the "Southern groaning boards" with heaping platters of steaming fried chicken. Even though evidence has been garnered in support of these assertions, scholars and lay people alike often attempt to discredit these contributions.[24]

Some White people will go to any lengths to distance fried chicken and other "Southern-identified foods" from the culinary repertoire of Black people. Take for instance this anecdote from the 1998 American Studies Association Annual Meeting. Following the presentation of a similar argument about the "particularistic" relationship between fried chicken and Black people, one audience member vehemently exclaimed, "fried chicken is not African American food, it's Southern food."[25] This assertion begs the question of why White people find it necessary to distinguish foods eaten in the South from those prepared and consumed by Black people. If I had, for instance, written a paper on chit'lins or collard greens, I doubt that I would have met with the same resistance given that these are deemed "soul foods" –foods within my culinary boundary. However, to align myself with foods that are comfortably situated within the White Southern culinary repertoire is an invasion. This cultural demarcation becomes necessary for symbolically separating the domestic rituals of the South. As a Black woman, my cultural role was to prepare and cook fried chicken like the proverbial mammy or enslaved cook in the Big House. However, fried chicken is not mine to claim, less I blur the lines between the "symbolic separations [of] those who prepare the food and those who consume it" according to literary theorist Mary Titus.[26] This relationship reveals fried chicken as a "complex cultural text," a Southern food that emerged out of a social institution shaped by racial complexities. Therefore, keeping the symbolic mental distance between cook and consumer is necessary for White Americans to maintain the purity of Southern cuisine, but it is also complicated by the consumption of fried chicken by Black people. It seems here that words are being used to convey coded messages, namely, Southern is a code word for White, while "soul food" is decoded as Black.[27] I never conveyed that fried chicken "belonged" to Black people; rather, I explicitly argued that the relationship between Black people and fried chicken has to be considered in the context of the historical and economic circumstances of the South. This circumstance involves the creation of a national narrative that was in defense of a White Southern heritage—a heritage defined by food; indeed, one of the South's most prevalent defining characteristics.

Implicit in this illustration is a repetition of the genre contained in many White cookbooks—recipes contributed by Blacks, yet culturally robbed by Whites. Taking the illiteracy of Blacks for granted, many White women took the recipes of Black women and used them for their own pecuniary gain and acclaim. This practice was still taking place as late as the 1940s when Marjorie Rawlings wrote *Cross Creek Cookery* using many of the recipes created by Idella Parker. In her biographical account, Parker states:

> Many of the recipes in the book were mine, but she only gave me credit for three of them, including "Idella's Biscuits." There were several others that were mine too, such as the chocolate Pie, and of course it was me who did most of the cooking when we were trying all the recipes out. All I ever got from the cookbook was an autographed copy, but in those days I was grateful for any little crumb that white people let fall, so I kept my thoughts about the cookbook strictly to myself. [28]

This practice has occurred far too often to enumerate. It is, I believe, one of the ways that White people have been able to claim and reclaim Southern foods like fried chicken for their own. Diane Spivey has labeled this phenomenon, "Whites Only Cuisine" in her recently published book, *The Peppers, Cracklings, and Knots of Wool Cookbook: The Global Migration of African-Cuisine*. She says:

> The end of the [Civil] war also signaled the beginning of the redefining of southern white heritage. The "Lost Cause," or southern white elites' efforts to hold on to their old way of life, centered around food. Cooking and cuisine were remade to look uniquely southern. . . . Asserting that the recipes were "southern" made these cookbooks exclusionary, and therefore racist, because the cookbooks and recipes contained therein were heralded as the creations of elite southern white women. In an attempt to promote southern white culture, therefore, the concept of "southern cooking" started out as *Whites Only Cuisine*.[29]

This concept of *whites only cuisine* seemingly remains today in the subconscious minds of many White Americans undergirded by a need to control most aspects of American cultural life.

This concept is another one of the propelling forces that has produced and shaped the stereotype surrounding Black consumption of fried chicken. This stereotype has left such an indelible imprint that some African Americans refuse to consume the food in public. According to a survey I conducted in relationship to another research project, many Blacks in corporate settings—particularly those between the ages of 29 and 35—refuse to eat chicken in the presence of White co-workers. As one informant said, " I don't even want my co-workers to get in their minds that whole stereotype thing of [fried] chicken and watermelon, you know?" This feeling suggests that these African Americans understand the ideology of racism and how it is deeply embedded in many White Western minds so as to make stereotypical comments commonplace. On the other hand, their resistance to eating chicken may suggest an uncomfortable feeling with being associated with this aspect of their food heritage and identity. Still others celebrate this aspect of the stereotype by acknowledging it as a part of their identity as African Americans in a racist society. Nowhere is this more evident than in Black churches where chicken is affectionately called, the "gospel bird" or the "preacher's bird."[30]

RESISTING THE STEREOTYPE

It is in African American churches where the oppressed have taken an active role in the social process of cultural identification. In this arena, fried chicken has been and still remains a visible part of the expressive culture of African Americans and a useful tool in social action. An examination of its role in the process of collective self-help and racial uplift will delineate the ways in which Black women have used chicken—despite the stereotype—to construct parts of their cultural identity. In their discussion of the material expressions of culture, archaeologists Mary Beaudry, Lauren Cook, and Stephen Mrozowski, argue that the use of objects and their symbolism in the process of constructing cultural identity is "first and foremost a public act of mediation between self and other."[31] They suggest that through an analysis of material items we can begin to understand the ways in which individuals used objects important to self-expression and self-definition in the construction of this identity. Borrowing from Mihaly Csikszentmihalyi and Eugene Rochberg-Holton, they further suggest that individuals and members of a "subculture" will create their identity by using "object[s] or sign[s] that [allow] a person to 'make his self manifest'"; a process that generally occurs through leisure or during off-work hours.[32] What this suggests, then, is that when Black women congregate in church kitchens, cooking, networking, and "strifing," they are building upon an integral part of the Black communities' cultural identity.

Many Black religious activities like the new minister's induction, funerals, homecomings or revivals, women's day, men's day, and youth day are replete

Figure 9.3.   "Get Thee Behind Me Satan," ca. 1905 author's collection.

with food. Black women (and men) "light up more stoves" and "grease more frying pans" in an attempt to feed congregations while asserting and maintaining their heritage and culture through the tradition of selling fried chicken dinners. For instance, Workman Memorial AME Zion Church in Hartford, Connecticut, made news in *The Hartford Courant*, with the headlines declaring, "Church to Have Soul Food Benefit." The article indicates that the church is ninety-eight years old and has been selling fried chicken dinners for as many years. With a global mission of "help[ing] in poor parts of Africa" the church has its annual "Soul Food To Go" dinner selling: "southern fried chicken, collard greens, candied yams, macaroni and cheese and corn bread." According to the pastor, Rev. Shelley D. Best, "you don't get soul food in Connecticut. . . . There's something to be said for the food—It's not Kentucky Fried Chicken. . . . Every item is an art form. It's part of the African American tradition."[33] These acts of resistance against the narrative put forth by White America can perhaps be considered unconscious; however, the constant use and reuse of fried chicken as a tool for social action might suggest otherwise. African Americans have used fried chicken to symbolize self-definition, self-expression, and celebration. Food identifies those who belong to the "in-group" and as Beaudry, Cook, and Mrozowski suggest, is "occasionally [used] as a weapon to annoy those who do not" [belong].[34]

Food as emblematic of culture and as a weapon of resistance has long been utilized in the Black community and in particular in our formal institutions like the church. Just after Emancipation when Black people were in need of a "safe space" to structure and organize their lives, the church provided this support.[35] It has been a mainstay in the Black community as a haven for social, political, and cultural expression. Though many White Southern families would also engage in preparing chicken on Sunday when the preacher came, for African Americans this ritual dates back to Emancipation when the church became the center of Black community life. It was during this period that Black people could construct lives consistent with being freed women and men and removing themselves from the controlling presence of White churches. In selecting their own preachers they no longer had to hear sermons of White masters who admonished them "don' steal f'om you' marser an' missus" among other things. In Black churches of this period, parishioners could hear messages of equality and social action. The minister was their spiritual leader and motivator. To show their gratitude and fondness for the minister, parishioners would take turns inviting him to their home for Sunday dinner and the hostess would excitedly engage in the labor-intensive process of cleaning, catching, killing, plucking, and cooking a chicken for the occasion. Nowhere is the excitement of the occasion captured more euphorically then in the autobiographical narrative of Sara Brooks. In illustrative detail Brooks recalls how her mother hustled to prepare a "big meal" for her preacher:

> My mother would fix a big meal . . . so they could have fried chicken for the preacher cause the preacher love fried chicken . . . and she'd clean the chickens out by givin em cornmeal—wet it and put bakin soda in it—and that would clean the chickens out. So my mother'd have fried chicken and she'd

cook vegetables and cakes and pies. The preacher and my daddy would eat
first; then we'd eat what was left.[36]

Numerous anecdotes and jokes in African American folklore detail stories
about the preacher and fried chicken. Because the pastor is considered to hold
the position of highest esteem and "cultural power" in the church, and often
the community, it is considered a privilege to serve him the choicest pieces of
chicken. Marvalene H. Hughes indicates, "whether on the church ground or
in the Black home, the Black preacher is the first to choose his food."[37] So
powerful is this object to the Black community that it has become associated
with our folklore. In a recent church service, one minister suggested that
chicken is one of the four Cs that could "bring the preacher down." As the
saying goes, the Cs represent, "cash," "chicks," "cadillacs," and "chicken." For
the preacher to praise one parishioner's chicken over another can result in
gender conflict resulting in ostracism and internal strife among the women
known for cooking the best fried chicken. His open acknowledgment and
praise of one sista's fried chicken over another suggests that he is enjoying
something at that sista's house other than just the "preacher's bird."[38]

Strife over who cooks the best bird on Sundays is one of the many feelings
engendered by fried chicken consumption. It is so central to many church
functions that its absence can also arouse the displeasure of parishioners with
savoring tongues. I recall one year I decided to fast on chicken beyond the
Lenten season. Mother was used to my whimsical ever-changing dietary
habits, so she asked what foods I preferred for the post-Lenten meal. Though
I knew the meal was going to be openly shared by everyone after church service, I never thought that what my mother prepared for *me* would be shared
as well. So, in the absence of this morsel of knowledge, I boldly exclaimed,
"baked fish. I'm still fasting from chicken and fried foods." She said, "Fish?
Aw, you've gone and messed up my dinner. I had a menu all laid out. All
right." And, of course, she was right. I had, in fact, "gone and messed up her
dinner." What I had not anticipated was the relative badge of cultural shame
I brought to my mother, who, as a preacher's wife, had a certain expectant role
to play in the culinary expose of the after-church meal. During the course of
the meal, more than one parishioner commented, "Sista Williams you didn't
cook any chicken this year? Umph, that's not like you. I just knew I was gonna
have some of your chicken." In an effort to support my resolve and quell my
temptation, my mother had all but violated one of the unspoken principles of
food consumption within the Black church—she, a preacher's wife, had left
out the chicken!

Black women have been gracing tables in the church with fried chicken for
a long time. Like the present-day benefit held at the Workman Memorial

AME Church in Hartford, Connecticut, churches during the latter part of the nineteenth century would often have church fairs and bazaars to raise money. Overlapping with mutual aid and benevolent societies, church institutions—as a venue for cooperative economics—relied upon the leadership of women in varying roles ranging from the Sunday school teacher to the kitchen cook. Using the proceeds from church lunch and dinner sales, Black women were able to assist in building baptismal pools, edifices, sanctuaries, and contribute to other church needs. This creative consciousness combined with spirituality, camaraderie and cooking imagination imbues chicken with polysemic meanings. These meanings exceed the obvious notion of food as nutritive; they also reflect ingenuity and creativity wrought by the historical circumstance of living gendered lives in a racist society.

Historically and in contemporary society, for many African American women cooking in the church not only offers an opportunity to provide sustenance, but also a time for networking "in the name of the Lord." Though women were often denied the status and power afforded men, they were able to carve out an alternative space of power in the microcosmic arena of the kitchen to provide their pecuniary contributions. The kitchen afforded Black women a level of "cultural authority" and "financial autonomy" as described by Doris Witt, wherein they could exercise a modicum of power by contributing to the campaign of racial uplift. In the microcosmic "safe space" of the kitchen, they could engage the macro space of the Black church to explore and validate expressions of the self even as the wider American culture issued assault. In her discussion of the women's movement in the Black Baptist Church, African American religious historian Evelyn Brooks Higgenbotham contextualizes Black women's involvement in the church from the perspective of the larger racial struggle. With a focus on "racial solidarity" and "racial self-determination" they operated out of a "paradox of opposition": male domination/racial cooperation; White control/collaboration. This "amalgam of separatist leanings" was "inspired by the nexus of race and gender consciousness."[39]

This "nexus of race and gender consciousness" operated out of the context of W. E. B. DuBois' "double consciousness" to form what Higgenbotham calls, "double gender consciousness," which blurred the lines between Black women as "homemakers and soldiers." Black women were doing more than merely frying chicken in the kitchen to "raise a little bit o' money." These collective efforts forged from "separatist leanings" were assaulted by varying degrees of opposition and conflict including Black men, White Baptist women, and sometimes each other. These conflicts notwithstanding, they were also engaged on a larger scale in redefining their expressions of self for themselves and for the larger American society who sought assiduously to subjugate and

Figure 9.4.   "My Old Kentucky Home," ca. 1908, author's collection.

oppress them with negative stereotypes. Working "under siege," Black women were burdened with the task of not only procuring, preparing, and presenting foods like fried chicken for consumption, sustenance, and economic gain, but also, they were challenged with the task of teaching and conveying "respectable behavior" in all forms of expression, particularly table manners. Working against demeaning caricatures and icons in popular culture and academic discourse, like the "Coon" or the physically deviant Hottentot Venus, Black women resisted these depictions by emphasizing an air of respectability. They believed that proper adherence to manners and morals would negate the claims of racial and gender inferiority and give rise to social acceptance.

This goal notwithstanding, these assertions brought with them class and status implications that manifested themselves most assuredly during mealtimes. Aimed in large part at the Black working-class poor, these edicts found expression in most of the major newspapers, magazines, church sermons and cookbooks/self-help guides of the period. For example, in *The Correct Thing to Do—To Say—To Wear*, Charlotte Hawkins Brown advocated the proper rules for presenting a dining room that creates an atmosphere that appeals to the eyes as well as to the taste" inasmuch as each meal should be "conducive to harmonious social intercourse."[40] Instructions were given on the proper way to use a fork and knife, including how the tines should be held when food is being carried to the mouth. Chicken, in any form, is absent from the menu. Rather, foods like "stuffed tomatoes in Aspic," "Cheese and Jelly Sandwiches," and "Celery Hearts" are among the delicacies. Of course, it is not surprising that fried chicken is not mentioned among the offerings given the assimilationist intent of these self-help manuals. In this context, Brown's "harmonious social intercourse" could not be obtained while eating fried chicken—a practice performed sans utensils—because this form of eating replicated an element of barbarism left over from the colonial past when tableware was scarce or nonexistent.

These edicts aside, among the working poor and middle-class Blacks, fried chicken was a constant. Few written documents of the Black middle class make note of its appearance at gatherings not wanting to associate themselves with foods or other acts of "barbarism" that would reduce their social acceptance in the eyes of the larger White society. The Black middle class often maintained a code of silence about the everyday lives of the Black working class for fear that *all* Black people would be subjected to the humil-

Figure 9.5.   "Bird in de han," author's collection.

iation and economic despair that accompanied second-class citizenship. Yet, anecdotes and oral histories tell the story of how fried chicken was and continues to be a steady survival food among most African Americans.

Big boxes of fried chicken packed neatly for the Northern journey, rent parties where fried chicken dinners sold for a dollar, juke joints where fried chicken flows like the whiskey and music, all reflect spaces where African American culture, community, and history can be expressed. Even the metaphorical "chicken bone express" is celebrated in the folklore of Black people to describe the days of segregation when travelers would carry shoeboxes full of food to sustain them on their journey because White food establishments were inhospitable to Blacks. As the saying goes, you could identify the travel route of Black folks by following the trail of chicken bones along the highway or the railroad track. Norma Jean Darden recounts similar travel experiences in her family memoir and cookbook, *Spoonbread and Strawberry Wine*:

> These trips took place during the fifties, and one never knew what dangers or insults would be encountered along the way. Racist policies loomed like the unidentified monsters in our childish imaginations and in reality. After the New Jersey Turnpike ended, we would have to be on the alert for the unexpected. So, as we approached that last Howard Johnson's before Delaware, our father would make his inevitable announcement that we had to get out, stretch our legs, and go the bathroom, whether we wanted to or not. This was a ritualized part of every trip, for, although there would be many restaurants along the route, this was the last one that didn't offer segregated facilities. From this point on, we pulled out our trusty shoe-box lunches.[41]

Listed first on the menu of foods found in those "trusty shoe-box lunches" was fried chicken accompanied by peanut butter and jelly sandwiches, deviled eggs, carrot and celery sticks, salt and pepper packets, chocolate layer cake, and a thermos of lemonade. Though negative and unwelcome at the time, experiences such as these are a part of the African American legacy of living in America. These experiences become a filter through which objects, like fried chicken, take on meanings that fashion a collective memory of resistance. These are also experiences through which Patricia Hill Collins' process of self-valuation—understanding and resisting the controlling images and then replacing them with more positive ones—takes place. As I think about the comfort foods of my youth I recognize my own memories as a part of this self-valuation experience. Traveling to Virginia with picnic baskets full of food were fun times for me. I always remember wanting to be the one to stay awake and help my father, "watch the road" just in case he needed my navigational *help*. Staying awake through most of the journey also entitled me to knowing when we were ready to eat. When we traveled to the South in the '60s and '70s my mother would prepare a big picnic basket with fried chicken, Vienna sausages, white bread (which was later replaced by wheat), fruit, juicy juices, cookies, and potato chips. This was the economy lunch for a family of five. I was always excited when it was announced that we were going on a trip. I couldn't wait; sleep was elusive. The combination of sightseeing, helping my father watch the road, and considering the contents of the picnic basket always kept me wide awake.

On the morning of our trip I vividly recall waking to the smells of chicken frying in the kitchen. I would usually be the first one awake and into the kitchen climbing up on the stool beside the stove to watch my mother deep fry chicken and gather foodstuffs for our trip. Sometimes she let me season the chicken (after I washed my hands of course). At first she used only salt, pepper, and a dash of paprika. Later she began to use garlic powder, an aroma I still love to smell. When the chicken was well floured, she lowered it into the hot and sizzling frying pan or pot filled with Wesson oil. As I got older and began cooking my own fried chicken—when I still cooked and ate chicken—I would add my own twist with cayenne to give it an extra spicy taste. These were fun times. My feelings about these times were slightly hampered, however, when I later learned the reasons we traveled with our own food. In part, it was economics. Feeding a family of five at every stop would prove to be very expensive. The other reason, it turns out, was the lack of eating establishments hospitable to African Americans. The 1970s were not far enough removed from the feelings of hostility surrounding the Civil Rights confrontations. To avoid these encounters, we stopped to use the restrooms and order food at places that served and catered to Black people. Understanding these circumstances and their social and political implications was turned into acts of agency by my parents who exposed us to the racism while simultaneously displaying tactics of resistance.

These displays of self-support and collective memory continue to exist—consciously or unconsciously—every time a kitchen fills with the smells of fried chicken, candied sweet potatoes, black-eyed peas, greens, and macaroni and cheese because somewhere nearby there is probably a Black woman. Through her double gendered consciousness of being Black and a woman in the United States, she brings to bear on the food she cooks the act of positive self-expression and self-valuation. It is usually through her that proper morals and manners of mealtime behaviors are instilled and executed, not necessarily to accommodate racial discourses as such, but to foster individuals imbued with a social and cultural history of African American struggle.

For some people, fried chicken may still simply suggest the presence of Southern culinary culture. But for many African Americans fried chicken is a symbolic icon of the African American struggle and survival. Foods like fried chicken, collard greens, deviled eggs, potato salad, macaroni and cheese, and corn bread are more than "soul food" or what Vertamae Grosvenor calls, "get down foods." For many Black people, these foods also reflect certain times and places in history when food choices and establishments were limited or inaccessible; when these foods provided a way to pay rent; and, when they offered a temporary safe haven away from the complexities of the urban landscape by being served at the chicken shack up the road.

Though many of these foods have been modified and adapted to include a number of ethnic and regional cooking variations, there still exists a solid link between fried chicken and African American history. Through the sharing of stories with elders and siblings, younger generations can come to understand the traditions and legacies that comprise these histories and life experiences. In this way, they can arm themselves with the knowledge of how negative controlling images creep into our psyches and slowly eat away at our self-esteem and cultural identity as Black people. We must never forget that we live in a society that espouses "liberty and justice for all" but fails in reality to live up to this enormous undertaking. It is, in part, out of this contradiction that African American women as survivalists generation after generation have used their "soulful creativity" to transmit cultural practices of food through their networks in the home, the labor market, and the community. Through their culturally sanctioned roles as nurturers and caretakers, African American women make food a major aspect of the expressive culture of the Black community. During times of economic despair, African American women create a big pot of chicken stew, or fry chicken backs and feet adding rice to make a meal. When the economic condition improves, chicken still may be fried, or steamed, barbecued, curried, eaten alone or with a host of side dishes to complete a dinner. Whether pilfering, borrowing, or sharing, African American women along with their men have insured that our heritage and history are present through the continued presence of these foods at almost every major family gathering. More importantly, Black women have manipulated fried chicken to serve as a weapon of resistance in repudiating the negative connotations and denigrating ideologies espoused in the image of "chicken eating Black folks."

NOTES

I am grateful to the Smithsonian Institute's Anacostia Museum and the Center for African American Life and History, specifically Portia James for helping to support some of the research for this chapter. I also wish to thank Sherrie A. Inness, Philipia L. Hillman, Doris

Witt, Donna Rowe, Shireen Lewis, Warren Belasco, and Lyllie B. Williams for their helpful comments and encouragement. I would especially like to thank my husband, Akai Kwame Forson, for sharing his Diasporic experiences and perspectives.

1. I wrestled with whether to use the prevailing term *African American* or to use the almost nonexistent *Black*. I decided that I would use the terms interchangeably and risk debate. It seemed that regardless of whether people were born in America and are, therefore, "African American" or if they have migrated to the United States from around the African Diaspora, they are considered "chicken loving darkies." See the comments regarding the Tiger Woods debacle.

2. At that time, scholarly work was scant. There were several cookbooks including Jessica Harris's *The Welcome Table* and *Iron Pots and Wooden Spoons*, and Vertamae Grosvenor's *Vibration Cooking*. Archaeological work about faunal remains and slave artifacts were also prevalent. However, little scholarly work had been completed that went beyond historical explanations to include interpretations and meanings. One of the most recent scholarly works to explore these domains is Doris Witt's *Black Hunger* (New York: Oxford University Press, 1999).

3. This discussion in no way attempts to negate the contributions of Black men to this negotiation process. However, if women are prescribed socially to undertake the cooking for and nurturing of the family, we can readily accept Quaggiotto's argument. See Carole M. Counihan, "Female Identity, Food, and Power in Contemporary Florence," *Anthropological Quarterly* 61 (1988): 52.

4. Harry Blauvelt, "Zoeller Says His Comments about Woods Made 'In Jest,'" *USA Today*, 22 April 1997, sec. 2C.

5. Witt, *Black Hunger*, 4.

6. I borrow quite loosely here from Witt, *Black Hunger*, who discusses this incident in relation to African American women, food, and masculinity. See in particular 3–5.

7. Patricia Hill Collins, "Learning from the Outsider Within: The Sociological Significance of Black Feminist Thought," *Social Problems* 33, no. 6 (1986): 516.

8. Collins, "Learning from the Outsider Within," 516–17.

9. Collins, "Learning from the Outsider Within," 516–17.

10. Some sources indicate that chicken started to become a mass-produced commodity around the year 1800, but travelers' accounts and planters records date the trading and bartering activities of enslaved Blacks to earlier periods. Phillip D. Morgan, *Slave Counterpoint: Black Culture in the Eighteenth-Century Chesapeake and Lowcountry* (Chapel Hill: University of North Carolina Press for the Omohundro Institute of Early American History and Culture, Williamsburg, Virginia, 1998).

11. Scholars have argued that chicken was a semiluxury item for plantation owners, relegated primarily to Sunday dinner or for the arrival of visitors; see Sam Hilliard's, *Hog Meat and Hoecake* (1972) and Joe Gray Taylor's, *Eating, Drinking & Visiting in the South* (1982). However, Hilliard also points out the frequency with which many enslaved people kept chickens and other poultry and would supplement planter's coffers when flocks were low. Southern Black and poor White families have always eaten what anthropologist Tony Whitehead refers to as "low status" chicken: necks, feet, giblets, and backs. The participants in his study refer to these items as "poor people's food" or "black people's food." See Whitehead's "Sociocultural Dynamics and Food Habits in a

Southern Community," *Food in the Social Order: Studies of Food and Festivities in Three American Communities,* ed. Mary Douglas (New York: Russell Sage Foundation, 1984), 115. My own research has yielded that fried chicken fat (the chicken butt) supplied an additional meat source as well as a source of cooking oil in lieu of traditional pork sources (fatback, lard, bacon). The chicken bones are often used to season soups and broths and then sucked dry to savor the seasoned marrow.

12. Anne E. Yentsch, *A Chesapeake Family and Their Slaves: A Study in Historical Ar-chaeology* (Cambridge, U.K.: Cambridge University Press, 1994), 242.

13. Morgan, *Slave Counterpoint,* 359.

14. Yentsch, *A Chesapeake Family and Their Slaves,* 245.

15. Yentsch, *A Chesapeake Family and Their Slaves,* 245.

16. Yentsch, *A Chesapeake Family and Their Slaves,* 244.

17. Morgan, *Slave Counterpoint,* 360.

18. Yentsch, *A Chesapeake Family and Their Slaves,* 248.

19. Eugene Genovese, *Roll, Jordan, Roll: The World the Slaves Made* (New York: Vin-tage, 1976), 606.

20. Charles L. Perdue Jr., Thomas E. Barden, and Robert K. Phillips, eds., *Weevils in the Wheat* (Charlottesville: University of Virginia Press, 1976), 116.

21. Kenneth W. Goings, *Mammy and Uncle Mose: Black Collectibles and American Stereotyping* (Bloomington: Indiana University Press, 1994), 4–7.

22. Goings, *Mammy and Uncle Mose,* 43–44.

23. Goings, *Mammy and Uncle Mose,* 47.

24. This debate is a highly contentious one among scholars of Southern and African American foodways. Since few references to fried chicken appear in Southern cookbooks prior to 1850, numerous scholars have attributed the technique of frying to West African women—this coupled with West African use to palm oil. However, another body of schol-ars suggests that the English made this contribution to New World cuisine. As Yentsch suggests, there was such amalgamation that true origins of some food practices are hard to pinpoint. See Yentsch, *A Chesapeake Family and Their Slaves,* 196–215; Jessica Harris, *The Welcome Table: African American Heritage Cooking* (New York: Simon & Schuster, 1995); Michael Krondl, *Around the American Table: Treasured Recipes and Food Traditions from the American Cookery Collections of the New York Public Library* (Holbrook, Mass.: Adams Pub-lishing, 1995); Sam Hilliard, *Hog Meat and Hoecake: Food Supply in the Old South, 1840–1860* (Carbondale: Southern Illinois University Press, 1972.

25. These observations must be attributed to Doris Witt who actually read the paper in my absence during the conference. However, any misrepresentations of the incident are mine.

26. Mary Titus, "'Groaning Tables and Spit in the Kettles': Food and Race in the Nineteenth-Century South," *Southern Quarterly* 20, no. 2–3 (1992), 15.

27. This notion of coding was suggested by Witt during comments on earlier drafts of this chapter.

28. Idella Parker and Marjorie Keating, *Idella: Marjorie Rawlings' 'Perfect Maid.'* (Gainesville: University Press of Florida, 1992), 69.

29. Diane M. Spivey, "Economics, War, and the Northern Migration of the Southern Black Cook," in *The Peppers, Crackling, and Knots of Wool Cookbook: The Global Migration of African Cuisine* (New York: State University of New York Press, 1999), 263.

30. See Jualynne E. Dodson and Cheryl Townsend Gilkes, "There's Nothing Like Church Food," *Journal of the American Academy of Religion* 63, no. 3 (1995): 523; and Helen Mendes, *The African Heritage Cookbook* (New York: MacMillan, 1971), 82.

31. Mary C. Beaudry, Lauren J. Cook, and Stephen A. Mrozowski, "Artifacts and Active Voices: Material Culture as Social Discourse," in *The Archaeology of Inequality*, ed. Robert Paynter and Randall H. McGuire (Oxford: Basil Blackwell, 1991), 154.

32. This is not to suggest that Black women's church work, including cooking, is "leisure" or "nonwork." To the contrary, it is important social work; however, for the purposes of this discussion, church activities are considered in addition to the formal production of labor.

33. Jill Storms, "Church to Have Soul Food Benefit," *The Hartford Courant* 1998, 16 November 1986, sec. B1.

34. Beaudry et al., "Artifacts and Active Voices," 156.

35. Farah Jasmine Griffin uses the term *safe space* to designate "spaces of resistance" which are by no means hegemonic but where "the South is evoked . . . the site of African American culture, community, and history." See Griffin, "Safe Spaces and Other Places: Navigating the Urban Landscape," in *Who Set You Flowin'? The African-American Migration Narrative* (New York: Oxford University Press, 1995), 110–11.

36. Thordis Simonsen, *You May Plow Here: The Narrative of Sara Brooks* (New York: W. W. Norton, 1986), 78–79.

37. Marvalene H. Hughes, "Soul, Black Women, and Food," *Food and Culture*, ed. Carole Counihan and Penny Van Esterik (New York: Routledge, 1997), 277.

38. I am grateful to Philipia L. Hillman for providing me with this observation. Dr. G. Martin Young, "Hold On Help Is on the Way." Sermon preached at Florida Avenue Baptist Church, Washington, D.C., 29 March 1998.

39. Evelyn Brooks Higgenbotham, *Righteous Discontent: The Women's Movement in the Black Baptist Church, 1880–1920* (Cambridge, Mass.: Harvard University Press, 1993), 50.

40. Charlotte Hawkins Brown, "At Mealtime," *The Correct Thing to Do—To Say—To Wear* (New York: G. K. Hall, 1995), 47.

41. Norma Jean Darden, *Spoonbread and Strawberry Wine* (New York: Doubleday, 1994), 291.

Index

About the Contributors

Benay Blend received a Ph.D. in American studies from the University of New Mexico. She is currently revising her dissertation on Mary Austin for the University of Iowa Press. Her research interests include Jewish women writers of New Mexico and Latin America. She has contributed chapters to several books, including *The Literature of Nature: An International Sourcebook* (1998) and *Writing under the Sign of Nature* (2000). Her articles can be found in *Critical Matrix*, *Bucknell Review*, *Southern Quarterly*, and other journals.

Paul Christensen is professor of creative writing at Texas A&M University. He is the author of *Charles Olson: Call Him Ishmael* (1979); *In Love in Sorrow: The Complete Correspondence of Charles Olson and Edward Dahlberg* (1990); *Minding the Underworld: Clayton Eshleman and Late Postmodernism* (1991); *West of the American Dream: An Encounter with Texas* (2000); and five collections of poems. He has published over one hundred essays in the United States and Europe. He is currently at work on an anthology of nineteenth-century American protest poetry for Oxford University Press. Christensen lives part of the year in southern France and is contributing editor on French culture to the journal *France Today*.

Elizabeth S. D. Engelhardt is an assistant professor of women's studies at West Virginia University. She received a Ph.D. in women's studies from Emory University. Her dissertation was "Southern Appalachian Ecological Literature and Feminism: Women Authors Address the Land, 1890–1910." She studies representations of women, nature, and feminist and environmental activism. Her writing can be found in the journals *Women's Studies Quarterly* and *Legacy* and in the *Oxford Companion to African American Literature*.

Patricia M. Gantt is associate professor of English at Utah State University. She is presently working on a book on Wilma Dykeman's fiction and nonfiction, as well as one analyzing women's oral histories from the Federal Writers' Project. Her published essays include work on regional women writers, August Wilson, William Faulkner, folklore, and teacher education.

Sherrie A. Inness is associate professor of English at Miami University. Her research interests include gender and cooking culture, girls' literature and culture, popular culture, and gender studies. She has published nine books: *Intimate Communities: Representation and Social Transformation in Women's College Fiction, 1895–1910* (1995); *The Lesbian Menace: Ideology, Identity, and the Representation of Lesbian Life* (1997); *Tough Girls: Women Warriors and Wonder Women in Popular Culture* (1999); *Dinner Roles: American Women and Culinary Culture* (2001); *Nancy Drew and Company: Culture, Gender, and Girls' Series* (editor, 1997); *Breaking Boundaries: New Perspectives on Regional Writing* (editor, 1997); *Delinquents and Debutantes: Twentieth-Century American Girls' Cultures* (editor, 1998); *Millennium Girls: Today's Girls around the World* (editor, 1998); *Kitchen Culture in America: Popular Representations of Food, Gender, and Race* (2001); and *Running for Their Lives: Girls, Cultural Identity, and Stories of Survival* (editor, 2000).

Virginia S. Jenkins holds a Ph.D. in American studies from the George Washington University. She is the author of *Bananas: An American History* (2000) and *The Lawn: A History of an American Obsession* (1994), which won the Ray and Pat Browne Award for the best book on popular culture, awarded by the Popular Culture Association. She is a scholar in residence at the Center for Chesapeake Studies of the Chesapeake Bay Maritime Museum studying the sea food industry of the Chesapeake Bay.

Traci Marie Kelly is currently teaching technical communication at the University of Wisconsin–Madison. She earned her Ph.D. in 1997 from the University of North Dakota with a dissertation entitled "Burned Sugar Pie: Women's Cultures in the Literature of Food." She also has a chapter included in the anthology *Kitchen Culture in America: Popular Representations of Food, Gender, and Race* (2001).

Kathleen LeBesco is assistant professor of communication arts at Marymount Manhattan College. She is coeditor of *Bodies Out of Bounds: Fatness and Transgression* (2001) and author of several scholarly essays about struggles to resignify the fat body. Her research interests include studies of sexuality, gender, and popular culture.

Jessamyn Neuhaus received her Ph.D. in history from the Claremont Graduate University. Her article "The Joy of Sex Instruction: Women and Cooking in Marital Sex Manuals, 1920–1963" appeared in *Kitchen Culture in America: Representations of Food, Gender, and Race* (2001), edited by Sherrie A. Inness, and she is currently revising her dissertation on cookbooks and gender in modern America for Johns Hopkins University Press. Neuhaus has taught at New College of California, California State University, Hayward, Oregon State University, and Lewis and Clark College.

Psyche A. Williams-Forson is a Ph.D. candidate in the Department of American Studies at the University of Maryland College Park. She is currently working on her dissertation, "Fried Chicken in the Kitchen: African American Women, Material Culture, and the Power of Food[ways]." She has taught material culture studies in the American Studies Department at the University of Maryland College Park and diasporic literature at Western Maryland College, where she is the Jessie Ball DuPont Visiting Scholar. She has also served as a consultant with the Smithsonian Institute's Anacostia Museum and the Center for African American History and Culture in Washington, D.C.

9 780742 515741